Business Relating Business

Acclaim for *Business Relating Business*

'The primacy of the view of the firm as a rational, or relatively rational decision-making entity, is increasingly irrelevant to the way in which contemporary business has developed older models of the firms as something deeply embedded in a network of local connections, as in areas such as the Birmingham Jewellery District, to the exigencies of contemporary and increasingly international organisational collaboration. Much of the material dealing with these developments has been scattered between different fields – some in marketing, some in supply chain management, some in strategy and organisation studies, and so on. In *Business Relating Business* Ian Wilkinson develops these fields to present a realistic, empirically grounded and theoretically fascinating analysis of the contemporary state of play and knowledge of collaborative and network business strategies.'

– Stewart Clegg, Research Director, Centre for Management and Organisation Studies, University of Technology, Sydney, Australia

'This book demonstrates that no organisation is an island, but is part of a complex structure composed of a myriad of other organisations. The author provides an analytical framework within which an organisation's marketing strategy may recognise the opportunities and challenges offered by the interrelated networks within which it operates.'

– Donald F. Dixon, Emeritus Professor of Marketing, Philadephia, USA

'With few exceptions, professors of marketing are balanced and diplomatic and avoid being personal or original. They hide behind references to *Journal of Marketing* articles; it makes them feel secure. Not so Ian Wilkinson. No doubt well-read, he explores the networks of B2B marketing on his own terms, with originality; business dancing is such a creative example. Read his book and learn to business dance!'

– Evert Gummesson, Professor of Marketing, Stockholm University School of Business, Sweden and author of *Total Relationship Marketing* and *Marketing as Networks: The Birth of Many-to-Many Marketing*

'Ian Wilkinson is a marketing scholar who has been an active participant in the scientific community regarding marketing and the function of markets for many years. He has become well known both for his way to challenge the existing thinking but also in his creativity to formulate and use new metaphors. All of this is also characterising this new book where he very much summarises his findings and thoughts. The ideas presented are interesting as they are not just representing a personal view but also a view of a specific position. As an Australian citizen Ian has kept his very close connections to Europe and the US but he has also managed to become highly involved in the economic development of Asia. In this way he can draw on examples and developments in the three major economic zones of the world. The result is impressive and, as typical for Ian, both challenging and creative. This book can be recommended to all those who are interested in the use of alternatives to the existing hegemony of more limited market models!'

– Håkan Håkansson, Professor of International Management,
BI Norwegian School of Management, Oslo, Norway

'This is a modern book on the modern ways business is done in the global economy and on how companies and people interact in it. The book gives fruitful insights for both practitioners and academics into recent developments in relationship management and marketing and it will help students to understand better the world they will work in in the future.'

– Professor Michael Kleinaltenkamp, Professor of Business and Services
Marketing and former Dean, School of Business Administration
and Economics, Freie Universität Berlin, Germany

'In this timely book Ian Wilkinson provides managers (and academics) with an insightful review of contemporary thinking about life in a networked world. Like it or not, we live now in a world where both our capacity and our need to interact with others in business relationships is increasing daily, under the combined effects of social, economic and technological change. Inevitably, networks based on trade, trust, mutual advantage and commitment have become part of everyday business life. This is a world where decisions have to be made by managers conscious of being part of an extended firm with commitments to networked partners, where the ability to access the resources, knowledge and skills of these partners is a critical competitive advantage. As Wilkinson comments, "the central strategic problem confronting firms in networks is developing, sustaining and protecting a firm's network position". His book explores these ideas and provides a valuable synthesis of research and practice in this challenging and important field. It is intellectually stimulating and a pleasure to read.'

– Roger A. Layton, Emeritus Professor of Marketing,
Australian School of Business, University of New South Wales,
Australia

'This book integrates Ian Wilkinson's extensive research on business relations and market networks. It is a thought-provoking and forward-looking book, accessible to both academic and business audiences. Wilkinson's analysis of contemporary markets as complex adaptive self-organising systems has important implications for business analysis and management as well as for government policy making. It is well fitted for use in advanced courses in marketing and strategy.'

– Lars-Gunnar Mattsson, Emeritus Professor of Business Administration,
Stockholm School of Economics, Sweden

'What I really like about Ian Wilkinson's book is that it deals comprehensively with the social phenomenon of commercial relationship – most other books on marketing relationships don't! This fresh discussion productively challenges any comfortable assumption that we know everything about relationships in commercial society, and will bring further economic sophistication to the study of marketing and marketing management. This is just the kind of market analysis that is sorely needed in the marketing field – and it can be read without dread. Many marketing students don't ever study markets, and, following Robert Bartels, it is important for society that we understand marketing as technique and as human interaction. Ian Wilkinson has succeeded in bridging the confusing gap between the everyday interpersonal sense of relationship and the business and work sense of relationship at the higher level of social organisation we call the firm or "organisation".

The discussion is founded on a wealth of intellectual development, scholarship, and experience as a researcher and educator. It is wide-ranging and comprehensive – importantly bringing forth the "big picture" of the social-economical-political market system within which the marketing process operates. Crucially, we learn about why as well as how commercial relationships arise – and why this matters in an era of post-industrial globalisation.

Yes, this is a highly readable book in that it foregrounds ideas and explanation, without defaulting to the cataloguing of accepted "facts". The author does this with engaging personality, and in doing so provides an expert portal to what matters in the vast and continuously growing literature that sheds light on marketing in society. I have little doubt that this will catalyse much needed further scholarship. I have already recommended it to my students of Relationship Marketing.'

– Dr Richard J. Varey, Professor of Marketing,
The Waikato Management School, Hamilton, New Zealand

Business Relating Business

Managing Organisational Relations and Networks

Ian Wilkinson

Professor of Marketing, Australian School of Business,
University of New South Wales, Sydney, Australia

Edward Elgar
Cheltenham, UK • Northampton, MA, USA

Published by
Edward Elgar Publishing Limited
Glensanda House
Montpellier Parade
Cheltenham
Glos GL50 1UA
UK

Edward Elgar Publishing, Inc.
William Pratt House
9 Dewey Court
Northampton
Massachusetts 01060
USA

A catalogue record for this book
is available from the British Library

ISBN 978 1 84542 539 5 (cased)

Printed and bound in Great Britain by MPG Books Ltd, Bodmin, Cornwall

Contents

To Louise

Introduction: relationships and networks are us

Relationships and networks are everywhere. In business and life we cannot exist without or avoid relations with others. We are born into a relationship with our biological mother as the product of interaction in a relationship, however temporary, between a male and female. The rest is our history.

We are enmeshed in relations in life and business life, and the two interact. This book is about relationships and networks, interconnected systems of relationships, in business. I am interested in the opportunities and problems, insights and blinkered vision that arise through and about interactions with others. From a business perspective the focus is on the way collaborative advantage underpins competitive advantage: the way we compete to collaborate and collaborate to compete. I examine how firms and managers do and should manage their interactions and relations with other people, firms and other types of organisations, both internally and externally, be they direct counterparts or indirectly connected others. Even decisions and planning processes themselves are the product of relations and interactions among interested parties.

A firm, clearly, is not an island; it is embedded in a set of ongoing business, professional and personal relations that shape and are shaped by its actions and responses. Indeed, the firm is really no more than a construction or derivative of the pattern of interactions in which it is involved over time – a kind of connecting unit. This is what Håkansson and Snehota had in mind when they wrote:

> A business enterprise looks more like a linking unit where its strategic attributes lie in how it connects other market participants to each other . . . The picture of both the possibilities and the means to manage the business enterprise become quite different. (Håkansson and Snehota 1995, p. 21)

Moreover, the firm itself is nothing more than a complex network of interactions and relations among people playing various roles, among departments and functional units, and among business units, subsidiaries and establishments.

The rich complexity and confusion of business networks is well illustrated in a depiction of the world's product exports that recently appeared in the journal *Science*. In this diagram, which is shown in Figure I.1, a product is a kind of tree and all products together form a forest. Products or 'trees' are interrelated in many ways. This includes the input or output connections involved as raw material from mines and farms, for example, is processed, combined and recombined, and worked on by people to form various types of intermediate products and services, such as bauxite, to aluminium, to pots and pans. Products are also related because they are produced, bought or consumed together, and/or because they require similar technologies, people or places to produce and work with them. Two products are similar if they require similar inputs and support systems to produce them; they will tend to be produced together. If products are dissimilar, they are less likely to be produced together.

The similarity of products is used to form a proximity matrix as illustrated in part A of Figure I.1. This shows that some products are very connected, while others are not connected at all or are hardly connected. The pattern of interconnectedness can be visualised as a very complex network, as shown in part B of Figure I.1. This reflects the economic and production logics of business and the way value is created and delivered to intermediate and final consumers. The network depicts the pattern of exports, from 1998 to 2000, for 775 different types of products, defined in terms of the 4-digit Standard Industrial Trade Classification (SITC-4), which is used to combine trade statistics internationally. Links are shaded according to their proximity value and the sizes of the nodes (circles) are proportional to world trade value. Only the strongest links among products are used to construct the network picture; the technical details need not concern us here.

The resulting network has a core–periphery structure, with a core of metal products, machinery and chemicals, and a periphery consisting of four groups of products, as shown in the figure.

What Figure I.1 shows is the interconnected nature of business and commerce as products and services are produced and used. Underlying all this and responsible for the activities involved are all manner of business firms and other organisations that carry out the necessary activities involved, and interact and trade with each other. These interactions and transactions matter a great deal in getting the goods and services we value designed, developed, produced and delivered. This book is about how these interactions happen and how business relations and networks are formed and re-formed from the ongoing patterns of action and interaction taking place over time.

My focus is the 'markets-as-networks' tradition developed in large part in Europe by the Industrial Marketing and Purchasing (IMP) group. Hence I

A

node colour (Leaner Classification)

①②③④⑤⑥⑦⑧⑨⑩

Petroleum | Raw Materials | Forest Products | Tropical Agriculture | Animal Agriculture | Cereals | Labour Intensive | Capital Intensive | Machinery | Chemicals

Proximity

0.9 0.8 0.7 0.6 0.5 0.4 0.3 0.2 0.1

Ink colour (proximity)

> 0.65 | > 0.55 | > 0.4 | < 0.4

node size (world trade [thousands of US$])

3.0 × 10⁶ | 1.5 × 10⁶ | 7.5 × 10⁵ | 3.7 × 10⁵ | 1.9 × 10⁰

B

Fruits · Oil · Vegetable oils · Fishing · Forest and paper products · Vegetables · Cereals · Coffee and cocoa products · Mining · Garments · Vehicles machinery · Metallurgy · Electronics · Textiles · Animal agriculture · Chemicals

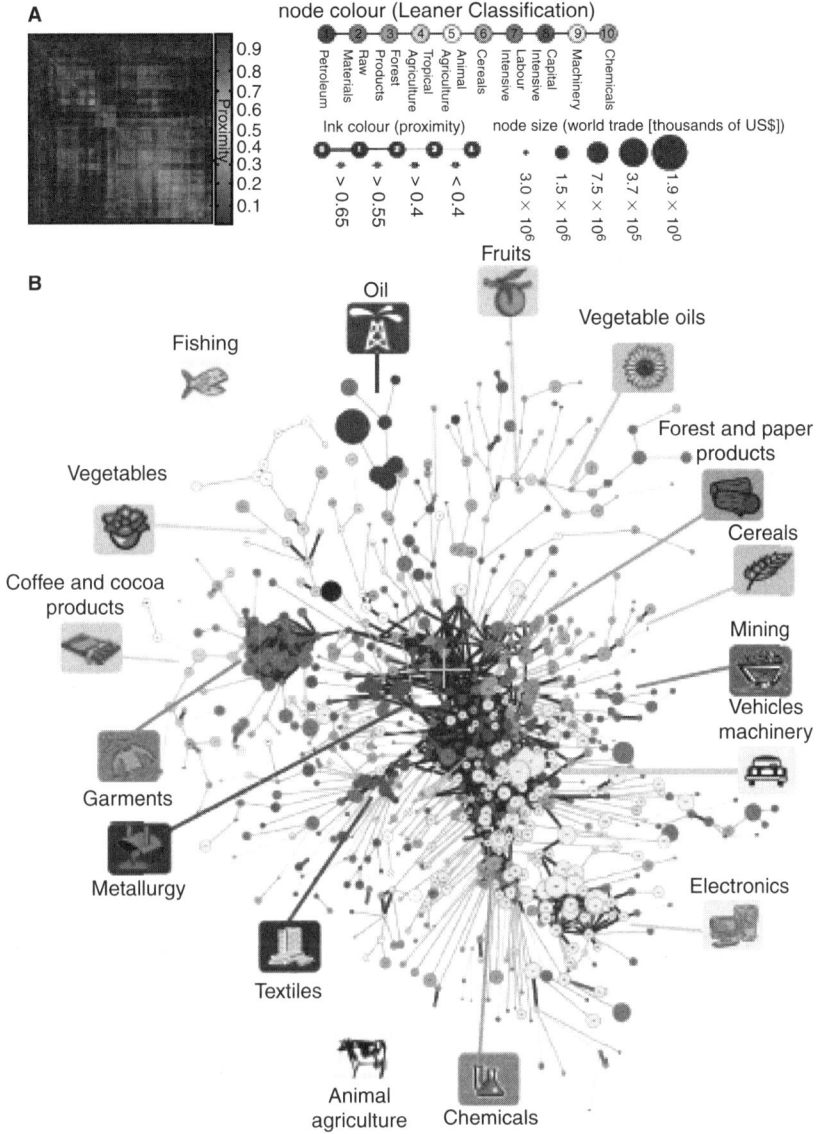

Source: Hidalgo et al. (2007).

Figure I.1 The world's export production network

view the problems of management in terms of relations and networks – whether one is a manager attempting to manage or being managed, a policy maker, a researcher or simply an interested observer. I will describe a framework of analysis and tools to aid decision makers, and link the discussion to developments in the business literature in marketing, management, economics, economic sociology, social psychology, philosophy and psychology. There is much communality here, even though cross-referencing among these separate domains and disciplines is often limited. In addition, there is a tendency among practitioners in different disciplines to use jargon and to attribute the origin of ideas and approaches to the founding mothers and fathers in their particular neck of the academic wood. I hope I can minimise this and draw on some of the best expositions of particular concepts from diverse fields – although I do not claim authority in all these areas.

I link ideas about business to biology and evolution because business is ultimately biological: it involves people doing things, thinking things and feeling things. None of us can avoid evolution: we are necessarily part of the ongoing process, both culturally and biologically, and theories and concepts from evolution and biology can inform and guide our thinking about business. These days models and concepts from many diverse disciplines are coming together in the form of complexity theory or the complexity sciences. This shows us, as general systems theory did many years ago, but limitedly, that the different worlds of ideas represented by different disciplines have a great deal in common. They face analogous problems and can use each other as metaphors to help advance thinking. As Steven Hawking says, this century is the century of complexity. And nowhere more so than in business.

In marketing, my home discipline, you are relatively free to read anything you want, because the boundaries around the discipline are rather ill defined; marketing is an example of applied social science. In other disciplines, such as economics (my original training), there seems to be much more emphasis on feeding on and developing ideas within more narrowly defined academic boundaries in terms of journals, books and authors. But the focus here is more concrete; it concerns the different types of relations and interactions in business.

The organisation of the book is based on a course I have taught over the years in marketing and business-to-business marketing, and more recently a course devoted specifically to managing business relationships and networks. The book is targeted at upper-level undergraduate and postgraduate courses in business or industrial marketing, supply chain management, customer relationship management, relationship marketing, marketing channels and the like. It is also relevant for courses in industrial sociology and economic geography.

I am unashamedly an 'IMPer' in outlook and philosophy. I go to most IMP conferences and have done much of my research with people associated directly and indirectly with this group. They have strongly influenced my thinking. But I do not claim that this book is an IMP book. It reflects my personal views developed over many years of teaching, researching and consulting in the area. I have a great respect for and am strongly influenced by many research streams from the North American tradition, and by researchers in other parts of the world, including in particular Asian scholars and ideas.

I like to think of Australians as the 'between' guys: friendly and non-judgemental, but robust thinkers. I have even drawn parallels with Australia and the Medici. The Medici, as John Padgett and Christopher Ansell (1993) tell us, married members of the aristocracy from different districts of ancient Florence. These were largely not the people from the same district as them. However, the Medici developed close personal and business friendships with people from the same district – merchants and others. I don't want to push the analogy too far, but Australians have until quite recently focused marriage links on Europe and North America, but to a large extent live and work in the Asian region. Here we have friends and business partners. Thus we are in a sense a link between East and West, not a threat to either and (I hope) trusted by both sides. This gives us many opportunities, but also problems and responsibilities.

This book is designed to bridge the gap or occupy the space between Eastern and Western, European and American, approaches to business understanding and practice. So I hope it will appeal to all these groups and not just other Australians. This is the very essence of the book – managing interactions and relations directly and indirectly with others.

Lastly, the writing style adopted here is not the usual formal style of a textbook. It is rather the style of serious but popular science, social science and economics books in an active and sometimes informal voice. To improve readability I have kept referencing to a minimum. I draw on many previous papers I have published and indicate in endnotes where sections are based on particular papers. Additional references not directly cited in the book are given in those papers and the bibliography.

I owe a great debt in writing this book to many who have influenced my thinking, educated and informed me. These include, in particular, and in no particular order, Don Dixon, Roger Layton, Geoff Easton, Stan Glaser, Fred Emery, Lou Stern, Stuart Kauffman, David Kipnis, Stu Schmidt, Jim Wiley, Håkan Håkansson, David Ford, Lars-Gunnar Mattsson, Thomas Ritter, Per Freytag, Michael Kleinaltenkamp, Jan Johanson, Bob Marks, Lawrence and Denise Welch, and of course all the IMPers I have debated and drunk with at numerous IMP conferences and meetings. My colleagues at the University of New South Wales have been a source of inspiration, information and friendship over the years, and have shaped my academic persona in many ways. I have also profited much from time spent at various universities discussing and refining my ideas. These include the University of California at Berkeley, Temple University, the University of Cincinnati, the Stockholm School of Economics, BI (Norwegian School of Management) in Oslo, Lancaster University, the University of Bath and in China at Fudan University and the University of International Business and Economics in Beijing. My students, especially the research students I have had the privilege of supervising, co-supervising or generally annoying, have been a constant source of challenge and inspiration over the years. Much of the development of the ideas in this book is due to them. I would like to single out a few who have made significant contributions to my thinking and whose research is reflected directly in chapters in this book. They are, again in no particular order, Catherine Welch, Van Nguyen, Gary Buttriss, Ross Cameron, Charles Wong, Baiding Rong, Stephanie Huang, David Darby, Virpi Havila, Pierra Morlacchi, Kevin Yeogh, Yanto Chandra, Marie-Celine Chery, Neeru Sharma, Georgina Georgieva and Sara Denize. I am sorry if I forgot a name or two – there have been so many!

But of course my greatest debt and gratitude and stimulation is to Louise Young, my wife, colleague, best friend and protector. Without her, life would be very different, and I dedicate this book to her and to our co-produced relationship asset Melanie, who continues to delight and surprise me, and to the relationship that conceived and raised the relationship-specific asset that is me.

1. The nature and role of relations and networks in business

There is a proliferation of books, articles, research and business advice that seek to address the issue of relations and networks in business life. This literature has been growing at an ever-increasing pace during the last decade. Different authors refer to fundamentally the same types of issues in many ways so as, it seems, to confuse us. There is talk about relationship marketing, supply chain management, customer relationship marketing, networking, partnering, strategic alliances, collaborative strategies, co-opetition and the like. Here I want to make sense of this profusion of terms and give a simple roadmap of what is meant by business relationships and networks, what types businesses are involved in and what their role and importance is. This sets the scene for developing tools and frameworks of analysis to help us understand how and why relations and networks develop and evolve over time, and the problems of managing them. I draw on a variety of literature but do not attempt to review or synthesise it in any comprehensive manner. Much of what I have to say draws on papers written over the years with many colleagues and students.

WHAT IS A RELATIONSHIP?

I began the Introduction with the point that all of us are the product of a relationship between our mother and father, and are born into a relationship with our biological mother. This focuses attention on the structural (biological) bonds or ties linking us and our parents. But we are the product of an active sexual dance between these people, not from mere propinquity – simply being there! In the same way our relationship with our biological mother comes through the *act* of birth and is an ongoing pattern of interaction that changes over time.

Relationships are patterns of interaction among those involved over time. They are not like marriages that exist until they are dissolved. They are more like a dance; they are actively reproduced through time or they cease to exist. At any given moment there is a history of interaction that shapes how we interact now and how we intend to interact in the future.

This shadow of the past is reflected in our attitudes, beliefs and the meanings we attach to ourselves and others and their interrelationships, including both negative and positive aspects, as we learn to trust or distrust, respect or disrespect, like or dislike others. The shadow of the past is reflected also in the resources and routines that have been co-developed. These are the remains of a unique history of interaction that can be a source of strength and/or weakness for those involved. Thus our actions, capabilities and values are path-dependent: they have been shaped and constrained by our history, by the sequence of events that have made us and our relationships what they are, not just the assortment of events that have occurred.

Not only do relationships have a history; there is also a futurity, a shadow of the future, that manifests itself in expectations of continued dealings and even valuation of the relationship for its own sake. An isolated transaction between anonymous players, who have no history to go on and who expect or desire no future transactions, is a non-relation and corresponds in many ways to the neo-classical 'perfect market' concept of a transaction. But most business, indeed any kind of social or economic transaction, is not like that. Transactions are embedded in ongoing relations of different characters with different histories and expectations. Market transactions are also embedded in non-market transactions and relations among the players engaging in a focal market transaction, as well as with others, that affect and are affected by a focal transaction or relation. When we trade with a particular firm or person over time, personal relations emerge that help or impede market transactions and the development of the market relation. It was Mark Granovetter (1985), a sociologist, who focused our attention on the socially embedded nature of economic action. But there is a far longer history of discussion and analysis of the way economic and social life are intertwined, going back to the origins of modern markets, as Don Dixon (2002) and other market and economic historians have shown. For a historical account of the development of relationship and network thinking in marketing in the last century see Wilkinson (2001).

The core message here is that a market relation does not develop in isolation from other relations in which the parties are involved. This includes other types of non-economic relations the parties have with each other and the economic and non-economic relations they have with third parties, both directly and indirectly. In short, transactions and relations are not islands.

Let me offer a definition of a relationship as an interconnected set of transactions over time involving at least two people. Market relations are sets of interconnected market transactions over time. A transaction in turn is the basic unit of analysis and involves, as the name implies, *inter-action* between two actors that results in an exchange of some kind. Such transactions can involve exchange of information, money, goods or services; a relationship develops over time as a result of a series of transactions. These transactions are both an expression of the attitudes and beliefs of the participants involved, or what we may loosely call the rules of the relationship, and are the means by which, at the same time, these attitudes and beliefs, or rules, arise. We may take stock of a relation at a particular point in time and measure various characteristics of it that have developed, such as the degree of power, conflict, trust, satisfaction in its performance. But a relation does not stop; it is in a continual process of expression, reproduction, change and evolution. A relationship is a pattern of behaviour over time, not a pattern of behaviour measured at a moment in time. This has important implications for the way we understand and attempt to manage the development of and our participation in market relations and networks.

WHAT KINDS OF RELATIONS ARE FIRMS INVOLVED IN?

The 'markets-as-networks' tradition sees markets in terms of relations and networks rather than as sets of autonomous actors vying for a place in some mass market (Johanson and Mattsson 1994). From this view we see firms embedded in networks of relations with other firms, including suppliers, distributors, customers, competitors and complementors. And the firm itself is constituted of a network of relations among the people, departments and units that comprise it.

Intra-firm Relations

A firm comprises a number of different people and departments performing various kinds of activities. These activities are involved in creating and delivering value to a firm's customers and shareholders in the form of products and services that return profits and allow the firm to survive. These value-creating activities have been summarised by Michael Porter in terms of the firm's value chain, which is depicted in Figure 1.1.

A sequence of primary activities lies at the heart of the value creation process involving inbound logistics, operations, outbound logistics, marketing and sales and service. These primary activities are supported by various types of activities that involve other parts of the firm. This interconnected system of activities is what together produces value and implies

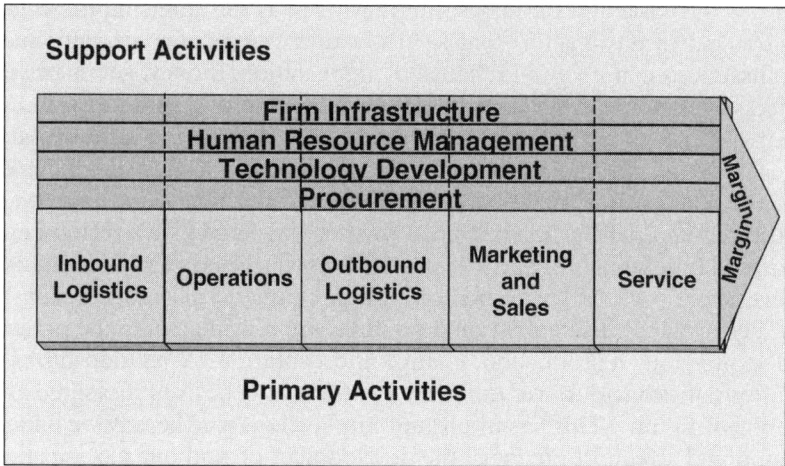

Source: Porter (1985, p. 46).

Figure 1.1   The firm's value chain

a network of intra-firm relations involved in this value creation process. As Porter comments:

> [T]he value chain is not a collection of independent activities but a system of interdependent activities. Value activities are related by linkages within the value chain. Linkages are relationships between the way one value activity is performed and the cost or performance of another. (1985, p. 48)

These interdependent activities are coordinated within firms by means of formal and informal relations. First, coordination takes place through the formal management hierarchy within the firm, which indicates who reports to whom and who can tell whom what to do. This formal structure is reflected in a firm's formal organisation chart, as illustrated in Figure 1.2a.

As anyone knows from working in an organisation, coordination is not simply achieved through the working of the formal structure; it is also achieved through an informal organisational structure. This refers to the pattern of interpersonal and cross-functional relations and interactions that take place among members of a firm in order to carry out their tasks and coordinate their activities. Figure 1.2b indicates the importance of these informal relations and interactions. It shows the pattern of emails taking place among members of the same firm as depicted in Figure 1.2a. We can see that the relations and interactions are numerous, and cut across formal lines of reporting and authority.

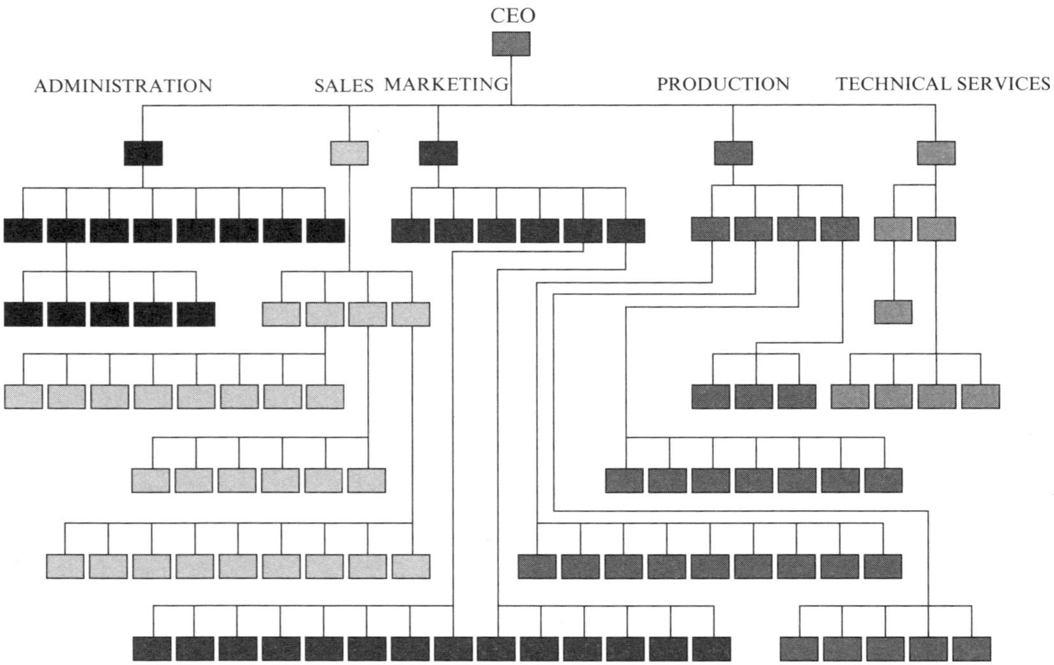

Source: By kind permission of Network Analytics.

Figure 1.2a   A firm's formal organisation

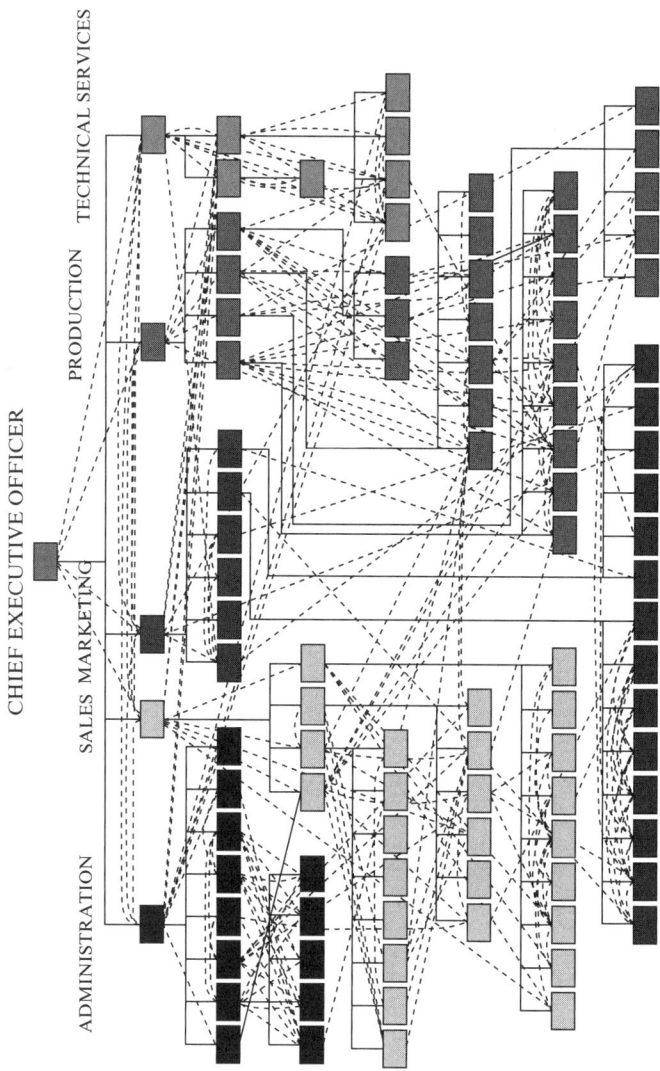

CHIEF EXECUTIVE OFFICER

ADMINISTRATION SALES MARKETING PRODUCTION TECHNICAL SERVICES

Source: By kind permission of Network Analytics.

Figure 1.2b   A firm's informal relations

A Firm's External Relations

A firm is simultaneously involved in many relations with customers, distributors, suppliers, competitors, technology partners, government instrumentalities, community groups and other types of organisations that comprise what may be called its relationship portfolio. These are sometimes referred to as stakeholders because they all have an interest or stake in the focal firm and can affect its operations. An example of the many types of relations comprising a firm's relationship portfolio is shown in Figure 1.3 for the Shouldice Hospital in Canada, which specialises in hernia operations.

A useful way of summarising the sets of relations in which a firm is embedded is in terms of its 'value net', as shown in Figure 1.4. The concept of a value net was proposed by Brandenburger and Nalebuff (1997) in their book *Co-opetition*, which focuses on the simultaneously competitive and cooperative nature of business and market relationships. We could group each of the relations for the Shouldice Hospital in terms of one or more of these four basic types of relations – suppliers, competitors, customers and complementors. Most of the relationship partners are self-explanatory, except perhaps for complementors, whom I describe further in the next section; here I want simply to depict the broad range of relations in which a firm is embedded.

I add a further dimension to that proposed by Brandenburger and Nalebuff, that of intra-firm relations. A firm interacts with other firms and organisations by networks of relations between firms, and an important strategic issue confronting management is the interfacing of intra- and interfirm relations.

Researchers have proposed various other classifications of relations in which a firm is embedded, but I prefer the value net concept, as augmented, because of the way it identifies the main strategic types of relations. It is not attempting to provide an exhaustive list of types of other organisations but to highlight different generic types of relationship partners.

Networks: Interconnections among Relations

The value net can be used as a simple way of classifying relations, but there is more to it than this: there are relations between the relationship partners as well, and what goes on in one relation affects what goes on in others. Such connections occur through the focal firm and its intra-firm relations, such as the way a firm's supplier relations affect and are affected by its relations to customers, competitors or complementors. They are also connected through the other players in the value net; for example competitors' relations with their suppliers affect relations between the focal firm and its suppliers and competitors.

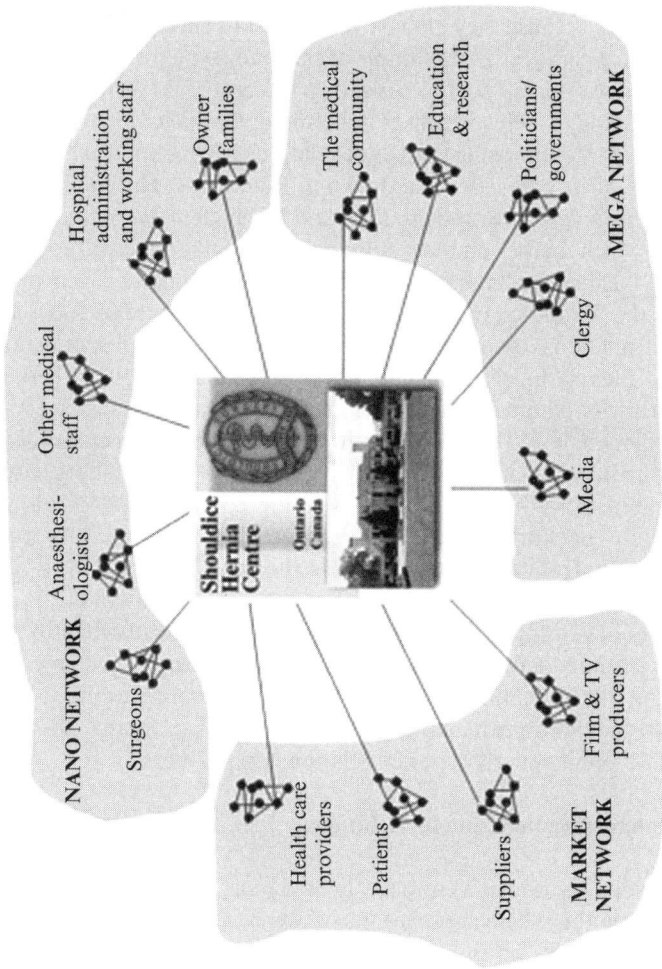

Nano Network

Owner families

Hospital administration and working staff

Other medical staff

Anaesthesi- ologists

Surgeons

NANO NETWORK

The medical community

Education & research

Politicians/ governments

Clergy

MEGA NETWORK

Media

Shouldice Hernia Centre

Ontario Canada

Health care providers

Patients

Suppliers

MARKET NETWORK

Film & TV producers

Source: Gummesson (2006).

Figure 1.3 Shouldice Hernia Centre's relationship portfolio

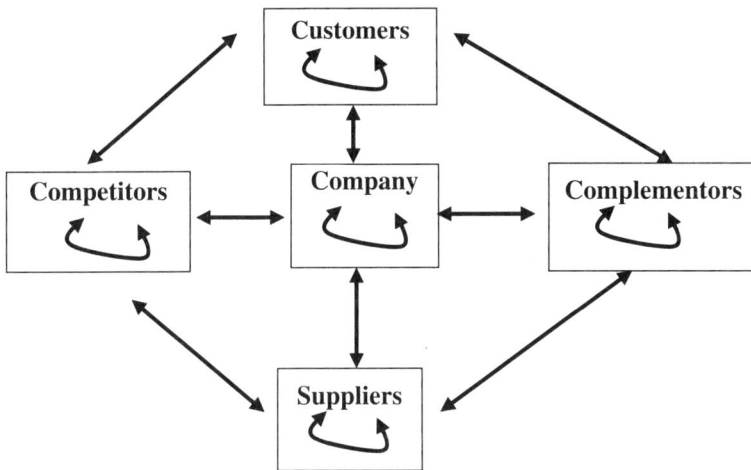

Source: Adapted from Brandenburger and Nalebuff (1997, p. 17).

Figure 1.4   A firm's value net

Relations with complementors arise because customers have other suppliers and suppliers have other customers. Another supplier is a complementor if your customers value your product or service *more* when they have this firm's products or services than if they have yours alone. In contrast, it is a competitor if your customers value your product or service *less* when they have this firm's products or services than if they have yours alone. Examples of such complementary products and suppliers are computer hardware and software suppliers, and red wine and dry cleaners. If supplying other customers adversely affects the way the supplier serves you, they are competitors. If supplying other customers helps the supplier serve you, they are complementors. Thus if a firm learns how to serve you better by serving other customers, or can offer you better prices because it has other customers, these other customers are complementors.

Another firm or organisation can be a complementor for some aspects of its operations and a competitor for others. Thus different mobile phone suppliers are competitors, but complementors, when it comes to the development of industry standards for mobile phone systems and in lobbying government. As a result, competitors sometimes cooperate in developing technology, opening up and developing markets, and in lobbying activities. Here the actions of one competitor help the position of other competitors, and the complementarity arises because competitors have the same suppliers and technology, and are subject to the same types of regulations.

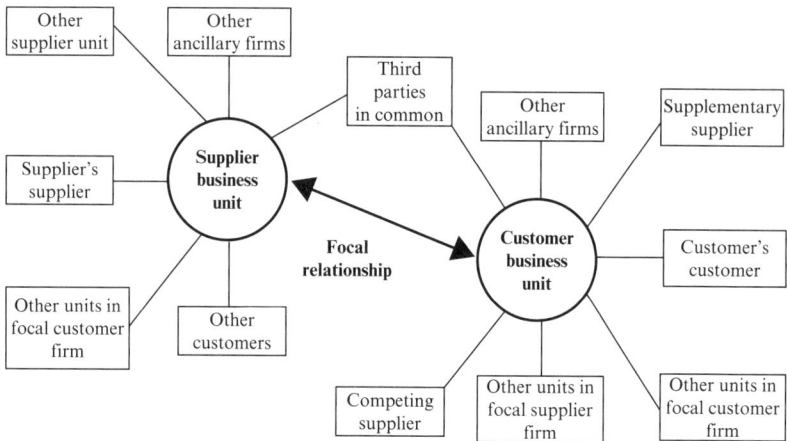

Source: Anderson et al. (1994, p. 3).

Figure 1.5   Connected relations

The other types of relations that may be connected to a focal relation between a firm and a customer are summarised in Figure 1.5. Depending on the particular industry or firm situation, any of these connections to third parties may be important. For example, the customer's customer is an important driver of the direct customer's demand and, when the customer's customer gets into trouble, this has repercussions for those indirectly connected. The activities of the sub-suppliers or the supplier's suppliers affect the ability of the first-tier suppliers to meet the demands of their customers.

Two examples of networks of firms directly and indirectly connected are shown in Figures 1.6 and 1.7, for Toyota's supply network and Mitsubishi Motors' production network.

The value net depicts relations from the perspective of a focal firm. But each type of organisation in the value net has its own value net and is only in part captured by the relations shown in one firm's value net. A firm's competitor's competitors include firms the original firm does not regard as its *direct* competitors. For example, a retailer serves a particular market area and competes with other retailers located within that area. But retailers located further away have market areas extending beyond the bounds of that served by the original firm, and this brings them into competition with yet other retailers, who are not direct competitors of the original firm and hence would not form part of its value net.

As we extend a focal firm's value net to include the value nets of those firms in the original value net, we begin to see the networks of business relations

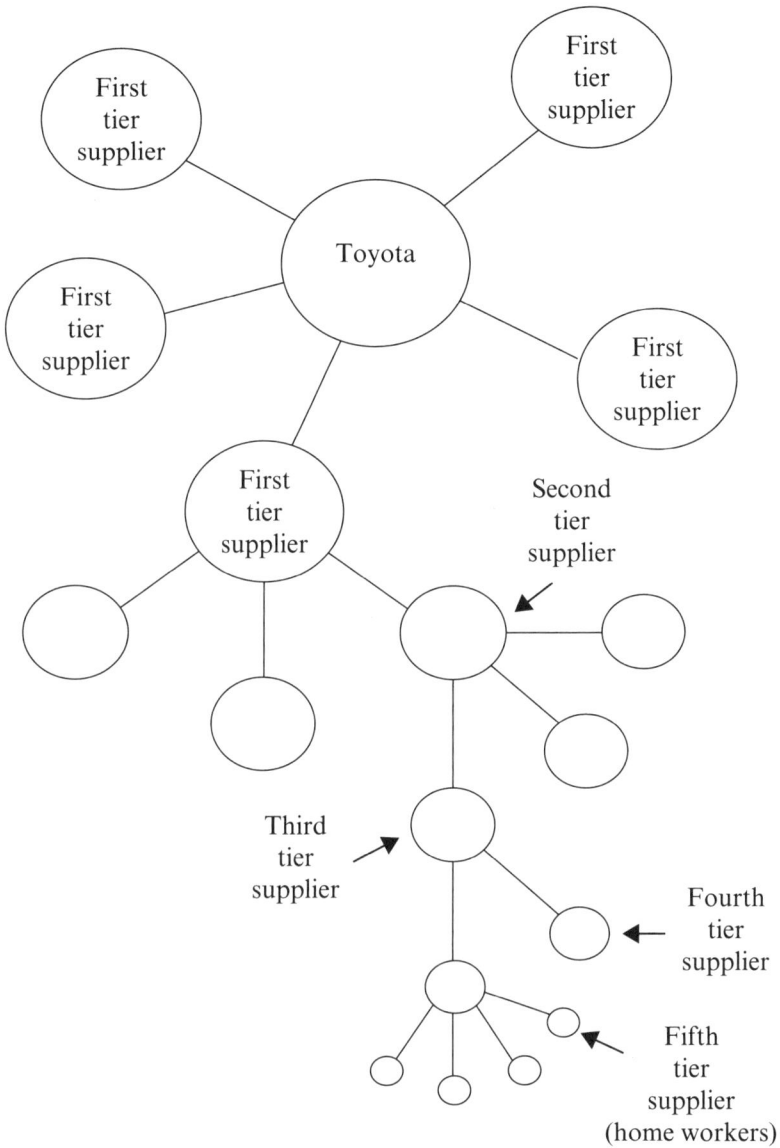

Source: Blenkhorn and Noori (1990, p. 23).

Figure 1.6   *Toyota's supply network*

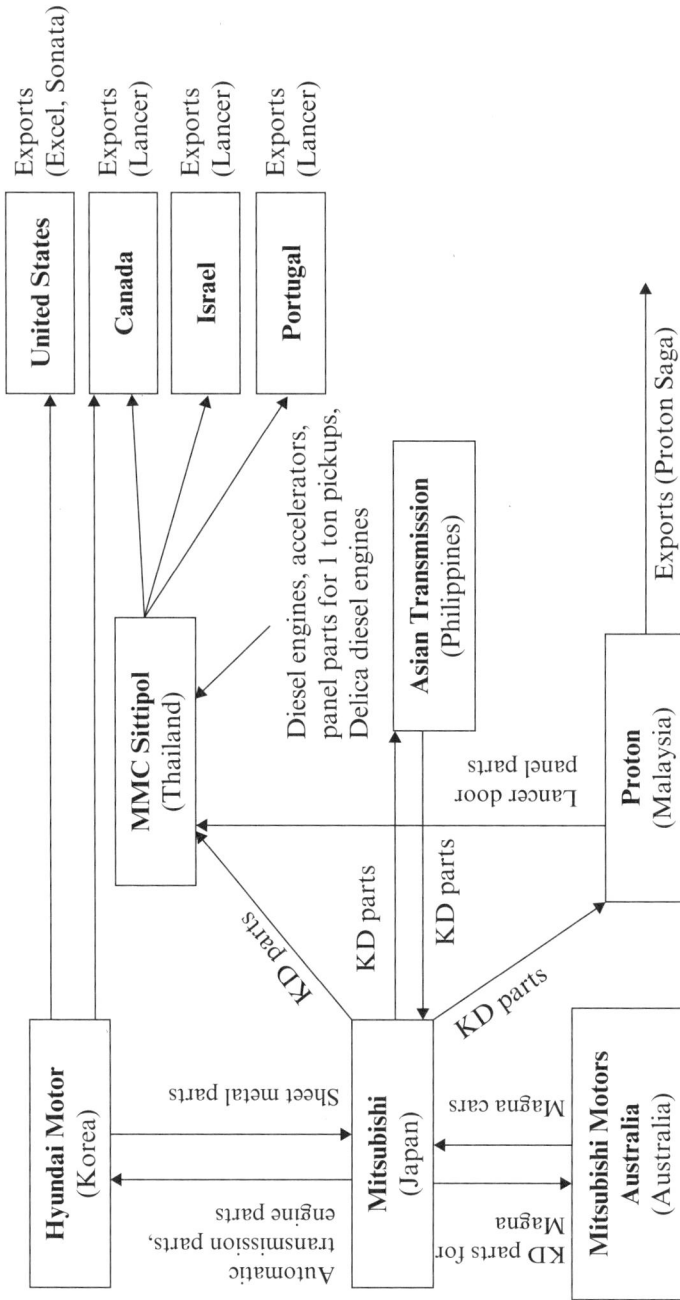

United States — Exports (Excel, Sonata)

Canada — Exports (Lancer)

Israel — Exports (Lancer)

Portugal — Exports (Lancer)

MMC Sittipol (Thailand)

Diesel engines, accelerators, panel parts for 1 ton pickups, Delica diesel engines

Asian Transmission (Philippines)

Proton (Malaysia)

Exports (Proton Saga)

Lancer door panel parts

KD parts

KD parts

KD parts

KD parts

Hyundai Motor (Korea)

Sheet metal parts

Automatic transmission parts, engine parts

Mitsubishi (Japan)

Magna cars

KD parts for Magna

Mitsubishi Motors Australia (Australia)

Source: Hatch and Yamamura (1996, p. 34).

Figure 1.7 Mitsubishi Motors' production network

in which a firm is embedded. Even this is incomplete because we are excluding non-business relations, such as social and family relations that may exist among people working in the same or different firms. In some cultures these types of relations have an important impact on business activities and relations, such as the role of *guanxi* in Chinese business relations.

Researchers have proposed various ways of referring to the networks of relations in which firms are involved. An early and important contribution is by Wroe Alderson (1957, 1965), the founder of modern marketing theory. He distinguishes between transactions and *transvections*. Transvections comprise systems of transactions, connected in series and parallel, that link an original source of supply to final demand or, according to Alderson's definition:

> A transvection is the unit of action for the system by which a single end product such as a pair of shoes is placed in the hands of the consumer after moving through all the intermediate sorts and transformations from the original raw materials in the state of nature. (1965, p. 86)

A transvection is a concept of action that involves many interrelated transactions among firms and other organisations required to bring it about. These transactions take place in the context of many types of relations between firms and other organisations that define the networks in which these firms operate. There have been few attempts to map the full set of transactions and the firms and organisations involved in completing a transvection. One attempt was made by Alderson and his colleagues in the 1950s for all products used in building a house in Philadelphia (Cox and Goodman 1956). This demonstrated the complex web of transactions and organisations involved. Another example is in Vaile et al.'s (1952) marketing text, *Marketing in the American Economy*. In one chapter they considered the complexities of breakfast and proceeded to trace the origins of all the food consumed by an American household for this meal. Another notable early example is the work of Ralph Breyer, who studied the distribution and production networks for a variety of industrial and consumer products and services in the USA in the 1920s. Figure 1.8 shows his mapping of the complex webs of relations among types of firms involved in the marketing of cotton textiles. While these early writers clearly understood the role and importance of the networks of relations in which firms are embedded, it was not until more recent times that the significance of these networks has been understood in mainstream business and marketing thinking.

Networks may be depicted in terms of linked sets of individual firm value chains, or what Michael Porter originally called value systems. A firm's value chain depends on inputs supplied by other firms that may themselves be intermediate components or raw materials that become inputs for still other firms' value-adding activities. In other words, a firm's value chain is

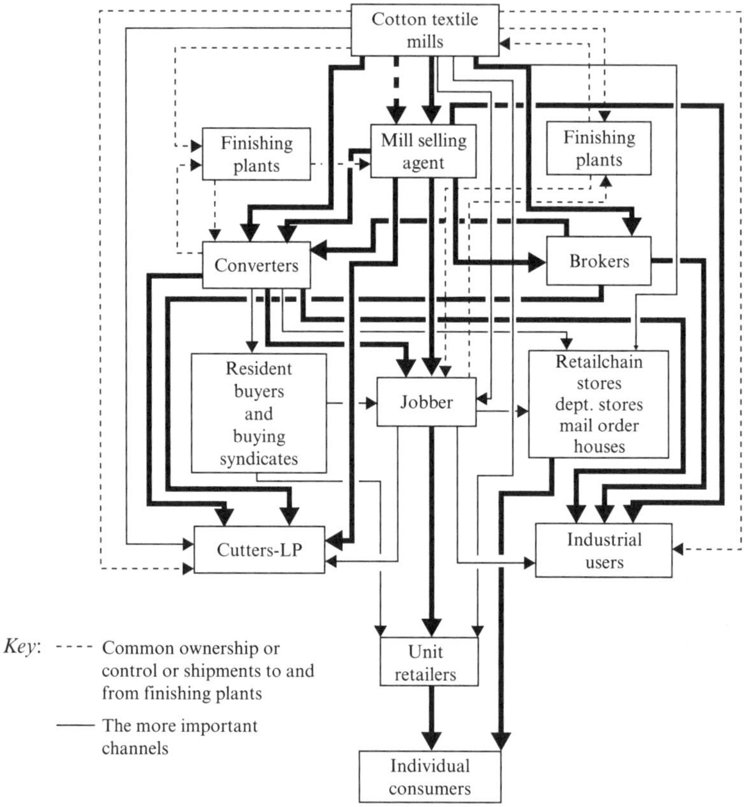

Source: Breyer (1931).

Figure 1.8   *The marketing system for cotton textiles in the USA in
              the 1920s*

embedded in a larger stream of value chain activities that involves a number
of firms and other organisations, as depicted in Figure 1.9. Porter (1985)
highlights many different types of potential linkages between and within
firms' value activities that serve to demonstrate the nature, role and importance of intra- and interfirm webs of relations among those performing
these interconnected value activities.

The concepts of value chains and value systems focus on the individual
firm and how it is linked to other firms in networks of relationships. We are
also interested in the networks of relations from a more macro perspective.
This is particularly relevant when issues of government industry and trade
policy are considered. For example, Porter (1990) has extended his depiction

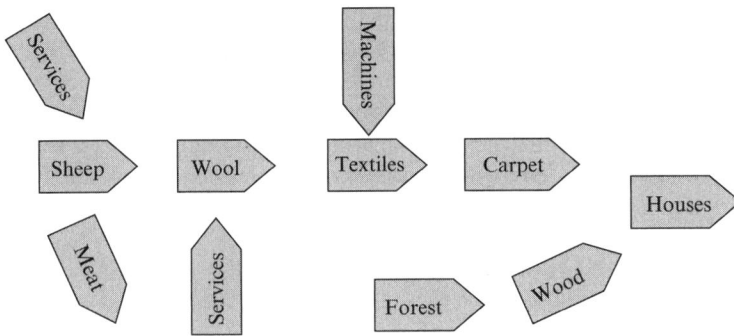

Figure 1.9   Linked value chains – the value system

and analysis of value chains and systems to the level of industries in his book *The Competitive Advantage of Nations*. This book describes the results of studies of the competitiveness of various nations' firms and industries. A particular focus is the role of industry clusters, involving closely competing as well as supportive industries, in driving and sustaining a nation's competitive strengths. The developing of industry clusters, such as in the computing industry in Silicon Valley in the USA and in the textile industry in Northern Italy, is seen as instrumental in galvanising technological development and international competitiveness. Porter's analyses have been influential in shaping many nations' trade and industry policies. Other researchers, including me, have studied the role and importance of interfirm and intra-firm relations and networks in supporting international competitiveness. I shall return to this topic in later chapters.

The point here is to demonstrate the rich networks of relations in which firms operate, and how the nature and development of these relations and the way firms attempt to manage themselves as participants of them is of fundamental importance to a firm's survival and growth.

I now turn to another basic question about relations. It is all very well to describe the range of relations and networks that make up a modern market economy, but why do such relations and networks exist? I provide some answers to this question in the next section. Chapters 2 and 3 deal with it in more detail.

WHY DO RELATIONSHIPS AND NETWORKS EXIST?

Relations are an inextricable part of our biology and the organisation of society. As already noted, we exist as a result of interactions between our mother and father, and are born dependent on others to rear us. But there are more than biological bases for relations – although sex helps. Humans are social animals. They live in families and communities in which there is specialisation and division of labour. Only Robinson Crusoe had to do everything for himself – until his man Friday came along. But even Robinson Crusoe relied on the efforts of others in terms of the material and equipment he was shipwrecked with, and the education and training he had received earlier in his life.

Relations and networks are important in stabilising markets and allowing economic actors to function effectively. Without such relations all would be a sea of chaotic, unpredictable mayhem in which little planning and efficiency would be possible, and complex structures of specialists impossible to establish and maintain. As Neil Fligstein, one of the important voices of modern economic sociology, argues: '[T]he search for stable interactions with competitors, suppliers, and workers is the main cause of social structures in markets. The tactics we observe in business are oriented toward producing stable social relations' (2001, p. 18).

But this still leaves unanswered the key question of why depend on others in the first place; why not avoid this altogether? Relations arise because of the division of labour that exists in social and economic life. This division of labour arises in part because we are social animals and need to interact to continue our existence. But specialisation also leads to economies or efficiencies in the performance of activities because of the economies of scale and scope that arise. We will explore these principles in more detail in Chapter 2, but once we divide up labour we must provide for its coordination, or we shall only be able to access the fruits of our own labour. The coordination of effort is an unavoidable consequence of the division of effort. Even when a single individual organises their activities so that they do not try to do everything at once, they need to coordinate the different activities to ensure that goals are achieved and conditions adapted to. But the situation becomes more complex when more than one individual is involved. Then we have to provide for the coordination of effort between minds and people.

Economists refer to the costs of coordination as transaction costs. And just as we seek efficient use of our resources in carrying out activities, or what we may refer to as reducing the costs of producing outputs, we also seek efficiencies in the coordination or governance of activities, or what we may refer to as reducing the transaction costs involved. The total costs of creating and delivering value to customers is the sum of production costs and transaction costs. Transaction costs relate directly to the issue of relationships and transactions among people and firms. It is through such relations that we get access to the resources and outputs of others, and through such interactions and relations we also co-create new resources. Moreover, in this way we also gain access to and co-create an important and invisible resource: knowledge. Relations and networks are both pipes and prisms: they are ways of creating and accessing resources, and they are also the lenses through which we view and make sense of the world. Of course, our relations and networks do not supply us with an unbiased reading of the world. It is a fundamental paradox that they both enable and constrain us. They enable us through creation of and access to resources and knowledge, and they constrain us through the limits of the resources and knowledge we are able to create and access. Every firm and person is embedded in a unique set of relations with their own history, which can be the source of competitive and cooperative advantages and weaknesses.

Transaction costs as well as production costs are the focus of much of economics, marketing and other business disciplines, and we will review the theories that have been developed in Chapter 2. But costs are only half of the problem; it is the values that are created as a result of incurring these costs that are of central interest to people and firms, not just the costs. It is to these values that I now turn.

THE VALUE OF RELATIONS AND NETWORKS

Approaches to Relationship Marketing

I want to make an important distinction between two approaches to what is often referred to in the marketing literature as 'relationship marketing'. I have pointed to the networks of relations in which firms are embedded and the important role they play in firm survival and growth. Marketing management from this perspective is about the development and management of a firm's relations with other firms, including customers and suppliers, and the marrying of this with the internal relations within the firm. This is a rather generic view of the link between marketing and relations and networks. But in the literature the importance of relations and networks has been emphasised in recent times by scholars coming from a variety of disciplinary perspectives. In marketing, relationship marketing concepts have emerged from three domains of marketing teaching and research: industrial or business-to-business marketing, consumer marketing, and services marketing. Writers from each of these areas bring particular perspectives to bear on the nature of markets and marketing and the role of management. In this book I try to incorporate each such view into a comprehensive overview, but some writers would want to maintain a greater separation and adversarial position with regard to the ideas and orientations of writers with other perspectives.

One division in particular is worthy of attention. It roughly corresponds to the distinction between consumer, including services, marketing and industrial marketing. Consumer marketing has tended to dominate the mainstream of marketing writing, even though business-to-business (B2B) transactions account for a far greater proportion of GNP in any economy than business-to-consumer (B2C) transactions. The term 'relationship marketing' has its origins in consumer marketing. The focus here is one-sided, in that the seller is assumed to be the active party in markets and the individual consumer is the target of the seller's attention. The kinds of relations that underlie relationship marketing here are similar to a fisherman's relationship to fish. Marketing is viewed as something that is done to or for the consumer. Relationship marketing has been described by some as a paradigm shift because it shifted attention from competing to gain customers to competing to retain customers. The importance of customer retention arose with the realisation that it often costs more to gain a new customer than to keep an existing one. Regular, loyal customers have additional value in that they can be a source of positive word-of-mouth advertising and could become customers for more value-added products and services with higher margins. But the essential idea is that relationship marketing is something sellers engage in in order to gain and retain customers and thereby form a relationship with them. This one-sided view of relations contrasts with the view emerging from B2B contexts.

B2B relations and networks play a role in consumer and services marketing. They include relations with distributors, advertising and research agencies, and complementary service and product suppliers. Even here, consumer-focused writers tend to emphasise a one-sided view. The focus is on developing partnerships or other types of cooperative relations to serve the overall goal of gaining and retaining customers. While I do not disagree with the underlying motives and rationale for this approach, it is too narrow-minded. It fails to address the role of non-cooperative relations and how they are managed, and it fails to recognise the role of the other party in actively shaping, co-producing and co-regulating relationships and their outcomes.

The 'markets-as-networks' tradition was born in a different context to that of the more dominant consumer marketing approaches. Its origins are mostly in Europe, where industrial, technology-based marketing is more prevalent – at least in terms of some of the better-known companies. And there is a long and deep history of business and business relations in Europe compared to the USA, where fast-moving consumer goods (FMCG) marketing has led marketing thinking by and large. International marketing is also more the norm as the diverse countries of Europe live close to each other and have a long history (not always congenial) of business, political and other relations and interactions with each other.

In such contexts the role and importance of often long-term business relations is difficult to ignore. It is this context that gave birth to the Industrial Marketing and Purchasing (IMP) group, originally made up of European-based researchers but now extending to all parts of the world. Its focus was on developing an alternative to the mainstream 4Ps (product, pricing, promotion and placement) approach to marketing that dominates marketing textbooks. I describe their thinking in more detail in later chapters. Here I want only to draw a sharp distinction between an approach to marketing and business arising in this context and that arising from a focus on fast-moving consumer goods (FMCG).

Collaborative Advantage

> People who declare that true intimacy means you don't have to worry about being polite will soon run out of people who want to be intimate with them.
> (Judith Martin, *Miss Manners' Basic Training: Eating*)

The struggle for survival in business has often been portrayed as a Darwinian struggle in which the fittest survive. Fittest in turn is interpreted in terms of the characteristics of the individual firms that survive. This has led many researchers in management and marketing to search for the key competences or skills or resources that distinguish successful from less successful firms. This type of reasoning plays an important part in our understanding of firm success. Just as in ecological systems, there is natural selection in which the fittest survive, but it is more complex than this suggests. First, what is fittest depends on the context of other players and strategies, what we may refer to as the game we are playing and, as a result, cooperative elements enter into the struggle for survival. We don't and firms don't survive on their own. They depend on other firms and organisations for resources and knowledge, and thus must consider their needs as well as their own if they are to survive and to have relation partners who want to continue to relate to them – as the quotation that began this section implies.

Firms are not islands. They are embedded in networks of business and non-business relations on which they depend for their survival. Firms exist and persist as much because they are chosen by others to interact with as because they are able to choose whom they interact with. The relevance and importance of this dimension of competition is reflected in the concept of 'collaborative advantage' first proposed by Rosabeth Moss Kanter (1994). Competition and cooperation are not alternatives or opposites; they are complementary concepts: we cooperate to compete and compete to cooperate.

We can see the role of cooperation in competition by building on Kenichi Ohmae's (1982) depiction of a market in terms of the strategic triangle of

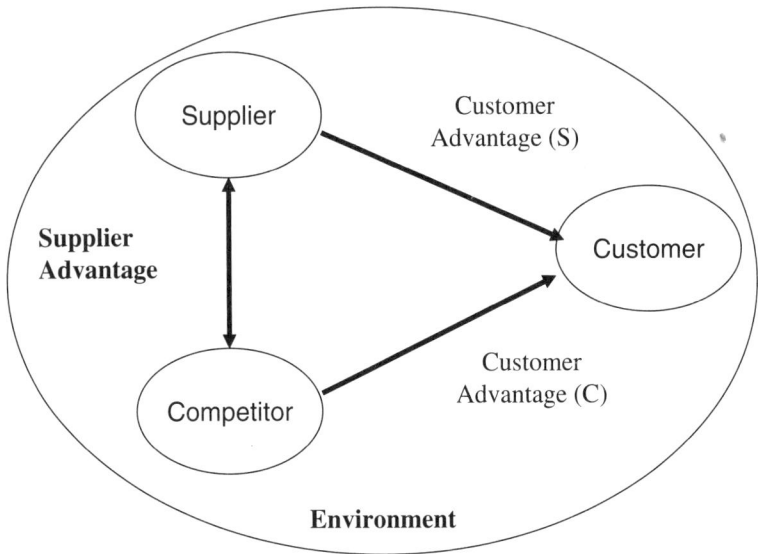

Source: Ohmae (1982, p. 92).

Figure 1.10   The strategic triangle

supplier, competitor and customer, as shown in Figure 1.10. Suppliers seek to develop and offer value to customers or advantages in using its market offerings. Customer advantage or value is in the eye of the beholder; it is perceived value that matters, as perceived by the customer.

For customers to perceive advantage, benefits must exceed costs, which may be summarised in terms of a market value equation as follows:

Customer-perceived value in using supplier X's offer = Perceived benefits of X's offer *minus* perceived costs of X's offer

But, in a competitive market, suppliers compete with other suppliers in offering customer advantage and, in order to survive, they must offer *competitive or differential advantage*. They must offer customer advantages greater than competition, as perceived by the customer. The ability to offer this depends on what Ohmae terms 'supplier advantage'. Supplier advantage in turn stems from the resources of the supplier relative to its competitors, or its *resource advantages*. But what are these resources, and what characteristics of resources give rise to competitive advantage? There has been much theory development and research regarding this in the resource-based theory of the firm. It has been recognised that the relevance

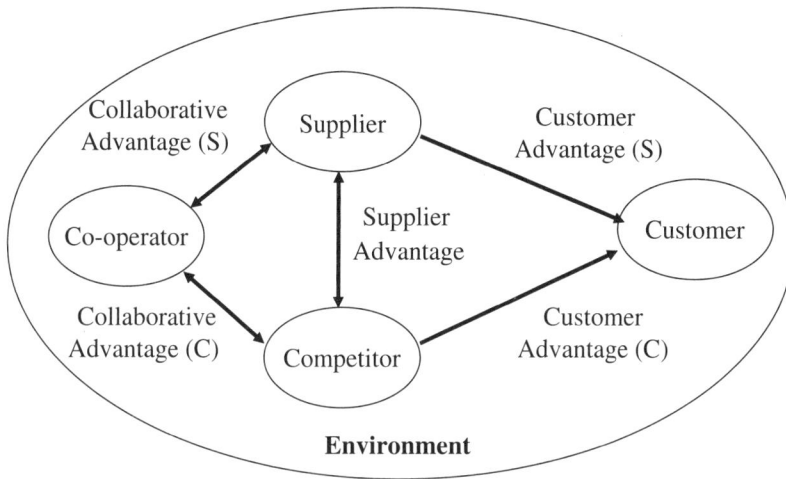

Source: Based on Ohmae (1982).

Figure 1.11 Collaborative advantage

and importance of different resources vary by competitive and customer context and over time – especially in a dynamic environment where needs, technologies and resources are continually changing.

Relationships can be an important type of resource, and the ability to develop, maintain and adapt relationships is itself an important type of resource or capability. This leads to an extension of Ohmae's triad by adding in a further element – cooperators. This is depicted in Figure 1.11.

A firm's source of competitive advantage depends on its collaborative advantage, and this in part depends on its competitive advantages. A supplier's, as well as a competitor's, ability to offer customer advantage depends in part on the resources and knowledge they are able to develop and access through their relations and networks. They compete to develop relations with the same or different cooperators, such as suppliers, distributors, complementors and even competitors. But a supplier's or competitor's ability to develop and maintain productive relations with others depends on the competitive advantages it is able to provide. Successful firms generally find it easier to find willing cooperators than less successful firms.

Relations and networks are different types of resources from those usually considered in resource-based theories of the firm. They are not controlled by the firm; they are co-produced and maintained through interactions over time, and there are potential conflicts as well as communalities of interests. For a firm to develop and maintain valuable relations with various types of cooperators, it must be able to offer value to the counterparts involved. In other words, there are many types of 'customers', or stakeholders, that are simultaneously involved in meeting a focal customer's requirements. This underscores the interconnections among relations and the way interactions and relations do not occur in isolation from other interactions and relations. Interactions in any focal relation are connected to, directly and indirectly, a network of interdependent relations spanning different industries, technologies and, increasingly, nations. This enables and limits management's ability to understand and control the factors and resources contributing to its own success and survival.

The problem is not hopeless and beyond our ability to cope. Obviously rich and varied business ecosystems have been developed by people over time and, by and large, we seem to succeed in navigating our individual ways forward through these complex, dynamic webs of business life. But there are winners and losers. Business ecosystems, like ecological systems, evolve. No amount of consulting advice from the best species around, we suspect, could have saved the dinosaurs. In the same way we must rethink what we mean by management theory, the role of consultants, and the role and value of management and marketing theory generally.

I shall return to these issues. But now let us consider what the nature and dimensions of market relations and networks are, how and why they come into existence, how they end, and how they operate, develop and evolve over time. Then we shall be in a position to see how best to manage or be managed by the relations and networks in which we operate and how to develop appropriate rules and regulations.

2. Why business relations and networks exist I: specialisation and the economics of insourcing and outsourcing[1]

INTRODUCTION

Why do business relations and networks exist, and what role do they play for firms and the economy generally? Much has been written about this, but it boils down to two basic reasons. First, they are the means by which the fruits of the division of labour in a society are realised: the way the activities, skills, resources and outputs of people and firms specialising in different tasks are accessed, combined, recombined and coordinated in order to produce and deliver value in the form of desired products and services. Second, they play a central role in shaping the way an economic system develops and evolves through their impact on innovation, learning and knowledge development. Through these roles business relations and networks extend what a firm can do, know and think. They act as both pipes and prisms, providing the means of accessing and using the resources, knowledge and skills of others, and the means by which the firm can know and understand the problems and opportunities it faces (Podolny 2001).

In this chapter I focus on the first of these reasons. Chapter 3 examines the role of business relations and networks in the development and evolution of an economy.

To appreciate the role that business relations and networks play in creating and delivering value in society we need to understand the work that has to be done to provide us with the products and services we use to live our lives. Many types of activities have to be undertaken, divided up among people and firms within and across nations. This division of work takes place because of the advantages of specialisation. By specialising in different activities, people and firms are able to carry out activities more efficiently. But once work is divided up in this way, the activities and outputs of the different types of specialists have to be coordinated and recombined in order to create and deliver value in the form of the products and services

demanded by society. Recombining and coordinating work is another type
of work that has to be undertaken, which itself can be divided up in various
ways.

Robinson Crusoe, alone on his island, had only himself to rely on and did
all the work, including recombining and coordinating different activities
and their outputs. Once specialisation takes place among people and firms,
recombining and coordinating work becomes more difficult, as it involves
interacting with other people and firms, and exchanging outputs of products and services. Business relations emerge out of the interactions and
exchanges taking place, and they can both help and hinder the processes
involved. Within firms, the work of recombining and coordinating the activities of people and departments is done through the formal relations
specified in a management hierarchy and the associated rules and procedures, as well as through informal relations that develop over time among
those involved. Between firms, recombining and coordinating is done via
market exchange agreements and through the development of various types
of formal and informal business relations.

In short, business relations and networks exist for two interrelated
reasons: (a) to enable the division of work – the patterns of specialisation among and within firms that improve economic efficiency; and (b)
to enable the recombining and coordinating of work – the way the activities of specialists are linked together to create and deliver value to
customers.

In this chapter I examine the economic reasons for specialisation within
and between firms, and the factors affecting firms' decisions about which
activities to insource, to perform within the firm, and which to rely on
others to perform – to outsource. I will show how various types of
economies of specialisation play a role and that individual firms are
limited in the extent to which they can take full advantage of them, no
matter how big they are. Specialisation between firms overcomes some of
these limits, permitting firms to gain further advantage of economies of
specialisation through outsourcing. However, relying on other firms is not
without its problems because of the need to recombine and coordinate
activities across firm boundaries, which in turn limits the nature and extent
of outsourcing and hence specialisation between firms.

The pattern of specialisation within and between firms changes over time
as new technologies for performing activities emerge, new resources are discovered, and demands for products and services change. As we shall see in
Chapter 3, business relations and networks play a key role in technological
development and in the discovery, creation and delivery of new types of
products and services.

THE WORK OF BUSINESS

The work of business begins with the original assortment of resources provided by nature, as a result of physical, chemical, geological and biological processes. From these, various types of intermediate assortments of products and services are created by the activities of people and firms. Extractive activities remould material resources into semi-processed forms such as iron ore, bauxite and coal; agriculture and aquaculture turn natural resources into milk, meat, fruit and vegetables; and education systems turn individuals into people who can perform useful tasks in society. These intermediate products are transformed and transferred in space and time in various ways and in various stages into the final assortments of products and services we consume. The work involved has to be done by someone if value is to be created and delivered, and is divided up among various types of firms and other organisations that make up the economic system of a society, including the final consumers themselves. This division of work in turn gives rise to various types of exchange relations as people and firms seek to avail themselves of the outputs of other specialists in order to carry out their own activities.

Wroe Alderson, one of the founders of modern marketing theory, characterised the work involved in creating value into four generic types of sorting activities – collecting, assorting, allocating and sorting out – based on two underlying dimensions. First, activities are involved either in building up assortments or breaking them down, and the assortments created or broken down are either qualitatively or quantitatively different. Quantitatively different assortments are homogeneous collections of such things as materials, information, funds, products and services, including the stocks of similar products produced by extractive industries and mass production, as well as the potential to offer similar services by specialist service firms such as transport, advertising and research firms. Qualitatively different assortments are heterogeneous in their value and use, including the assortment of products and services required by firms to produce goods and services, and households to meet a family's needs. The four types of sorting functions are summarised in Table 2.1.

THE ECONOMIES OF SPECIALISATION

Why don't firms perform all the activities involved in creating and supplying the products and services they offer for sale? Surely, if a firm could do the tasks just as well itself, it would do them, and not rely on others in respect of whom it may have only limited influence and understanding.

Table 2.1   Business activities as types of sorting

	Breaking down	Building up
Quantity: homogeneous	Allocating (e.g. distributing, communicating, diffusing, paying, financing, selling, leasing)	Accumulating (e.g. buying, renting, storing, saving, collecting, attending to)
Quality: heterogeneous	Sorting out (e.g. processing, timing, branding, segmenting, qualifying, grading, valuing, analysing)	Assorting (e.g. manufacturing, positioning, differentiating, promoting, packaging, assembling)

The economies or benefits arising from specialisation, the division of work among people and firms, explains why one person or firm can perform an activity better than another. Specialisation takes place at all levels of a business system. People, teams, departments, divisions and firms specialise in different assortments of activities. At the extreme, one person could specialise in one activity only, rather like the description of the pin factory in Adam Smith's classic *The Wealth of Nations*. Here, instead of each person making the whole pin, the task is divided into a number of activities and each person specialises in one of them. Why does this help? There are several reasons that are part of any basic economics course. People learn from doing one task many times and get better at it, even suggesting improvements; people naturally differ in their abilities to do different things and vary due to prior experience or education; there is no downtime when switching tasks and people get better at handing on tasks to each other. Of course there are downsides to this as people can become bored, their physical abilities may become damaged due to overuse, and there are other factors limiting the gains from specialisation.

Just as individuals can gain from specialising, so can groups of people, including teams, departments, firms and even networks of firms. A nice illustration of network specialisation is Toyota's car production system:

> Toyota's knowledge of how to make cars lies embedded in highly specialized social and organizational relationships that have evolved through decades of common effort. It rests in routines, information flows, ways of making decisions, shared attitudes and expectations, and specialized knowledge that Toyota managers, workers, suppliers and purchasing agents, and others have about different aspects of their business, about each other, and about how they all can work together. (Badaracco, 1991, p. 87)

Not only can people and groups of people gain from specialisation; so can machinery, buildings and land. Machinery is designed to do different things, and so are buildings. Land varies in its ability to support different types of activities, depending on the local climate, material resources and its position in relation to other resources and markets. There is also specialisation by time as well as place, including the seasonal patterns of agriculture, the man-made cycles of rest and fun, festivals, fashion and tastes, and the sequence effects that lead to some tasks being done before or after others. In short, all the resources required to carry out activities can and do specialise in various ways, and efficiency comes from appropriately matching resources and tasks.

What prevents a firm gaining fully from the benefits of using specialised resources such as people, machines and places? The reason is that, as Florence (1953) pointed out, the economies of specialisation are only potential economies. The conditions have to be right to enable them to be used effectively and efficiently without incurring additional costs elsewhere that outweigh any gains. There are three types of factors at work. First are the transaction costs, including the time involved in acquiring and using specialised resources that may outweigh the benefits. Second, a firm's ability to take advantage of specialised resources is limited by the size of its market. Third, the benefits or economies of different types of specialisation are sometimes mutually incompatible. I consider each of these in turn.

Transaction Costs

The division of labour necessarily requires the coordination of labour. Once activities are divided up among people, machines and places, some means has to be provided for their coordination and recombining in order to accomplish the overall tasks of which they are a part. The costs of coordinating and directing the contributions of the different parties and resources involved are known as transaction costs, i.e. *between* actions. Within a firm, transactions take place between people and units specialising in different activities, such as between purchasing and production, marketing and sales, engineering and production. These transactions are organised through the formal management hierarchy and the systems and procedures in place. An exchange agreement exists between the employees and the firm, whereby the former agree to provide their labour services in return for payments and rewards. In practice the processes of coordination within firms are more complex, with both formal and informal relations and communication systems playing an important role, as was pointed out in Chapter 1.

Coordination or transaction costs can exceed the benefits from additional specialisation. For example, if one person performs all the activities involved in supplying a product to a customer, they are coordinated through that person's mind, memory and actions. If we divide the task between two people, they have to coordinate their actions through one or more transactions between them. Three people results in three transactions (a–b, a–c, b–c), which are interconnected and have to be coordinated, four results in six transactions and so on, with the number of transactions given by the formula $n(n-1)/2$. As the number of specialists increases, the coordinating task becomes ever more complex because the number of transactions grows geometrically while the number of specialists grows arithmetically. Eventually transaction costs outweigh the benefits of more specialisation. Studies show how the number of people involved in coordinating or managing tasks within firms becomes an ever larger proportion as firms expand and coordinating costs become a larger proportion of total costs.

Managing and coordinating is another type of activity that must be done for an overall task to be carried out, whether within one person's mind and body in one place or among people, teams, departments or firms. Dividing up work creates coordinating work or, more precisely, changes the nature of the coordinating activities. Because the amount of coordinating work grows faster than the number of specialists to coordinate, average coordination costs tend to rise as firms expand. This means that coordinating costs are increasing cost activities. But be careful, this does *not* mean that managers are becoming less efficient; it is just that the amount of coordinating and directing work expands faster than firm size and output. Firms employ specialist managers, machinery and systems to improve coordination efficiency, but the underlying problem cannot be avoided. Specialisation results in efficiencies, as it does for any activity, and holds down coordination costs to some extent. It also creates additional layers of coordination and management in order to coordinate the coordinators!

The faster growth of coordination work as a firm expands is one example of the more general principle of non-proportional change identified by Kenneth Boulding (1953). As a firm or any system expands in one dimension, in this case the number of specialists used, the rate of growth of other dimensions will not expand at the same rate – in this case the number of transactions or the amount of coordinating work to be done. We shall come across other examples of this general principle, which creates both economies and diseconomies for firms, relations and networks.

To jump ahead in the argument, the problem of coordination is not solved by handing it over to the market, by outsourcing a specialist task such as production of a component or supply of a specialised service to an external supplier. The coordinating work cannot be avoided. A specialist supplier may be smaller than the contracting firm, as when a component supplier supplies a major car manufacturer, an advertising agency services a multinational firm, or a local retailer sells products produced by a huge food producer. The smaller specialist will therefore have lower average coordinating costs, as reflected in, say, its management overheads. However, the transactions and coordinating activities are not limited to coordination within the supplier and contracting firm. Interfirm transactions and coordination are required to complete the overall task. The firms have to make contact with each other, work out what each is to do, when and how, agree on prices and payments, draw up contracts, monitor performance, move the finished components to where they are required and fit them into the vehicle. If the relevant market for components resembles the economist's perfectly competitive market, then market transactions are a costless way of coordinating the activities of firms. All components are the same, all buyers and sellers are the same, information is complete and communication costs are zero, there are no transportation costs, markets set a ruling price based on aggregate demand and supply. But this ideal type of market does not exist in practice and this affects the costs of market transactions and how they compare with intra-firm transactions.

The costs and efficiency of market versus intra-firm transactions affect the net benefits of using a specialist supplier. We cannot avoid coordination and management costs by outsourcing; they can only be changed from one form of governance to another, as different people and organisations are used to carry out relevant activities. As I shall explain later, market coordination itself leads to the use of specialists in carrying out different subtasks, resulting in different types of specialist market intermediaries and market transactions.

Market Size

The second type of constraint on a firm's ability to gain from greater use of specialisation is the size of the market. There are several dimensions to this that tend to get ignored in marketing and management books but which are important to understand because they affect the economies of specialisation.

Market and firm size are multidimensional; the scale and scope of firms and markets can vary in many ways. Firm size can refer to the size of a department, an establishment or the whole enterprise. A market can be large or small in terms of total volume or amount traded, the number and types of buyers and sellers, the size of individual transactions and the frequency of purchase. As firms and markets expand, the dimensions of market and firm size change at different rates, giving rise to different types of potential economies and diseconomies – another example of Boulding's principle of non-proportional change. The following subsections introduce three economic principles, identified by Florence (1953), that underlie the economies of specialisation in firms and arise for different dimensions of size.

Principle of multiples

In order to perform any activity, a variety of inputs is required, depending on the type of technology used, including people, machines, land and other specialised resources. The resources used in carrying out activities come with characteristic operating capacities and limits, depending on the activities they are performing. For example, machines are designed to carry out particular tasks and to work most efficiently at particular rates or levels. Typically, a variety of machines is available to do a job, with different operating capacities and cost efficiencies. We can buy a photocopier or printer for our home that is not particularly efficient and operates quite slowly, but it meets our needs. We could also use a larger, more efficient machine that operates much faster but which would be lying idle most of the time and therefore not be very cost-effective. As technology has changed, especially computer technology, these types of machines have become more and more efficient and less costly, and their operating capacities and quality have improved, but the same types of differences still exist. Other factors of production come with characteristic operating capacities, limits and cost levels, including people, land, establishments, firms and enterprises, depending on the tasks they are required to perform and the technology used. People vary in their capacity to perform different activities depending on innate abilities as well as education, training and experience.

There is nothing in the laws of nature that says that the characteristic operating capacities of different factors of production required to perform a task are mutually compatible. Specialist inputs come in different shapes and sizes, with not necessarily the same efficient operating levels, or what is referred to as 'lumpiness in factor inputs'. This causes problems and limits a firm's ability to make full use of the most efficient specialised resources available. Just as you could not justify using a large, efficient copier or printer at home, because it would be standing idle most of the time, acting as a spare table, filing rack or plant stand, so a firm is unable to use more efficient machines that have higher operating capacities than it can use. As spare tables and plant stands in the workplace, large, expensive, specialised machines are not the most efficient thing to use. A simple table is cheaper, versatile and more efficient. The problem is illustrated in Table 2.2, which shows the different activities involved in building a lawn mower.

Table 2.2   The principle of multiples

Activity	Machine capacity	Number of machines	
		Sell 1000	Sell 2000
Engine	1000	1=1000 capacity	2=2000 capacity
Spark plugs	700	2=1400 capacity	3=2100 capacity
Frame	400	3=1200 capacity	5=2000 capacity

Source: Dixon and Wilkinson (1982, pp. 231–2).

Three activities are involved, building the frame, the engine and spark plugs, and each involves the use of a particular type of machine. Ignore all other costs. The efficient working capacity per period of the most efficient machine for each task is shown in column two. These differ and are not mutually compatible. If a firm can sell 1000 units in a period, it will need to use one engine-making machine, two spark plug machines and three frame-making machines. This results in underutilisation of the spark plug and frame-making machine, which drives up costs, as the cost of the machine or its lease costs have to be met from producing 1000 not 1400 spark plugs in the period, and 1200 frames. If a firm could double its sales to 2000 units per period, it would require another engine machine but only one more spark plug machine and two more frame-making machines. Here is another example of non-proportional change as firm size increases. With sales of 2000 per period there is proportionately less excess capacity and costs per unit sold are less. The minimum firm output at which all machines are fully utilised is 14 000 (14 engine machines, 20 spark plug machines and 35 frame machines), which is the lowest common multiple of the three machine capacities – hence the term principle of multiples. A firm could decide to produce 14 000 lawn mowers each period because that is the most efficient, but, unless it could sell that many at a price greater than costs, it would not be worthwhile. There could be other considerations, such as driving competitors out of the market or building future sales, but that takes us beyond the issues being considered here.

The same principle applies to all factors of production, including people, land and buildings. Salespeople have limited operating capacities in terms of the number and types of customers they can serve in a day or week; accountants can only handle so much accounting work efficiently in a period; market researchers can design so many surveys, analyse so many data, write so many reports. Buildings and warehouses have fixed capacities for storing products and handling different types of activities; managers can supervise so many people depending on the nature of the task.

In general, any system designed to carry out a set of activities has a most efficient operating capacity that depends on the technology being used and the inputs required. This is depicted in basic economics texts in terms of how the efficiency of a firm varies at different levels of output in the short and long run. As output expands, a firm exceeds the capacity of its existing resources and costs increase. But in time it can reorganise itself and use different technologies, specialist machines and people in order to be more efficient at the larger scale. If it had used this way of doing things at the lower scale of output, it would have been less efficient due to excess capacity and idle resources. The long-run average cost curve shows how a firm can adjust its technology and use of specialised machines, people and other resources to be most efficient at any given scale. This long-run cost curve shows decreasing returns to scale if average costs fall as the scale of operations increases. The principle of multiples suggests that increasing returns to scale are likely because of increases in the degree of specialisation of labour and other factor inputs that are possible as size increases. More specialised and efficient people, machines, plants and equipment can be more fully utilised the larger the scale of operation of the firm.

Do such economies of scale continue for ever? If so, we would expect a single firm eventually to dominate the production of each type of product or service. But typically this does not happen, and not because anti-monopoly laws prevent it. There are other constraints on the size of the firm, including market size, how much of a firm's output customers are willing to buy at a price that covers its costs, and the existence of increasing cost activities, i.e. average costs that increase with scale rather than decrease. We have already met one such activity – coordination and management activities or transaction costs. Marketing costs, as we shall see, are another type of increasing cost activity.

Market constraints on firm size are summarised in Adam Smith's words: 'The division of labour is limited by the extent of the market.' The economies to be gained from the use of specialised people, machines, plant and equipment are only potential economies, because they depend on a firm's ability to fully utilise the specialised factor inputs. A firm not only has to produce the output, but find customers for it. It is no good storing the output in a big warehouse in the hope that it will eventually sell.

There are two ways of thinking about market constraints. The first is reflected in many textbooks in terms of the demand curve limiting the output of the firm. Here the demand curve shows the amount people are prepared to buy at each price level. This is generally depicted as downward sloping,

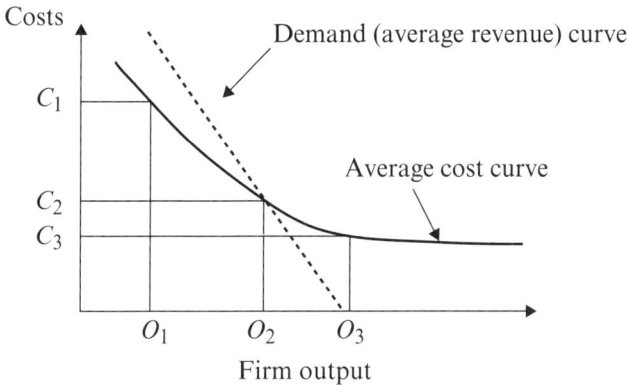

Figure 2.1   Firm cost and demand curves

with lower volumes demanded at higher prices. So long as average costs are less than average revenue or price, a firm is profitable. Maximum profits are made, as we learn in microeconomics, when marginal costs equal marginal revenue. However, managers generally have only a very vague idea about what these costs are and it is not relevant for the argument I wish to make anyway.

The situation is depicted in Figure 2.1, which shows a downward-sloping long-run average cost curve and a market demand curve for the firm's output. Costs decrease as the scale of the firm increases, such as from O_1 to O_2. The maximum output level the firm can produce and still cover costs is O_2. Beyond this customers are only willing to pay less per unit on average than it costs to supply the output. In other words, demand conditions stop the firm getting any larger, even though there may still be additional economies of specialisation to gain.

This is one way of interpreting the meaning of the phrase 'market size limits the division of labour', although it is rather simplistic. It ignores issues such as coordinating costs and marketing costs, and assumes that the demand curve is fixed and does not depend on the marketing activities of the firm. Firms can seek out additional customers by informing and persuading more people through advertising, salespeople and promotion, by reaching out to more distant markets and by adapting their products and services to reach additional market segments. How do we include these activities and what is the shape of the firm's cost curves for performing them?

George Stigler (1951), the distinguished economist, in a much-cited article on the way markets limit the division of labour and specialisation in firms, distinguished between increasing cost and decreasing cost activities. He was not too specific about what increasing cost activities are but, if they exist, they limit the growth of the firm. Figure 2.2 shows why this occurs.

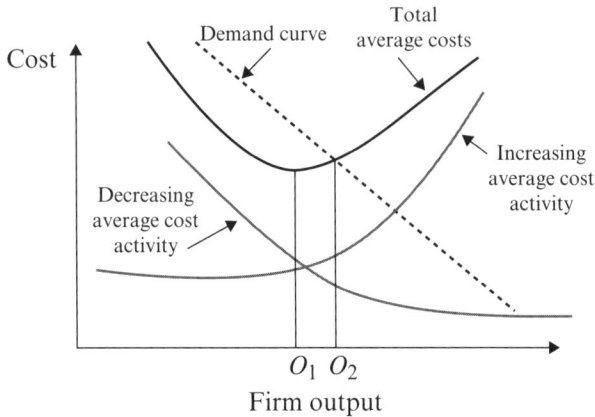

Figure 2.2   Increasing and decreasing cost activities

Increasing cost activities eventually make total costs rise. In Figure 2.2, minimum total costs occur at O_1 and the firm can expand to an output level of O_2 before costs exceed revenues. At greater levels of output further potential economies of specialisation occur, such as in manufacturing, but they are not viable because they are outweighed by increasing cost activities. Coordination and management costs (transaction) costs are one type of increasing cost activity, as was explained earlier. Such costs grow at a faster rate than the number of specialist people and other factors of production that have to be coordinated. Once again it should be noted that coordination activities are not being done inefficiently. Far from it, because, as the scale of such activities increases, more and more specialist people, machinery and systems can be fully utilised, resulting in economies. It is just that the *scale of the activity* expands faster than the scale of the firm, pushing up coordination costs per unit of output – an example of the principle of non-proportional change.

Marketing processes are another type of activity whose scale expands faster than the scale of output of the firm, resulting in increasing costs. Shove (1930) was one of the first to point this out clearly in his discussion of obstacles to the growth of a firm's market share:

> The two most important types for our present purpose are the increases in the cost of *transport* and *marketing* (competitive advertisement and so on) which a firm is liable to encounter as it advances further into its competitors' territory or markets. Singly or together, these diseconomies may well offset the economies of mass-production in the process of manufacture. (Ibid., p. 105)

Transportation costs eventually rise per unit of output because of the greater distances involved in delivering products and services to customers further away from the home base of the firm. For example, as a firm expands its markets beyond its own region to interstate and international markets, average transportation costs will rise. Once again this diseconomy is not due to inefficiencies but to the greater distances involved. As the scale and reach of their transport activities increase, firms will be able more fully to employ specialist personnel, systems and equipment and thereby reap more of the benefits of specialisation. But this will not be able to stop the eventual rise in transportation costs per unit as distance to market increases.

Marketing activities will tend to rise faster than a firm's output as a firm moves further away from its core market. Additional customers come from finding and attracting customers away from other firms through additional advertising and sales efforts for existing products and services and/or through product and service modifications and enhancements. As the scale of a firm's marketing activities increases, it can fully utilise more specialised marketing personnel, systems and equipment, taking further advantage of the principle of multiples. However, such efficiency gains cannot prevent an eventual rise in average marketing costs per unit sold as a firm expands.

In sum, coordination, transport and marketing costs are the types of increasing cost activities depicted in Figure 2.2. They arise because the scale of these activities expands faster than the scale of the firm in terms of sales volume. They are examples of the principle of non-proportional change. They are the source of the diseconomies of scale that limit a firm's ability to expand and take full advantage of the efficiencies of specialisation.

Specialisation among firms can help overcome some of the market and cost limitations on firms' ability to gain from specialisation. But a necessary consequence of this is the dependence of firms on other firms for inputs and services, which creates additional types of problems associated with interfirm transactions and coordination. These are considered below, but first I want to introduce two other principles underlying the benefits of specialisation identified by Florence. They play a part in explaining the benefits of specialisation and lead to the identification of further types of constraints on a firm's ability to exploit fully the benefits of specialisation by itself.

Principle of bulk transaction

Transactions refer to the actions involved in linking and coordinating the actions and contributions of different actors, including people, groups, departments and firms. *Trans*actions result in the exchange of information, ideas, money and material things between actors across time and place, and the costs of carrying out these activities are known as transaction costs, as already noted. Internal transaction costs occur within firms to coordinate and control the people and units of the firm specialising in different parts of the overall value production process, and market or external transaction costs occur with other firms and organisations such as suppliers, distributors and customers.

Transactions have contactual, contractual and material dimensions. Contactual dimensions refer to the communication and search processes by which actors find each other, negotiate agreements as to who is to do what, and monitor and control the transaction. Contractual dimensions refer to transfer of promises, rights and obligations between the parties, their enforcement and the settling of disputes. Material dimensions refer to the transfer of material objects, including people, through time and place, i.e. transportation and storage activities.

The principle of bulk transaction is that the cost of a transaction does not rise in direct proportion to the scale of the transaction, be that an internal or market transaction. It is another type of scale economy, this time linked to the scale of the transaction rather than the scale of the firm. Costs do not rise in direct proportion due to the benefits of specialisation, the ability to make fuller use of specialised people, machines and other factors of production.

As an example, consider the costs involved in negotiating the sale of products or services to another firm. Negotiating time does not rise directly in relation to the total amount bought or sold: the fixed costs of setting up a meeting time, finding out about the other's requirements, establishing rapport and so on are done only once, no matter how large the sale. The negotiation process will vary depending on its complexity, but not directly on the number of units sold, the period of the contract, the money value of the order, and learning curve effects will serve to reduce the costs per unit sold or bought. In addition, only one delivery and payment is required. These economies are a special case of the principle of multiples because the specialised personnel (salesperson and buyer) and systems (delivery and payment) are not being fully utilised by either party to the extent that they negotiate a smaller order than they otherwise could have in the same time. Another way of looking at this is that market constraints limit the potential benefits of specialisation because of the mix of products and services that are demanded and sold. The offering of discounts for bulk purchases is an everyday example of this type of economy. The same principle applies to transactions and negotiations within a firm. The employment contract is a type of specialist 'bulk' contract or transaction by which employees agree to abide by the rules of the firm and the directives of their boss, thereby saving the costs of many smaller individual negotiations. Transportation and storage costs do not rise in direct proportion to the amount transported or stored. The capacity of a truck, warehouse or connecting pipe depends on volume, which increases faster than length, breadth or diameter. Big trucks and buses still require only one driver even if they are paid more and require more training. These are yet more examples of the principle of non-proportional change.

A firm cannot decide to sell (buy) the particular assortment or amount of products and services it finds most efficient to sell in one lot (or buy in one lot) unless a customer requires or is willing to buy that assortment and quanitity (or a seller produces or offers that assortment for sale). But, as we shall see, specialisation among firms can in part overcome some of these limitations.

Principle of pooled risk or massed reserves

The third principle deals with the costs of handling risks such as bad debts or variable demand and supply. It has two names because the same principle has been described in different ways by Florence and later by Stigler (1946, 1951). The basic idea is that things become more predictable in the aggregate, which is essentially the same principle that underlies the central limit theorem in statistics and the principle behind insurance systems. It is very difficult if not impossible to predict individual events such as whether a particular machine will break down, a worker will be ill on a certain day, a particular customer will default on their payment or whether demand in a particular market will be the same as it was last period. But if firms have a large number of machines of a similar type, a sizeable workforce, a large number of customers, or sell to a large number of markets, these types of events become more predictable. This is another type of scale economy, but here the relevant scale dimension is the number of independent variable events of a similar type a firm has to deal with. As this number increases, the degree of risk and associated costs involved decrease as a proportion of the total.

A simple example is given in Table 2.3. This shows the sales of one firm's product at five retail outlets over time in a particular region. The sales for each vary over the four periods but in different ways because of differences in their local markets. If each retailer kept its own buffer stocks, equal to the maximum expected sales in any period, it would incur excess carrying costs due to unsold stocks at the end of some periods. But if a warehouse were set up close by to serve these retailers, the pattern of demand for the warehouse would be as shown in the final row of the table. The degree of variation in total demand is not the sum of the variations in each retailer's sales, because of cancelling-out effects, which reflect economies due to the principle of pooled risk. Because stocks are held centrally, or massed, this principle is sometimes described as that of massed reserves. Holding central stocks or reserves may result in additional efficiencies due to the principle of multiples

Table 2.3   Pooled risk and massed reserves

Firm	Sales per period				
	T1	T2	T3	T4	Max
1	90	30	40	60	90
2	50	90	60	70	90
3	60	90	50	30	90
4	30	40	70	90	90
5	90	60	80	70	90
Total	320	310	300	320	320

and bulk transaction. The warehouse operates on a larger scale than the individual retailers and can better utilise specialised workers, machinery and systems and can gain from volume-to-floor-space efficiencies.

A firm is limited in its ability to gain from this type of economy depending on its ability to pool or aggregate these types of risky but similar events but, through specialisation between firms, these limits can be reduced.

Tradeoffs among Economic Principles

The principles of multiples, bulk transaction and pooled risk are similar in that they all are examples of how the scale of a firm affects the efficiency of performing activities. But each principle focuses on a different dimension of the scale of a firm – the total output of the firm, the size of transactions and the number of independent risky events it deals with. Firms cannot be bigger in all these dimensions at once. Thus a firm that produces and sells a given amount of a product can either have more customers and smaller average transactions or fewer customers and larger average transactions. In the former case it benefits more from the principle of pooled risk in terms of variability in individual customer demand and bad debts, for example, but it is limited in its ability to gain from the principle of bulk transactions because average transaction sizes are small. In the latter case the situation is reversed.

As firms grow, they grow more in some dimensions than in others. This includes changes in the overall output of the firm, the output of different types of products and services, the scale of different activities, the number of customers and the average size of different types of transactions both internally and externally. As a firm grows, it will be able to gain more from some of the principles we have described than others, and this will vary by firm, market, industry and circumstance.

EXTERNAL ECONOMIES: SPECIALISATION AMONG FIRMS

Thus far I have shown how firms gain from economies of specialisation but that they are limited by various dimensions of the market in which they operate. In this section I show how specialisation between firms can alleviate some of these market constraints because specialist firms perform activities and produce and supply products and services on behalf of a number of other firms. From a firm's point of view it gains *external economies* by outsourcing activities that can be done more efficiently by other firms. The same principles underlie the efficiencies of specialisation between firms as the efficiencies of specialisation within firms.

An additional problem arises in that now activities have to be coordinated across organisational boundaries, i.e. through market transactions, rather than within one firm. The relative costs of market versus internal transactions and their effects on the structure and organisation of business is the central focus of transaction cost economics, an important area of research in economics and business generally.

Before we examine the types of efficiencies arising from interfirm specialisation and the effect of transaction costs, we must first distinguish between two important characteristics of activities – *similarity and complementarity* – a distinction first clarified by Richardson (1972). Similar activities are those that require common inputs and technologies and can be performed together by a firm, whereas complementary activities are those that have to be coordinated in order to complete a larger task or function, such as the creation and delivery of products and services to end consumers.

Similar Activities

Firms specialising in a set of similar activities on behalf of other firms gain economies of scale and scope that are not available to the firms they serve. A simple example is that of a specialist supplier of a raw material, component or service required in order to produce and supply different types of products or services. Economies of scale arise from performing the *same* activity on a larger scale such as organising to manufacture the same product on larger scales. As we have seen in the previous section, these economies arise from various economies of specialisation. But, to reiterate, such economies of specialisation are only potential economies in that a firm has to be able to operate at the right scale in terms of the relevant activity in order to take advantage of these economies. And scale here can refer to the scale of the enterprise, establishment or unit, scale of production and sales volume, transaction size and the number of risky independent events (e.g. bad risks) it handles.

If activities are not identical but are similar, there are still potential economies to be gained from carrying out these activities together, or what is called joint production. The resulting economies of specialisation are referred to as *economies of scope* rather than scale because they arise from a firm taking on different activities that require common inputs. The same principles underlie economies of scope and scale. By expanding the scope of its output to include activities that require common inputs not fully utilised by any one type of activity, a firm gains from the principle of multiples. It is able to utilise more fully specialist inputs by spreading their use across similar activities. By transporting different products from a common origin to a common destination, a firm gains from bulk transactions; by buying or selling an assortment of products and services that can be bought or sold together, a firm can gain from the use of specialised people, places, systems and equipment that would otherwise be underutilised. By producing and selling a portfolio of products and services to customers in a variety or markets and countries, a firm spreads its risks and gains from the principle of pooled risk. In general, we may refer to the economies arising from firms specialising in different assortments of similar or identical activities as various types of *aggregation economies*. Figure 2.3 shows how specialisation between firms alters the size of the market or demand function facing a specialist firm compared to those it serves because it is able to aggregate the demand for the same or similar products and services that allows it to gain economies of specialisation its customers cannot. Hence its customers have an incentive to outsource these activities to the specialist.

This applies to decreasing cost and increasing cost activities. For example, the supply of particular components such as spark plugs or frames in our earlier lawn mower example may be outsourced to firms specialising in their production and who supply other lawn mower companies as well as producers of other products requiring the same or similar products. In Figure 2.3(a) this is shown in terms of a specialist supplier operating at a larger-scale O_2 compared to an individual customer who operates at output O_1.

Firms outsource marketing activities, an increasing cost activity, for the same reason. They use specialist research firms and advertising agencies, who work on behalf of a portfolio of clients and can fully utilise specialist inputs; they use distributors, wholesalers and retailers who handle an assortment of products and services that are similar in that they call on common inputs such as people, places and equipment to store, display, buy and sell. This is shown in Figure 2.3(b), where the aggregation of demand by a specialist marketing intermediary offers savings to those using its services that reduce the marketing costs per unit supplied compared to the case of a firm performing the same activities for itself.

(a) Decreasing cost activity

Costs and revenues

Demand curve for one firm

C_1

Demand curve for specialist supplier

C_2

O_1 O_2

Firm output

(b) Increasing cost activity

Costs

Total average costs

Average cost reduction

Marketing costs for firm

Intermediary's costs

Firm output

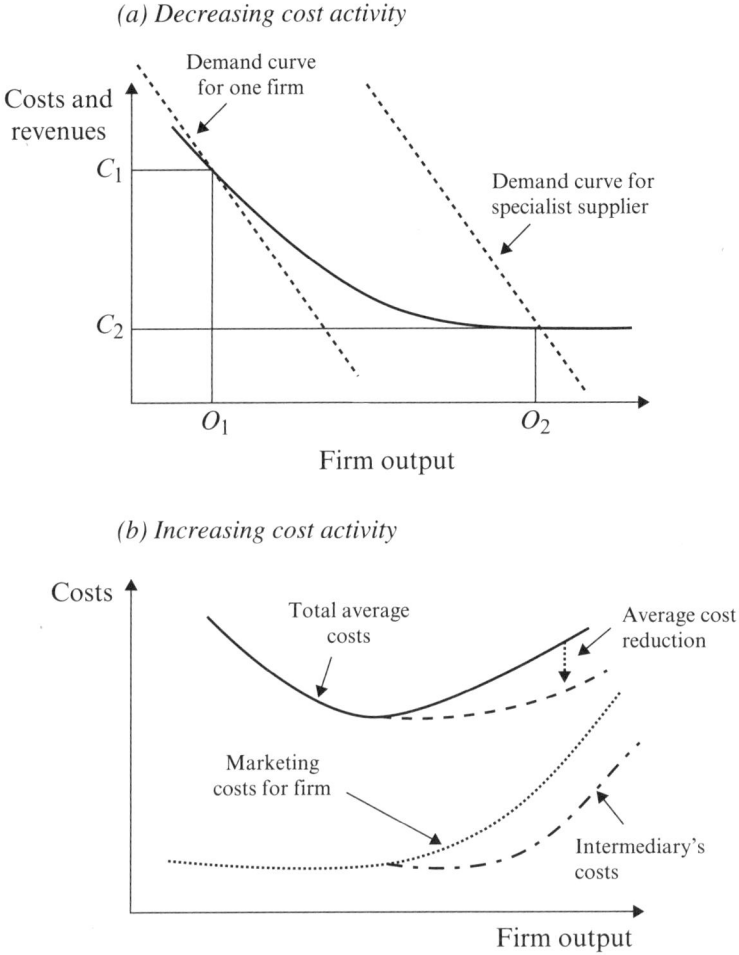

Figure 2.3   The external economies of specialist suppliers

Coordination costs as well as operating or production costs have to be considered. Once we divide up work between firms we have to provide for the coordination of their outputs. There are two aspects to this: that which takes place within firms and that which takes place between firms. Specialisation between firms creates the additional problem of interfirm coordination or market transactions.

In 'perfect market' situations, where all products and services are the same, all buyers and sellers are small and the same, and there are no communication and transport costs, the market is a highly efficient, indeed costless, means of coordination. Firms simply sell all they can produce at the market-determined price and firms specialising in different activities are coordinated in this way across linked sequences of such markets. But real markets are imperfect: they involve heterogeneous and changing sellers and buyers, with limited and asymmetric information, conflicting as well as complementary interests, and uncertainty, and there are communication, negotiation, transport and storage costs. In short, market coordination costs or market transaction costs are not zero, and can be an important cost element.

The costs of market transactions compared to intra-firm coordination costs is the foundation for the theory of the firm developed by Ronald Coase, for which he was awarded a Nobel prize. The essential argument is that, when the costs of market transactions are high due to market 'imperfections' of the type described, firms can gain by internalising the relevant activities, i.e. insourcing, rather than relying on external suppliers. Oliver Williamson has further developed Coase's theory and this has led to considerable research in marketing and business using transaction cost theory to explain industry and channel structures in domestic and international markets.

Coordination costs cannot be considered in isolation from production or operating costs. The efficiency of a firm depends on gaining economies of specialisation in performing both activities and, as I shall show shortly, there are tradeoffs to be considered between coordination and production costs. A firm may choose to insource an activity rather than rely on a specialist supplier, even though the supplier has access to economies of specialisation not directly available to the firm itself. It does this because the costs and risks associated with finding and using such a supplier outweigh the gains. Or, a firm could outsource an activity to a specialist that offers little if any additional economies of specialisation in carrying out the activity but provides significant economies in terms of coordination costs. An example of the latter is when a firm uses a specialist agent in a foreign market because of the market connections they already have with potential customers, and their efficiency and effectiveness in carrying out the various types of relationship functions. These include being a source of market information, a means of local innovation/adaptation, local image enhancement and as a source of referrals and introductions. I discuss these functions of relations in more detail in later chapters. These functions involve various types of interfirm coordinating activities. They are the means by which customers and suppliers are identified, and exchange relations are developed and sustained. If the firm were to take on these activities itself, it would be far less efficient and effective in carrying them out. It would have to find and hire local specialists, and develop its own local connections and image. If the costs and risks of using a specialist local distributor were too high, then a firm might decide to insource these activities by setting up its own local organisation.

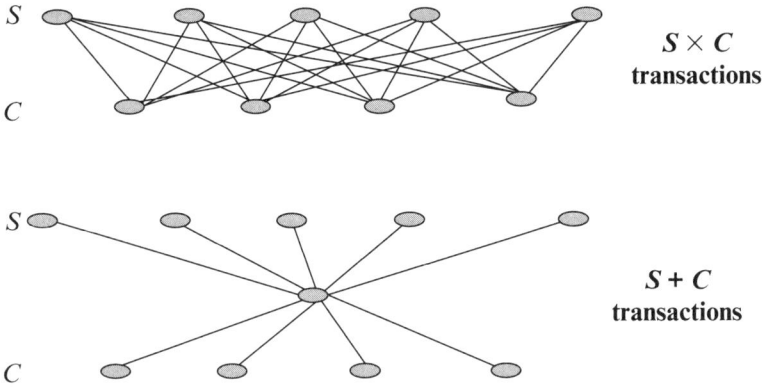

Figure 2.4   The economy of reduced transactions

Figure 2.4 illustrates some of the tradeoffs involved between production and coordination costs. It is a familiar diagram used in many marketing textbooks to show the economies of intermediaries. But the analysis is usually incomplete. In this example there are five firms supplying products to four customers. In the top network each supplier (*S*) supplies directly to each customer (*C*) and incurs all the costs in producing and supplying the products and services, including the transaction costs associated with dealing with each customer. Ignore other costs for now, such as those associated with suppliers and customers outsourcing other activities to specialist suppliers or what happens after customers buy the products and use them. The suppliers may be in direct competition and the customers spread their purchases among them over time, or they may be supplying complementary products and services that each customer requires.

In the bottom network a specialist intermediary is introduced to whom the firms supply all their products or assign service responsibility. The intermediary in turn supplies to each customer the assortment of products and services they demand. A new type of economy of specialisation arises, which has been called the principle of reduced contacts (Hall 1949). Without the intermediary there are $5 \times 4 = 20$ individual transactions to complete, involving communication, negotiation, transportation, payments, before- and after-sales service and so on. With the intermediary the number of transactions has been reduced to $5 + 4 = 9$, and this presumably results in some cost savings. Moreover, the transactions between the intermediary and the firms and customers are much larger, because the intermediary buys all the products and services required by all the customers from each supplier and sells to each customer an assortment of products obtained from different suppliers in one bulk transaction. It is the same situation when we do the weekly shopping at the supermarket. We buy an assortment of products that have been produced by many different firms in one bulk transaction.

Notice that the introduction of the intermediary also ameliorates the effects of the tradeoff between bulk transactions and pooled risk. In the example, suppliers continue to sell the same total amount to the same number of customers, but now these transactions are aggregated across suppliers for each customer, resulting in bulkier transactions than was previously the case.

Given that there are two sources of economies, reduced contracts and bulk transactions, the introduction of an intermediary must be cost-efficient. Or must it? A simple example will help make the point. Suppose 100 firms supply three products each to each of 150 customers. To simplify matters, assume each firm and customer has identical costs, and demand is of the same size. The costs of supplying a customer comprise a fixed cost of $5 per customer and a variable cost per unit supplied that varies depending on the size of the transaction, which is given in Table 2.4.

Without the intermediary, the cost of supplying one customer is $5 + $10 $\times 3 = 35. The total cost for one firm is therefore $35 \times 150 = 5250. What happens when the intermediary is introduced? Each firm now sells all its products ($3 \times 150 = 450$) to the intermediary, which costs $5 + 7 \times (450) = 3155. This is much less than the firm's total cost without the intermediary, even if the fixed costs increased to some extent, which is likely given the different nature of the transaction. The economy is in part due to bulk transactions, as reflected in the variable costs per unit sold decreasing from $10 to $7.

But the products have reached only the intermediary. The intermediary will charge for its services in selling the firm's products to the customer in

Table 2.4   An example of variable costs per transaction

Variable cost per unit sold, $	Total number of units sold per transaction
10	<50
9	<100
8	<400
7	<750
6	<1000
5	<1500
4	<2000
2	≥2000

the form of a discounted or wholesale price or a negotiated fee for service. The intermediary sells three products on behalf of each of the 100 suppliers to each customer, so the cost per customer is $5 + 8 \times 300 = $2405. The intermediary gains from the economy of bulk transactions as the variable costs are $8 compared to $10 without the intermediary. The intermediary's total costs are $150 \times 2405 = $360 750$ and to cover these costs it must charge $360 750/100 = 3607.5 to each firm. The total costs for each firm are now the costs it incurs to sell to the intermediary, $3155, plus the intermediary's charge of at least $3607.5, which totals $6762.5. This is more than the costs it incurred without the intermediary, i.e. $5250! How can this be, given the economies resulting?

This is what most textbooks do not make clear. The problem is that we have substituted two transactions for one. Instead of a direct transaction between the firm and its customer, we now have two transactions, one between the firm and the intermediary and one from the intermediary to the customer. Costs increase because the variable cost for the first transaction is $7 per product and for the second $8 per product, which in total is $15, not $10 as it was with a direct transaction.

Does this mean that there are no economies of intermediaries, and that arguments to cut out the middleman are right? No. In this case the gains from the principle of reduced contracts and bulk transaction were not sufficient to outweigh the additional costs of adding an intermediary. The intermediary had to at least halve costs to make it attractive for firms to outsource their business to it. The existence and persistence of various types of intermediaries around the world, both bricks and mortar and online, is testimony to the potential economies that can result.

In addition, every firm is a type of intermediary in the sense that it gets inputs of materials, components, equipment, land and people from specialist suppliers and combines them through various types of production processes into various types of outputs of value to others prepared to outsource these processes to it. The difference between marketing and other types of intermediaries is that they are not so much involved in production and transformation processes as in marketing processes, linking and combining products and services. Marketing activities are coordination activities and are the source of market transaction costs.

In the foregoing example we showed how the dividing up of activities between firms creates additional work in the form of market transaction costs that may outweigh the economies to be gained from specialisation between firms. This tradeoff depends on the extent of the economies of specialisation to be gained and the costs of market versus intra-firm transactions. Various factors play a role in affecting these economies and costs. The gains from specialisation between firms depend on how similar different activities are, which depends on the types of technology in use, the ability to fully ultilise specialist factor inputs, and the various types of market size constraints already referred to. These conditions will change over time as new technologies emerge, as economies and industries grow and decline, as tastes change and as regulations permit or constrain the emergence of different types of firms. The advent of computer technology and more recently the Internet has had a profound effect on the structure of industries and value chains, giving rise to new patterns of specialisation between and within firms. Activities that were previously quite dissimilar, such as banking and shopping, have become similar due to computer technologies, and supermarkets can now act as mini-banks. The contacts that can be established and maintained over the Internet, as well as the increased speed and comfort of travel, have enabled firms to develop global partnerships and supply chains that would have been impossible to conceive of or coordinate previously.

Coordination and marketing activities are also subject to economies of specialisation, and computer technology, the Internet and revolutions in communication and transport systems have led to different patterns of specialisation and coordination among firms.

Complementary Activities

So far we have shown how specialisation within and between firms can result in various types of economies, but that these may be tempered by the costs of coordinating the specialist. I focused on the aggregation economies that arise through firms specialising in similar activities, whether these be production or coordinating activities. Once we divide up work we have to provide for its coordination because the different activities are necessarily complementary to some extent. If a firm outsources a component or a service, it has to coordinate the work of the supplier with the rest of its activities in order to produce its output.

There are four types of coordination situations, depending on whether the activities to be coordinated are similar or complementary, as shown in Table 2.5.

Table 2.5   Coordination situations and types of activities

Complementarity	Similarity	
	Similar	Dissimilar
Complementary	Intra-firm coordination	Interfirm coordination
Non-complementary	Aggregation	No coordination

Complementary activities that are similar are generally coordinated within a firm unless they can be divided into component activities that are not similar and outsourced to a specialist, or because a firm is subject to market constraints that limit its potential to gain economies of specialisation internally. Non-complementary but similar activities create opportunities for aggregation economies, whereby specialist suppliers can gain economies of scale and scope. In a sense, the potential for gaining such economies makes these similar activities complementary because it is only by doing them together that economies arise. Further, in order for a firm to create aggregation economies it must persuade relevant firms to outsource these similar activities to it, and this involves market transactions and coordination between firms. For example, in Figure 2.4 the intermediary would not be able to provide external sources of economies for firms or customers unless a number of them agreed to outsource the selling of their products to it and customers were willing and able to buy their products from the intermediary. If just a few firms used the intermediary it would not gain much in the way of additional economies of scale and scope, and would eventually go out of business. Once sufficient numbers of firms begin using the intermediary it becomes increasingly attractive and a positive feedback process ensues, with more customers and suppliers leading to additional economies, which in turn attracts still more customers and suppliers. A specialist component supplier also needs to coordinate the demands of different firms requiring its input in order to gain the potential economies of specialisation.

Coordination of complementary but dissimilar activities creates probably the greatest difficulties. Their dissimilarity calls for specialisation between firms or units of a firm but their complementarity requires coordination. The costs of coordination depend on how closely they have to be coordinated, and this depends on how standardised the activities are and the extent to which they and their outputs have to be finely matched in terms of quality as well as quantity and in terms of the timing of each activity. Close coordination is required in just-in-time delivery systems, which attempt to match outputs and inputs in order to minimise stockholding. But standardised material inputs may require little coordination between firms, as they can be bought in bulk to minimise transaction costs.

Other things being equal, activities that require close coordination are more likely to be coordinated within firms because, according to transaction cost theory, coordination tends to be carried out more efficiently within firms than between firms. This is based on three arguments. First, firms are able to exercise greater control and to monitor performance better than is possible in markets, and are thus able to detect and curb opportunism more effectively. Second, firms can provide longer-term rewards in the form of promotion and other incentives that reduce the likelihood of opportunistic behaviour. Third, the atmosphere or organisational culture tends to align more closely the interests of members of the firm. Hence firms are preferred when the reduction in transaction costs arising outweighs the benefits of any economies of specialisation between firms.

The actual form of internal coordination mechanisms, or governance modes, includes work groups, teams, various types of hierarchical structures, decentralised and centralised structures, multidivisional and unitary structures. These will vary in their inherent efficiency and suitability for performing different types of coordination tasks, and transaction cost logic may be used to examine their relative efficiencies. But the details of these various forms need not concern us here; for a more extended analysis refer to the works of Oliver Williamson. In this chapter I am concerned with the costs and efficiency of coordination between versus within firms in various market situations.

DIMENSIONS OF TRANSACTIONS AFFECTING COORDINATION COSTS[2]

Williamson identifies three key dimensions of transactions that affect the nature and extent of the coordination problem confronting firms and the efficiency of market versus internal transactions. These are asset specificity, the size and frequency of transactions, and uncertainty. We consider each in turn. In general, the greater the coordination task due to asset specificity, transaction size and frequency, and uncertainty, the more likely are firms to favour internal organisation within a firm.

Asset Specificity

This refers to durable investments in the form of specialised products and services, plant and equipment, or expertise tailored to the needs of a particular customer or supplier, which have value in the relevant transaction or relation but have limited or no value elsewhere. Such assets mean that a firm is vulnerable to opportunistic behaviour on the part of the exchange partner and, in order to protect them, various types of safeguard mechanism can be introduced that drive up transaction costs. Contracts cannot exhaustively predict every contingency and, furthermore, enforcement of contract provisions, especially in international markets and between geographically distant parties, is not cost-effective. Under these conditions transaction cost analysis (TCA) argues that the activities will be insourced rather than outsourced, in order to reduce transaction costs and risks of opportunism. The freer flow of information within a firm, the existence of a common organisational context that tends to align interests, and the formal power structure that can be used to overcome conflicts contribute to this. Also, adaptations to unforeseen conditions can be made sequentially without the need to renegotiate agreements. When such assets are unimportant, market transactions will be more attractive, and studies of industry structures provide support for these arguments.

An alternative perspective is to see such assets not as something firms have to invest in *before* a transaction or relationship with a particular partner can proceed and which need protection, but as an *outcome* of transactions and relations. Firms that have been trading with each other for some time have a shared history, a shadow of the past, through which they develop various types of actor bonds, activity links, resource ties and schema couplings that represent assets co-produced by the relationship, rather than something that pre-exists and needs safeguarding. I discuss these dimensions of relations in the following chapters. Such assets are a property of the relationship, not the firms, and cannot be transferred easily to other relations and transactions, although some elements of the learning and adaptation taking place may be a source of value elsewhere.

One of the most important types of assets co-produced by transactions and relations are human assets. Personal bonds of trust, respect and even affection can develop, as well as forms of tacit knowledge, as a by-product of operating over time in a particular relationship or extended transaction. Such knowledge is 'sticky' and difficult for outsiders to see and replicate. It is developed and embedded in people's unconscious habits and routines, in the interactions and relations among people and work groups, and in the interactions and relations among firms. These assets are unpatentable, uncodifiable and untradable. Furthermore, co-produced specific assets are *mutual assets* that make each party vulnerable to and dependent on the other to some extent; they reduce the chance of opportunism, depending on the nature of the atmosphere that develops. They act in the same way as economic hostages are used to balance investments and commitment to relations in TCA, such as prepayments.

There is also a shadow of the future which affects the atmosphere of a relationship, and the problems and efficiency of coordination between trading partners. It affects firms' expectations about the amount of business an exchange partner represents and hence its likelihood of investing in relationship-specific assets. Studies report that partners who commit specific investments to a strategic alliance expect that alliance to continue for longer. The shadow of the future also promotes the development of more cooperative norms and reduces the likelihood of opportunistic behaviour. A high probability of future association makes people not only more likely to cooperate with others; they are also willing to punish those who do not cooperate. Cooperation emerges out of mutual interests and behaviour based on standards that no one individual can determine alone. As a result of these mechanisms, the difficulty of coordination is reduced, as is the need for more specialised governance mechanisms such as detailed monitoring of each other's activities and outputs. The development of cooperative relations is taken up again in later chapters.

Frequency and Size of Transactions

As Oliver Williamson argues, 'the cost of specialized governance structures will be easier to recover for large transactions of a recurring kind' (1975, p. 65). In other words, specialisation, in this case in performing coordinating activities, depends on the size of the 'market' for coordination, which is determined by the amount and frequency of transactions to be coordinated. We are back to where we started: the division of labour is limited by the extent of the market, and this applies to all kinds of activities, including production and transaction activities, including coordinating. The arguments developed above about the economies of specialisation being only potential economies applies just as much to transaction work, and the same underlying principles described can be used to understand the sources of these economies of specialisation, i.e. multiples, bulk transactions and pooled risk. If transactions can be aggregated over time and over different products and services for the same customer or supplier, firms gain from these principles.

Intermediaries gain economies because they reduce the number of transactions in a system by aggregating them into larger transactions with each party. This of course is limited by the extent of asset specificity for each type of transaction, or whether they are similar or not, in Richardson's terms. They are potentially complementary activities if they can be aggregated and gain from economies of specialisation, and also generate additional value to customers and suppliers in the form of pre-mixed and assembled products, components and subassemblies or synergistic assortments of services and information.

The development of exchange relations between firms in effect aggregates transactions over time and thus allows those involved more fully to utilise specialised equipment, people and places to carry out the transaction activities required. Within a firm, longer-term relations are created among the units and people in the firm than might occur through market transactions, and this allows firms to invest in more specialised internal government structures and gain efficiencies.

From the foregoing we can see that the size and frequency of transactions, and how similar they are, will affect the extent to which economies of coordination can be obtained in market transactions. This in turn will affect the costs of insourcing versus outsourcing. The greater the size and frequency of transactions between trading parties, the more likely it is that they can establish efficient means of coordination and, over time, the shadow of the past may serve to further reduce market transaction costs.

Uncertainty

Two types of uncertainty can be distinguished. *Environmental uncertainty* relates to the risks associated with developing market transactions with customers and suppliers in countries, cultures and markets that are geographically, psychically, technologically and culturally distant. In these circumstances communication delays and distortions are more likely to arise, information is harder to get and interpret, and understanding and monitoring each other's behaviour is more difficult. This increases the extent and costs of creating and coordinating transactions.

Behavioural uncertainty relates to the behaviour of a supplier or customer: will they do what is necessary to create and deliver the value expected from the transaction? Behavioural uncertainty stems from the character of the exchange partner and how well the parties know and trust each other, and from the nature of the products and services involved: how easy or difficult is it to evaluate the performance of another firm and its outputs. Such uncertainty is greater when firms trade for the first time and are unfamiliar with each other, as when they enter new international markets and territories. Uncertainty is also greater the more important are the experience and credence attributes of the products and services being traded.

Three types of product or service attributes may be distinguished in terms of their ease of evaluation – search, experience and credence (Nelson 1970). Search attributes can be known before purchase, as when products can be tested and their dimensions, price and warranties determined. Experience attributes are those that are known only after purchase, when the products and services are used. These include processing and running costs, interaction effects on other activities and products, and how they affect the value of the outputs of a firm. Credence attributes are the most difficult to assess because a firm cannot be sure about the value provided even after purchase and use. The evaluation of professional services such as consulting and legal services involves these kinds of attributes, with the quality of the advice given being hard to determine even after it has been used. So many factors affect the resulting outcomes, including how such advice was acted on and implemented, what other factors were relevant, and what other types of advice could have been offered. More complex technology and knowledge-intensive products and services will also involve greater behavioural uncertainty because of the difficulty of assessing all three types of attributes.

TCA argues that the greater the environmental and behavioural uncertainty, the more likely firms are to insource the relevant activities, especially when transactions and relationship-specific assets are involved, such as when specialised and tailored expertise and understanding are required, and the adaptation of products, services and systems. Uncertainty will diminish over time as firms become more familiar with each other and with new environments, which can give them the confidence to outsource activities in order to take advantage of specialist suppliers. In transaction cost parlance market transaction costs have decreased, and this permits additional outsourcing. But the key issue is not reducing transaction costs but being able to create and deliver the value required for the targeted customers as efficiently as possible. A firm is required to trade off the potentially higher transaction costs of outsourcing a component or service against the gains in efficiency and value it gets from using a specialist external supplier.

A further consideration is the efficiency with which the coordinating activities can be done internally versus externally. TCA assumes that within-firm coordination is more efficient than between-firm coordination, for the reasons given above. But in some situations this may not be true. One reason is that over time firms build relations that reduce transaction costs as they get to know and trust each other. Another reason is that external agents and service providers may be required to undertake some or all of the coordination tasks, especially when entering new and distant markets. Hence firms exporting to foreign markets use local agents and distributors to manage the relations with customers and to help develop and adapt a firm's market offer. Such market specialists are akin to specialist managers in a firm. They specialise in particular types of coordinating activities, such as monitoring markets and competition, linking other firms to important local networks, government and other institutions. They can serve as sources of information and introductions to potential partners in other markets. For example, serving the needs of a division of a multinational firm in one market may lead to opportunities to serve other divisions in other markets. Such market specialists are able to offer efficiencies in doing this work because they specialise and aggregate the tasks of a number of firms on whose behalf they act. They gain efficiencies from the principles of multiples, bulk transactions, pooled risk and reduced contracts in performing the relevant activities that are not available to the firms they serve. A further reason for using external specialists is that it is easier and less costly to change external suppliers than to restructure firms. Instead of investing in the fixed costs associated with maintaining a facility to carry out the necessary activities, a firm substitutes a variable cost in the form of payment for services rendered by the external supplier.

An additional problem arises when specialist market coordinators or managers are used. This is the problem of coordinating the coordinators. This is the same problem as we encountered in explaining the costs and benefits of market intermediaries. Once a specialist intermediary is used, two transactions are created, not one: one between the originating firm and the intermediary, and one between the intermediary and its customers or suppliers. If the additional costs of adding layers of transactions are outweighed by the cost savings and value created elsewhere, then it is worthwhile using the intermediary. Equivalent problems arise within firms, leading to hierarchies of specialist managers each managing subordinate managers with, it is hoped, some people, machines and equipment at the bottom of the hierarchy actually performing the value-creating tasks efficiently and effectively, and linking these tasks with other complementary activities.

TOTAL COSTS OF INSOURCING VERSUS OUTSOURCING

So far I have described the principles underlying the efficiencies of specialisation within and between firms. In both cases the costs and efficiency of (a) performing the focal activities and (b) the transaction costs associated with coordinating these activities with other activities that are similar or complementary, are relevant, and there are tradeoffs between these two types of costs, as well as between some of the principles involved.

Figure 2.5 depicts all costs of insourcing versus outsourcing an activity. This activity could be producing or supplying a component or material input, providing a marketing, business or financial service, or providing a distribution or sales service. Two types of costs are involved: those associated with performing the relevant activity and those associated with coordinating the performance of the activity with other complementary or similar activities. These activities are either performed by the firm itself (insourcing) or by a specialist provider (outsourcing). For the purposes of illustration we assume certain cost levels and patterns of change in average costs as the output of the firm changes. A more complete treatment would require a detailed activity-based costing analysis that shows how costs vary in response to changes and interactions among all the activities of a firm. Here we assume that we can separate out the cost of one activity and relate it to total output.

Consider first the costs of performing the focal activity, what I call here production costs. Figure 2.5(a) depicts the costs of internal production as a decreasing cost activity subject to economies of scale as the firm's output

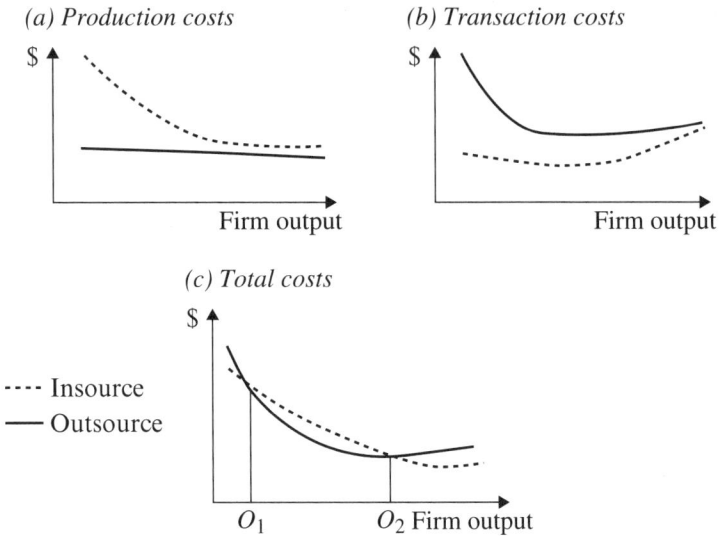

(a) Production costs

$

Firm output

(b) Transaction costs

$

Firm output

(c) Total costs

$

---- Insource
—— Outsource

O_1 O_2 Firm output

Figure 2.5   The costs of insourcing versus outsourcing

expands. The same type of analysis can be done for increasing cost activities, but I leave this up to the reader. The costs for a specialist supplier are assumed to be lower because of the greater economies of specialisation available to it. The cost curve is slightly downward sloping because the firm, by buying from the specialist supplier, increases the scale of production of the supplier and hence reduces its costs to some extent. The firm may also be able to buy in bulk as it gets bigger, but this is a transaction costs saving, not a saving in production costs.

Figure 2.5(b) shows the transaction costs for insourcing and outsourcing. This assumes that internal transaction or coordination costs are lower on average but the difference between the costs of internal and market transaction costs decreases as the output of the firm expands. The costs of outsourcing are high to begin with as a specialist supplier has to be identified and evaluated, and a contractual arrangement negotiated. As a firm's output expands it can spread these relation establishment costs over a larger output volume, hence reducing average transaction costs per unit sold. In addition, as output expands, the firm may be able to gain from bulk purchases and, as the size and frequency of transactions with the supplier increase, the ability arises to develop more elaborate and efficient governance structures, which are a form of asset specificity. This includes the development of a collaborative relationship atmosphere between the firm and the supplier that further reduces transaction costs by creating trust and more open communication and reducing the risk of opportunism. Other types of transaction costs are assumed to be reflected in the production or transaction costs shown, including those for the specialist supplier coordinating the serving of the focal firm with other customers to achieve economies of scale and scope. For example, conflicts can arise among different customers' demands which limit scale efficiencies or the ability to serve one customer as well as another.

The second type of transaction cost is that associated with the firm coordinating the supplier's contributions with other activities and other suppliers' efforts. Conflicts and incompatibilities can occur among suppliers' inputs and may affect the costs of supply and serving the focal firm's other customers. In other words, the costs and benefits of one transaction cannot be considered in isolation from other connected transactions and relations. But for the sake of illustration I assume that these costs are reflected in those depicted. I also assume that the value provided internally or externally is the same, i.e. the value of the product or service provided and the direct and indirect benefits of the internal and external transactions.

The total costs of insourcing and outsourcing are shown in Figure 2.5(c). In this case the two cost curves cross at two points. Up to output O_1, the firm insources the relevant activities as the costs of finding a specialist supplier outweigh any gains. From output O_1 to O_2, the gains from using a specialist supplier outweigh any additional transaction costs of market transactions. Beyond O_2 the firm is able to gain many of the economies of specialisation available internally and, even though market transaction costs are now not much greater than internal transactions, greater control and flexibility internally allow the firm to reabsorb the activity.

The position of the cost curves for insourcing and outsourcing will vary by activity, market and technology, among other things. Some examples are shown in Figure 2.6. In (a) the firm will never consider outsourcing because the activity is too firm-specific for outside specialists to gain any further advantages in performing it, it has to be closely coordinated with other activities, or market coordination costs and risks are too high. In the case of (b), the firm would never consider insourcing the activity because the costs of production would be prohibitive, e.g. the supply of utilities, media outlets, supermarkets, unless the firm were to expand the scope and scale of its own activities dramatically. Other examples are services that are public goods supplied by governments such as road, rail, airports and legal systems. Outsourcing standardised products and services also minimises the costs and risks of market transactions, as suppliers are readily substituted.

Case (c) is a firm that outsources until its gets large enough to perform the activity efficiently internally. Some firms are able to support their own advertising, marketing research and transportation systems; others have distribution outlets owned and controlled by the firm. Case (d) represents

(a) Make only

$

(b) Buy only

$

(c) Buy then make

$

(d) Make then buy

$

—— = Transaction plus production costs of outsourcing
···· = Transaction plus production costs of insourcing

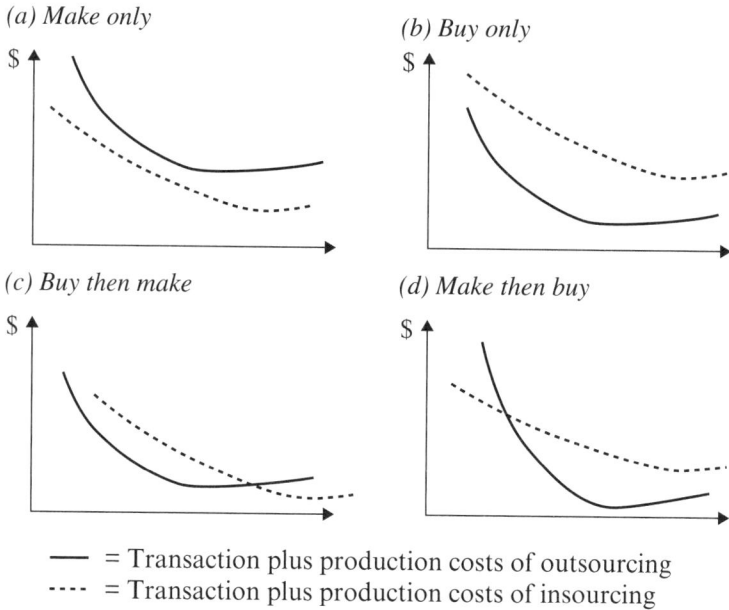

Figure 2.6   Four types of insourcing and outsourcing situations

the case of a firm that insources until an output level at which it finds it more economical to outsource the activity. Firms that expand from local to regional to international markets may begin to outsource key activities and components as they do so. They do this in order to avail themselves of the specialised knowledge, experience and contacts of local market suppliers, distributors and research firms, or to gain from international differences in production costs and efficiencies.

COMPETITION AND THE DEVELOPMENT AND EVOLUTION OF BUSINESS NETWORKS

Up to now we have analysed why firms form relations with other firms in order to gain external economies of scale and scope that they could not achieve by themselves. This provides the basis for explaining why relationships exist in business, both within and between firms. But we have to go further in order to explain how the complex, multi-layered networks of directly and indirectly connected business relations we observe in real economies arise. In this section I provide an economic analysis of the basis for such networks. In Chapter 3 I consider the development and evolution of business networks in more detail, including an examination of factors other than the economics of efficiency and effectiveness that colour and shape the business networks we see around us, and how and why they change.

The two main economic drivers of the development and evolution of business networks are specialisation and competition, and the way they affect each other. Specialisation between and within firms, as I have shown, depends on the nature of the activities to be performed, the technology involved and market factors that enable or constrain firms to gain full economies internally. It also depends on whether specialist firms, by aggregating activities on behalf of other firms, are viable and attractive to use. Conditions change over time, altering the most efficient and viable ways of organising activities between and within firms.

But managers and firms have limited and imperfect information, and are unable to identify optimal ways of organising activities. Moreover, the development of specialists requires some amount of coordination among firms because, unless firms outsource similar activities, there will be no market to support the specialist. Once again we can say that the economies of specialisation are only potential economies. The opportunity to gain economies through performing similar activities on behalf of a number of other firms requires that other firms do outsource these activities. We have seen how specialists can offer cost savings to their customers, but these cost savings depend on how many firms are using the specialist, and this depends on the differential advantage it offers. We are back to Ohmae's basic strategic triangle described in Chapter 1. Specialist suppliers are firms that seek niches in markets where they can perform activities and deliver value to targeted customers better than the competition.

When opportunities exist for specialist firms to offer cost savings or additional value, by getting other firms to outsource activities to them, firms are sooner or later going to discover this. An existing customer or supplier may start to perform some activities for other suppliers and/or customers and gradually refocus its business on these activities. For example, a firm could start to provide transport and sales services in some markets for firms offering complementary products that operate close by. The firm gains economies of scale and scope by expanding these activities through more fully using specialised resources such as trucks or salespeople (principle of multiples) or through bulk transactions with customers in the relevant market. Once begun, such a process is self-reinforcing as by offering the services to others it gains further economies which enable it to offer better value. Eventually it may become a specialist intermediary or a new kind of supplier serving various types of firms.

In their continuing search to establish and maintain differential advantage in serving their customers, firms carve out different niches in the

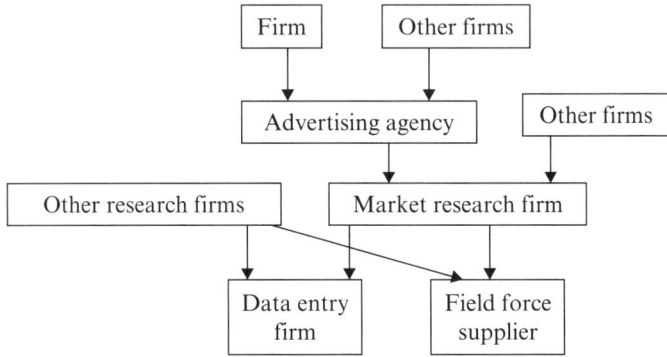

Figure 2.7   An example of a network of specialist suppliers

marketplace, which involves them in aggregating activities on behalf of others because of the benefits they can offer. What matters is if the activities are the same or similar, and so economies of scale and scope can be gained from performing them together. So long as customers demand the same or similar activities, they can outsource to the same specialists, even though these customer firms may operate in quite different industries and markets. Figure 2.7 gives a simple example of this in terms of the existence of a variety of specialist firms serving the research and advertising needs, directly or indirectly, of firms that operate in various industries. Firms from different industries, usually not competing directly, outsource advertising activities to agencies that specialise. Advertising agencies and other types of firms require market research to be undertaken and outsource this to specialists who aggregate this demand and gain economies of scale and scope. Market research firms and other types of firms in turn outsource some of their activities to other types of specialists, such as data entry bureaux or field force suppliers, who manage and train teams of interviewers. Through a system of linked transactions and relations, a complex network of suppliers, sub-suppliers and other specialists arises. In each case market size constraints and tradeoffs among the principles underlying their efficiency lead firms and specialist suppliers to outsource various activities to others.

But any specialist will face competition from both its own customers and suppliers, who could insource the activity, and from rivals that can set up in business and offer similar services (Baligh and Richartz 1967). Depending on the potential economies available and the size of market demand, a number of competing specialists may come to exist. A simple example is given in Figure 2.8 in terms of marketing intermediaries.

Figure 2.8(a) shows how a specialist intermediary reduces the number of transactions from 42 (7×6) to 13 ($7 + 6$). If the intermediary is viable, it

(a)

(b)

Total number
of contracts =
$(S+C)I = 39$

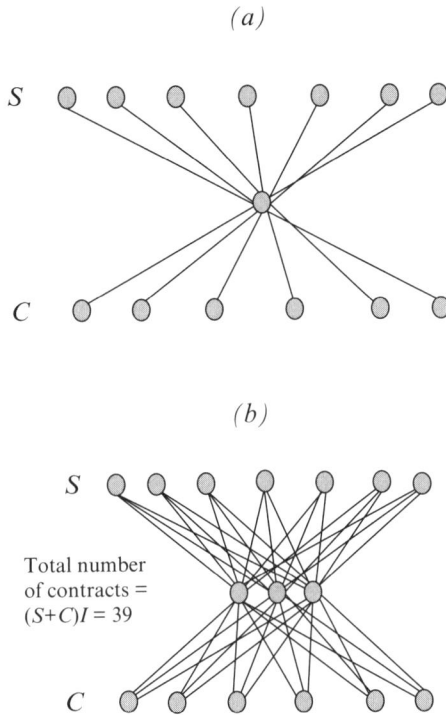

Figure 2.8   Specialist marketing intermediaries and competition

may attract competitors to set up, which may hold down prices but also means that customers must either choose among the intermediaries or spread their business among them. Assuming firms spread their business among competitors, how many intermediaries can survive? Each new intermediary adds another set of transactions between it and the suppliers and customers. The total number of transactions becomes $(S+C)I$, where I is the number of intermediaries. In Figure 2.8(b), with three intermediaries the total number is 39, which is still less than the 42 with no intermediary.

However, the economies of bulk transactions and reduced contracts that underlie the efficiency of the intermediaries are reduced. If firms spread their business, each intermediary is not able to gain the same economies of scale as a single or fewer intermediaries. For simplicity let's assume that only the fixed costs of a transaction matter. In this case the total number of intermediaries that can exist before the number of transactions exceeds the number without any intermediary is when $(S \times C) = (S+C)I^*$. The maximum number of intermediaries that can be supported then is $I^* = (S \times C)/(S + C)$. In our example this is $(7 \times 6)/(7 + 6) = 3.23$ and, because we cannot have part of an intermediary, the maximum is 3. If we take into account constraints on the economy of bulk transactions and other scale and scope effects, the number would be less.

In real economies there are very large numbers of suppliers and customers, and consequently opportunities for many types of specialists and their competitors to emerge. Indeed, the whole basis of a market economy is the specialisation between demand and supply, and the transactions that necessarily result. With numbers of competing specialists, further levels of outsourcing can arise, as in the example given in Figure 2.7. Furthermore, the economy never settles down to some kind of equilibrium network structure in which the benefits of specialisation within and between firms and the competition between rival specialists is optimal in some sense. There is a continual dynamic process going on, as opportunities to specialise in different assortments of activities and to produce different types of products and services are recognised and acted on, as new ways of doing business change the demand for and opportunities for different types of specialists, as new technologies alter the types of activities to be performed and how to perform them, changing the degree of similarity and complementarity among them, and as market conditions and knowledge change, altering demand and supply conditions. Out of this emerges the complex business network of interconnected and interdependent firms, and transactions of many types we see in the world. And it is continually being made, remade and changed through the actions and interactions taking place within and between people and firms. No firm is in control of more than a small part of the overall system. Each depends on others for needed inputs and activities. How firms deal with the problem of forming trading relations with each other and developing and managing their interactions within and among different such relations are matters I take up in later chapters.

NOTES

1. The chapter is largely based on Dixon and Wilkinson (1986) and draws on Dixon and Wilkinson (1982, Part IV).
2. This section is based on Wilkinson and Nguyen (2003, pp. 45–50).

3. Why business relations and networks exist II: value creation and innovation

INTRODUCTION

The previous chapter described how relations and networks arise in business because of economies of specialisation; how they are the means by which the fruits of the division of labour in a society are realised. This focused on the role they play in accessing, combining, recombining and coordinating the activities, resources and outputs of people and firms specialising in different parts of the overall process of value creation and delivery. In this chapter I describe the second basic role of business relations and networks in society: to shape the way an economic system develops and evolves through their impact on innovation, learning and knowledge development. While Chapter 2 focused on the role of business relations and networks in delivering a standard of living to a society given existing production logic, this chapter is about the way the standard of living delivered and the associated production logic change and evolve.

Business relations and networks play important roles in the development and evolution of the value-creating process. First, they contribute to the generation of new ideas, to learning, knowledge development and innovation. They are the means by which knowledge and ideas move around in business systems; the way ideas confront each other, are adapted, integrated, combined and recombined in new ways. Both functional and dysfunctional consequences can result, as we shall see. Second, they are the means by which new ideas are taken up and used. They are the means by which the knowledge, skills and resources required to develop, exploit and commercialise new ideas are marshalled and coordinated. In other words, they help people and firms see more, know more and do more.

New ideas, including ideas about new types of products and services, new ways of doing business and new types of technology, do not emerge out of nothing, like manna from heaven. Instead they emerge from developing, combining and recombining existing knowledge and ideas in new ways. The division of work in society results in a division of knowledge.

As Douglass North, a Nobel prize-winner in economics, summarises the problem:

> [B]ecause the division of labour produces a division of knowledge and different kinds of knowledge are organized in different ways, the coordination of knowledge requires more than a set of prices to be effective in solving human problems. The implication is that the institutional structure will play a critical role in the degree to which diverse knowledge will be integrated and available to solve problems as economies become more complex. (2005, pp. 72–3)

People and firms specialising in different activities come to understand what they do more deeply than others and encounter different types of information and ideas through the work they do and the people and firms they interact with. Within firms, those specialising in particular functions are selected according to their expertise and training, and develop a particular orientation, language and culture associated with their group and the type of activities they engage in that differentiates them from others. For example, engineers and technical personnel have different backgrounds and experience compared to those in marketing or finance and, as a result, see and understand the world differently. In the same way, firms specialising in particular types of products and services develop their own particular assortments of knowledge, expertise and understanding.

Business relations and networks are the primary institutional structures by which knowledge and ideas are integrated and reintegrated, and contribute to solving a society's economic problems. They both enable and constrain: they help identify and open up new opportunities but they can also blinker us by distorting, biasing and limiting the flow of information and ideas among and within firms.

TOWARDS A TYPOLOGY OF RELATIONSHIP AND NETWORK FUNCTIONS[1]

Various types of functions have been ascribed to business relations and networks in the literature (Walter et al. 2001, 2003). These are summarised in Table 3.1. *Direct functions* focus primarily on the economic logic of exchange relations linking firms specialising in different activities. These were the subject of Chapter 2. For customers, this involves gaining access to valued inputs and back-up suppliers, and taking advantage of bulk transactions and relationship-specific investments to reduce transaction costs. For suppliers, the direct functions comprise the means of serving and keeping important customers, as well as back-up market outlets, for their products and services.

Table 3.1   Functions of business-to-business relationships

Customer relations	Supplier relations
Direct	**Direct**
Profit – revenue greater than costs to serve	*Cost reduction* – working with suppliers to reduce costs and price
Volume – help use capacity and achieve economies of scale and scope	*Quality* – improving customers' value creation and costs
Safeguard – relations maintained as an insurance against crises or difficulties with other customers	*Volume* – single sourcing to gain influence, consistency and reduce communication costs
	Safeguard – parallel supplier
Indirect	**Indirect**
Innovation – source of new product and service ideas	*Innovation* – access to new ideas and technology
Market – support development of new markets through referrals or reputation effects	*Market* – bridge to other suppliers, industry associations, government and reputation effects from supplier inputs
Scout – source of market information	
Access – bridge or go-between to gain access to relevant organisations	*Scout* – source of market and technical information
	Social support – mutual support and working atmosphere, personal bonds

Source: Wilkinson and Young (2005a).

The indirect functions of business relations reflect the roles they play in the integration and development of knowledge and ideas, and the way they are exploited and commercialised. Within a business relation the problems, knowledge and ideas of the people and firms involved confront each other and become adapted, interrelated and combined through their interactions. This in turn leads to the development and adaptation of new products, services and processes.

In addition, through a business relation, access is gained indirectly to the knowledge, skills and resources of third parties. This is because business relations do not operate in isolation from each other; they are parts of networks of interconnected relations linking firms and organisations involved in various aspects of the value creation and delivery process. Knowledge and ideas are unevenly spread among the people and firms comprising the network as a result of the work they do and their experience and training. But, through the interactions taking place within and between business relations, people and firms gain access to the knowledge and experience of others, and to their resources and skills. Firms can learn about emerging new technologies in source industries from suppliers, who are more in touch with these developments. They can learn about the activities of their competitors through customers and distributors, and about developments in end-use demands from distributors and industrial customers.

Business relations can provide firms with information about new market opportunities or new supply relations, and facilitate market entry through reputation effects and referrals. They connect firms to the relations and networks of their relationship partners, which can be a valuable source of introductions and access to key economic and government actors. The term *relational or network capital* is used to refer to these types of firm resources. Lastly, business relations can be a means of direct social support, a friend and ally, which is another type of communication function but also reflects the intrinsic value of some business relations.

Not only can business relations and networks be a source of value to firms; they can also be a burden and limit what a firm can do, see and think. The types of business relations and networks people and firms are involved in and their position and role in them opens up sources of knowledge, ideas and resources but closes down and distorts others. People and firms in well-established relations and networks are already steeped in the current ways of seeing and doing things with each other, and are less likely to be receptive to ideas that undermine these relations and practices. They can become core rigidities limiting rather than enabling action and thought. As Hargadon (2003) puts it, the ties that bind are also the ties that blind.

It is for these reasons that the history of industrial innovation is replete with stories of firms from the periphery of existing industries and networks being the source of major innovations. For example, car producers did not arise from firms catering to the horse-drawn vehicles that preceded them; the emergence of xerography was ignored by firms already established in the copying industry.

This effect is demonstrated in research by Clayton Christensen (1997), who has shown how a firm's knowledge and evaluation of potential innovations can be distorted and limited by its established network of business relations; he calls this the innovator's dilemma. He shows that working with and listening to the views of *existing* customers and suppliers can be quite misleading in assessing and pursuing different types of innovation. He distinguishes two types: those involving convergent and those involving disruptive technologies. *Convergent technologies* are those that reinforce and build on existing skills, knowledge and competences, and sustain existing business relations and networks. *Disruptive technologies* do the opposite: they undermine the value and relevance of existing skills and resources and existing relations and networks. Using the knowledge and skills of existing customers and suppliers, and working with them to develop and implement new technologies, is helpful in the case of convergent technologies but not for disruptive technologies. Christensen illustrates the differences between convergent and disruptive innovations in terms of developments in disk storage technologies for computers. Radical and incremental innovations in head and disk technologies (ferrite oxide, thin film, magneto-resistive) and product architecture (removable disks, internal drives) are examples of sustaining or convergent technologies, whereas moves from larger to smaller disk storage technologies are examples of disruptive, divergent technologies. Innovations of the former kind are dominated by existing players in the industry, whereas in the latter case they invariably involve new entrants.

A good example of disruptive technological change is that of the waves of innovations that have taken place in hard disk storage systems for computers, starting with the large disks used for mainframe computers and moving through the hard drives used in mini-computers, work stations, desktop and laptop computers, and eventually in digital cameras and hand-held personal digital assistants and mobile phones. In each case the new technologies were at first inferior to existing technologies and not valued by customers. As a result, existing suppliers of the older technologies were influenced by their customers not to invest in the newer technologies, even though, in the early stages of development, they were quite capable of doing so. Instead, the newer technologies were first developed by new firms, sometimes started by people leaving existing suppliers, who worked with different types of customers and suppliers. Eventually, the newer technology overtook the older technology and the incumbent firms were replaced or threatened by firms using the new disk storage technology.

The disruptive innovations were technologically quite straightforward and were sometimes even originally developed by existing suppliers in the industry. But they offered a new package of product attributes that was not easy for existing customers to understand and appreciate. Initially, smaller storage disks did not perform as well on attributes that were considered very important by existing customers, but they performed far better on other attributes considered important by other types of customers. Firms producing large mainframe computers were not interested in smaller 8-inch disks because of their limited capacity, and so new entrants emerged (e.g. Shugart, Micropolis, Priam, Qantum) to supply producers of mini-computers such as Wang, DEC, Data General Prime and Hewlett-Packard, who were interested in smaller disks with less capacity. Eventually, the capacity of the smaller disks improved to rival the larger disks, a story that was repeated for still smaller disks. Moves to 5.25-inch and 3.5-inch disks were taken up by new entrants serving emerging desktop and laptop producers, once again because, to begin with, these types of disks offered no advantage to mini-computer producers. The same story was to be repeated for flash memory systems, originally developed for digital cameras and electronic organisers. These were not of interest to PC and laptop producers until their capacities came to rival the larger disk storage systems, as do the memory sticks of today.

In all these cases, existing suppliers had the capacity to develop and supply the smaller disks but were advised against it by their existing customers. They were in effect held captive by their existing customers. Both types of innovation, convergent and disruptive, can involve radical and complex forms; the difference is in terms of the value and relevance to the innovation of existing resources and skills, and ways of doing business. When new types of business models and new types of skills and resources are required, existing relations and networks can get in the way. Existing customers and suppliers in the industry may not be able to understand or appreciate the value of the innovation or may resist because their future is threatened. In these circumstances, listening and responding to ideas and information of incumbents may be counterproductive.

RELATIONSHIP STRUCTURE AND FUNCTION

The functions and dysfunctions of business relations and networks depend on their structure, which may be described in terms of the activity links, actor bonds, resource ties and schema couplings that emerge over time from the experience and outcomes of the actions and interactions taking place (Håkansson and Snehota 1995; Welch and Wilkinson 2002).

People and firms involved in business relations and networks act and interact in various ways using their resources. These actions and interactions are guided by the ideas and beliefs they have about each other, which I shall refer to as their relational and network schemas, and the bonds that exist between them. Schemas are the theories in use, sense-making, or mental models people and firms have regarding the nature and role of a business relation or network, including what they hope to get out of it, their ideas and beliefs about themselves and the other actors involved, and their expectations regarding each actor's behaviour and contribution.

Bonds refer to the emotions and feelings that arise between people and firms that affect their goals and behaviour, including affection, trust, dependence, commitment, respect and sympathy – feelings that may or may not be reciprocated. The experience and outcomes of the actions and interactions taking place over time in a business relation shape the activities, resources, schemas and bonds of all actors involved. Actors gain and lose resources; their knowledge, ideas and interpretation of each other and the relation and network develop and adapt, and the bonds between them are strengthened or weakened.

At any point in time a particular pattern of activity links, resource ties, actor bonds and schema couplings exists among the people and firms involved, which is the result of history. This pattern is the existing structure of the relationship or network, and it enables and constrains what the people and firms involved are willing and able to do. In this way the existing structure underlies and determines the functions and dysfunctions of a business relation or network. It affects the extent to which people and firms will or will not share information, act opportunistically towards each other, help each other and collaborate with each other. But the structure is not fixed; it is continually being reproduced and changed through the experience and outcomes of the ongoing actions and interactions taking place.

The relationship between the structure and functions of business relations is summarised in Figure 3.1 in terms of the constructive and deleterious effects of the activity links, resource ties, actor bonds and schema couplings that exist in business relations and networks.

Constructive effects refer to the positive functions of relations and networks for those involved (Anderson et al. 1994). *Resource transferability* refers to the ability to use, develop and combine the resources, knowledge and skills of others involved in a focal relation or in connected relations. *Activity complementarity* refers to the positive effects of the activities of a relationship partner or of actors in connected relations. This includes reducing costs or adding benefits, as when economies of scale gained in serving one customer reduce the costs to supply others, or when the

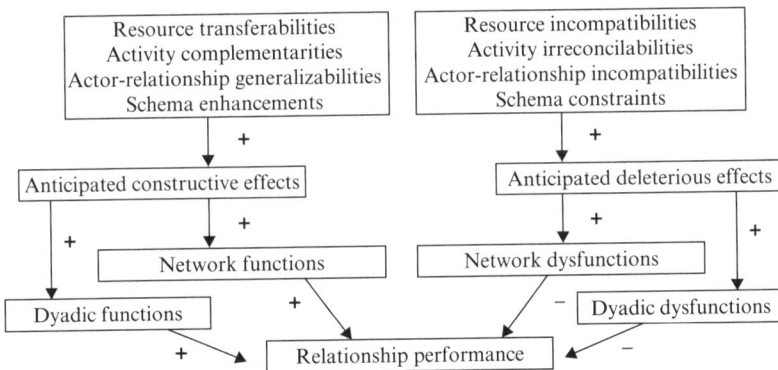

Source: Wiley et al. (2006, p. 4).

Figure 3.1   The functions and dysfunctions of business relations and networks

efforts and activities of suppliers enhance the quality of products and services offered to customers. *Actor-relationship generalisability* refers to the strengthening of actors' bonds through reputational and referral effects. The bonds developed with particular people and firms carry over into other relations through introductions and recommendations, and because they signal to others a willingness and capability to cooperate. Social balance processes also affect the kinds of bonds that can develop and persist among people and firms. I discuss this more fully below in terms of the deleterious effects of actor bonds. Lastly, *schema enhancements* refer to the way the ideas and beliefs developed in one relation can be used to enhance the vision and understanding of others in a focal relation or in connected relations, as when the benefits stemming from collaborating in one relation lead to changes in ideas about how to operate in other relations.

Deleterious effects refer to the negative effects or dysfunctions of relationship and network structures (Anderson et al. 1994). *Resource particularity* refers to the way resources tied up in a relation cannot be used in other relations or the way resources adapted for use in one relation have adverse effects on other relations, such as components and systems designed to serve one customer that all other customers have to use. *Activity irreconcilability* refers to the difficulty of meshing the activities of relationship partners or integrating activities across connected relations due to differences in technology and the way they are tailored to different relations.

Actor-relationship incompatibility refers to the negative reputation effects that may stem from dealing with particular people and firms. Social balance processes refer to the way people and firms seek balance in the way they act and feel towards each other. They codify the intuitive notion that 'a friend of my friend, as well as an enemy of my enemy, is my friend; and a friend of my enemy, as well as an enemy of my friend, is my enemy' (Antal et al. 2006, p. 130). Within a relation, balance depends on reciprocity or mutuality of feelings, i.e. A likes B and B likes A, or A doesn't care much about B and B doesn't care much about A. Here balance can mean mutually positive bonds, such as attraction, trust and sympathy or mutually negative bonds, such as dislike, hatred and distrust, or simply the absence of any bonds as in arm's-length market transactions.

In connected relations, issues of balance become more complex. The rules were worked out some time ago by the psychologist Fritz Heider (1958). When three actors are interacting, balance exists when all three pairwise relations in the triad are balanced and positive, or if one is positive and the other two negative. Different types of balanced and unbalanced relations among three actors are shown in Figure 3.2.

Attempts to achieve balance in particular dyads and triads can have repercussions elsewhere because they disturb balance in others' relations. This can

Four balanced triadic configurations

Four unbalanced triadic configurations

⟶ Positive   ------▶ Negative

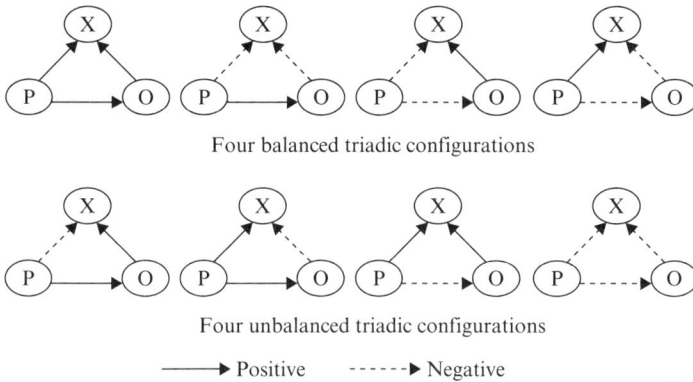

Source: Hummon and Doreian (2003, p. 19).

Figure 3.2   Balanced and unbalanced sets of relations

be both positive and negative. Deleterious effects arise when problems in dealing with one person or firm create problems with third parties, as when a firm switches suppliers and this affects the relations the supplier has with existing customers that compete with the new customer. Constructive effects can also arise, as when the mutual dislike of a supplier or distributor creates bonds between people and firms that otherwise would not exist.

The last type of deleterious effect stems from *schema constraints*, which refer to the conflicts of interests and ideology that arise between people and firms, making it difficult for them to work together effectively or to even get together at all. However, such conflicts are not always bad; they can be a source of stimulation and innovation, as is discussed later. Ideas and beliefs developed in one relation can limit and disrupt operations in other relations if they serve to undermine existing collaborative efforts, for example.

To understand more fully how and why these functions and dysfunctions of business relations arise, we need to draw on various theories of entrepreneurship and opportunity recognition, concepts of open innovation and lead users and social network theory.

INNOVATION, AND BUSINESS RELATIONS AND NETWORKS

[E]ntrepreneurs and inventors are no smarter, no more courageous, tenacious, or rebellious than the rest of us – they are simply better connected.

(Hargadon 2003, p. 11)

Innovation involves the development of new ways of doing things, including new types of products and services, new types of markets and new types of market organisation. Much early work on innovation focused on the lone genius inventor and the characteristics of innovative people or firms. Innovativeness, entrepreneurship and creativity were thought to result from a person's personality, intelligence, education, skills and resources. Thus we have all been taught about the genius of people such as Alexander Graham Bell, Henry Ford, Bill Gates or Thomas Edison, and the great inventions they are responsible for.

But more recent research on the processes of innovation, entrepreneurship and opportunity discovery show that this view is incorrect, and that innovation is more a process taking place through relationships and networks, in which knowledge and ideas flow backwards and forwards, confront each other and are developed and recombined in ways that have productive value. Old ideas and ways of doing things are challenged and come under scrutiny, which leads to the opening up of new possibilities, including both incremental and radical innovations. But not all business relations are engines of innovation; much depends on the knowledge and resources each party brings to a relation, and their ability and willingness to share information and to absorb and act on new ideas, with all the risks involved. This will depend on the character of the relation, including the degree of trust and commitment each party has, issues considered in more detail in subsequent chapters.

The main argument here is that new ideas do not arise through the genius of a lone inventor, instead they result from combining, recombining and adapting existing knowledge and ideas in new ways. For this to happen a person or firm has to have access to the relevant assortment of knowledge and ideas to recombine and the ability and willingness to make the necessary connections. The prior knowledge of a person or firm, which results from their history of activities and experiences, is one source of knowledge and ideas, and access to the knowledge and ideas of others is another source, which of course depends on the business and non-business relations and networks a person or firm is involved in. The role of relations and networks in generating and shaping innovation and patterns of technological development is becoming ever more important with the increasing complexity and variety of technologies and disciplines being combined and used in business today. No one person or firm can be familiar with all that is going on that is potentially relevant.

Discovering opportunities for new types of products, processes or services is one thing; exploiting and commercialising them is quite another. This requires the marshalling of relevant resources to develop the opportunity into a commercial form and to market it successfully. Once again relations and networks play an important role, as they are the means by which valuable skills and resources are accessed, developed and used. And the relations and networks that led to the opportunity being discovered are not necessarily those required for exploiting it. For this reason people and firms may sell their ideas to others to exploit in return for royalty or other payments.

The role of relations and networks in discovering and exploiting new business opportunities is well illustrated in the case of Thomas Edison, who is credited as the genius behind many important inventions, including those related to the development of the telegraph, telephone, phonograph, generators, light bulbs and vacuum pumps. A closer inspection of the sources of these inventions reveals the role played by networks linking people, ideas and objects together that Edison and his fellow researchers at his Menlo Park laboratory were part of.

> To single out Edison from this growing web is to record one truth – that Edison was quite remarkable – and in the process experience many lies: Edison neither invented the lightbulb nor acted alone in improving it. The web around Edison was thick with ties to other people, ideas and objects that together made up his particular 'invention.' Who Edison knew, what he and his engineers learned from the existing technologies of the day, what they believed possible, and who they convinced to join in their ventures all created the landscape in which his innovations took shape. (Hargadon 2003, p. 7)

The kinds of opportunities people and firms are able and willing to see depends to a large extent on their prior knowledge and motivations. A nice illustration of this comes from a study of the commercialisation of a new technology invented at MIT carried out by Scott Shane (2000). He interviewed those involved in eight new venture opportunities designed to exploit a three-dimensional printing process (3DP^{TM}) invented at MIT in 1989. It is a process for rapid and flexible production of three-dimensional objects using a computer to control the depositing of successive layers of a fluent powder in a mould and binding them together. He found that the number of opportunities identified was limited because the opportunities are not obvious from simply observing the 3DP^{TM} process, and entrepreneurs tended to discover only one opportunity each. The identification of attractive opportunities was not a matter of searching for information and evaluating alternative opportunities, but more a process of discovery and recognition. The entrepreneurs tended to recognise the opportunity immediately on seeing the 3DP^{TM} process. As one commented, 'When Ely Sachs showed me MIT's 3DP^{TM} process, I just saw immediately that there was an opportunity to make functional metal parts directly from a computer' (ibid., p. 457).

What appeared to be going on was the linking of prior knowledge and interests with the new knowledge of the 3DP^{TM} process. Prior knowledge and interests reflected the firm and industry background and experience of the people involved, and this enabled and constrained the types of potentially productive links they could make with the new information. This led an industrial designer with experience in architecture to see opportunities to produce cheap, fast on-site concept models; a pharmaceutical manufacturer to see an opportunity to design and develop drugs with special micro structures that improved their performance; a metal-casting firm to see an opportunity to manufacture metal parts without expensive tooling; an orthopaedics firm to better design and fit artificial prostheses; and an art dealer to develop three-dimensional sculptures of people from photographs.

So far I have shown how relations and networks play a key role in the innovation process, both in terms of the discovery of opportunities as well as in their further development, exploitation and commercialisation. I now consider various theories and concepts that have been proposed to explain some of the mechanisms underlying this. First I focus on business relations and the way the interactions taking place can stimulate the development of new ideas; then I turn to the nature and structure of networks and how they influence the types of knowledge and ideas people and firms have access to.

Relations, Interactions and Innovation

Various theories and concepts have been proposed to help explain the link between relations and innovation. All focus on the way interactions taking place in relations between people and firms lead to innovation through the confronting, combining, recombining and adaptation of the knowledge, ideas, skills and resources of those involved. 'Creative abrasion' is a term coined by Leonard-Barton (1993, 1995) to refer to the way we learn about each other's needs and capabilities in relations, and how interactions among technical personnel from buyers and sellers can lead to knowledge creation and innovation. The term 'productive friction', suggested by Hagel and Brown (2005), is similar and has been used to refer to the productive effects of conflict and disagreements among firms and their partners in generating new ideas and ways of doing things. The concept of *transformational outsourcing* (Linder 2004) shifts attention away from reducing costs and increasing efficiencies through outsourcing activities and processes, to the role these relations can play in identifying and co-developing valuable and innovative products and services, production processes and types of organisation.

Tacit and Non-tacit Knowledge

Innovation and knowledge development come from interrelating different types of knowledge from diverse sources, some of which is more easily communicated than others. Two types of knowledge are commonly distinguished – tacit and non-tacit. Non-tacit knowledge is more explicit and codifiable. In other words, it is easier to summarise in words and diagrams and to communicate to others. This is the type of knowledge that can be patented and is described in technical books and articles. Tacit knowledge is like know-how rather than know-what, and is much harder to communicate because it is less codifiable and tends to be embedded in a person or organisation, as well as in relations and networks. This type of knowledge is built up over time through practice and experience, and is of the type that a great artist or artisan possesses. Tacit knowledge can only be passed on through direct interaction with a person or organisation, as when an artist or experienced artisan tutors an apprentice. This type of information is 'sticky' because it is difficult to share with others, yet it plays an important role in technology and technological development (von Hippel 1994).

Relations and networks are the means by which both tacit and non-tacit knowledge is developed, shared and recombined. Over time firms learn more about each other, and develop and adapt their products and processes to meet their respective needs, resulting in the co-creation of various types of relationship-specific assets or resources. These represent types of innovation tailored to and embedded in a relation. They cannot be communicated to or duplicated easily by other firms and relations, and can be an important source of competitive advantage.

Another reason for the difficulty of sharing knowledge among people and firms is the nature of knowledge itself. In order to tell people what knowledge you have, you give away the knowledge or you have to be so guarded in your description that the potential recipient cannot evaluate it properly. Moreover, once information is shared it cannot be taken back. This type of problem is particularly acute in high-tech industries, where proprietary technology is closely guarded. A firm with a new idea may approach another suggesting that there are opportunities to be had by combining their idea with the resources and expertise of the other firm. But in order to share this information they usually first need the other firm to sign a non-disclosure agreement. But the potential partner may not be able or willing to sign such an agreement, as this may compromise research already under way in their own firm. In order to sign a non-disclosure agreement the potential partner needs to be convinced of the potential value of the new idea and how it relates to their own knowledge and resources. But to provide such information may reveal the new idea before a non-disclosure agreement can be signed!

It was this type of problem that led John Wolpert, who used to run IBM's Extreme Blue incubator programme in the USA, to develop a new way for firms to identify potential technical development partners and to build relations between them. His idea was to develop trusted intermediaries that could act as an executive recruiter for innovation. These trusted intermediaries are people with relevant expertise who have signed agreements not to disclose or use any of the ideas they learn about themselves, except as a means of identifying and introducing new potential technical partners to each other. The aim is to create intermediaries with whom firms are able to share more of their proprietary information in order to detect potential synergies of ideas among firms. Groups of firms are established that focus on particular types of industries and technologies, and participating firms agree to communicate more openly with one of the intermediaries. The intermediaries can also talk to each other and other firms involved in order to identify potentially productive relations. Several case studies are described on their website (www.ixc.com.au/intermediary.html), including a multinational firm seeking to acquire new technologies and to engage in joint R&D with Australian firms and research institutes.

Lead Users

Because tacit, embedded knowledge and resources cannot be readily duplicated by others, the only means of accessing and using it is through the development of relations with those people and organisations in which it is embedded. An example of this is the way firms have tried to develop relations with lead users of their types of products and services as a means of tapping in to lead users' tacit and embedded knowledge about relevant products, services and processes, including how they have adapted them in use.

The concept of lead user was first proposed by Eric von Hippel (1988, 2005) after he conducted a study of the sources of firms' product and service innovations. The original source of the ideas could often be traced to the consumer rather than the producer. Producers had often played a role in developing and adapting the original idea in order to commercialise it, but the original idea came from consumers. The same pattern was found in many different types of industries, as is shown in Table 3.2.

Building on the earlier research, researchers have continued to identify many examples of user-led innovation and to understand how and why it takes place. This has led to the development of various ways of identifying lead users and facilitating the development of productive relations and communication with them.

Table 3.2   Users as innovators in different industries

	Number and type of users sampled	Percentage developing and building product for own use	Source
Industrial products			
1. Printed circuit CAD software	136 user firm attendees at PC-CAD conference	24.3	Urban and von Hippel (1988)
2. Pipe hanger hardware	Employees in 74 pipe hanger installation firms	36	Herstatt and von Hippel (1992)
3. Library information systems	Employees in 102 Australian libraries using computerised OPAC library information systems	26	Morrison et al. (2000)
4. Surgical equipment	261 surgeons working in university clinics in Germany	22	Lüthje (2003)
5. Apache OS server software security features	131 technically sophisticated Apache users (webmasters)	19.1	Franke and von Hippel (2003)
Consumer products			
6. Outdoor consumer products	153 recipients of mail order catalogues for outdoor activity products for consumers	9.8	Lüthje (2004)
7. 'Extreme' sporting equipment	197 members of 4 specialised sporting clubs in 4 'extreme' sports	37.8	Franke and Shah (2003)
8. Mountain biking equipment	291 mountain bikers in a geographic region	19.2	Lüthje et al. (2002)

Source: von Hippel (2005, p. 20).

Users of products and services live in different worlds from those that produce and sell them. They therefore know more about the way products, services and processes are used, with what and by whom in particular contexts. This can be a source of knowledge for suppliers that they cannot duplicate for themselves. Lead users are a special type of user that can play an important role in innovation. They are a source of innovation in part because they are at the cutting edge in terms of experiencing a particular type of problem or need; hence they are motivated to adapt and improve the products, services and processes available to them. In other words, necessity is the mother of invention. But they also have considerable experience and know-how about the products and processes they use, and how they do or do not meet their requirements. They are therefore in a good position to identify improvements. For example, leading surgeons have been the inventors of many types of surgical tools because they faced particular types of problems and had to deal with them.

While all users have a more complete and deeper understanding of their own requirements and circumstances, not all are lead users. Lead users face problems that most consumers may not be aware of or have not yet confronted. But the solutions to these problems offer ways of improving products and services more generally, now or in the future. Some examples include the development of antilock braking systems by airline manufacturers that were then adapted for cars, the development of high-performance windsurfing equipment by lead enthusiasts, and innovations in machine tools have often come from the firms using the tools rather than the producers. A careful study was conducted for 3M comparing innovation projects based on identifying and building relations with lead users to more traditional in-house methods. This showed that projects developed by working with lead users tended to be more innovative and yield better returns than those developed using more traditional methods (Morrison et al. 2000).

NETWORKS AND INNOVATION[1]

So far I have discussed the way innovation takes place in and through relations because they are the means of accessing and confronting new types of knowledge, problems and perspectives, which result in the creation of new knowledge through the recombining and adaptation of existing knowledge. Here I consider how the networks of relations among firms affect the flow of knowledge and thereby enable or constrain the innovation process.

The structure of networks affects how easy or difficult it is to combine different types of information and expertise that is dispersed throughout the network, particularly tacit forms of information that require more direct forms of interaction among people and firms to develop, access, share and use. While non-tacit types of information may be transmitted and bought and sold easily, tacit information depends more on the channels of communication afforded by personal and professional business relations and networks.

The study of social networks, including business networks, has become a significant focus of scientific attention in recent years, in part because computers have enabled the development of more sophisticated ways to measure and analyse them. An early result to capture attention was the work of a sociologist, Mark Granovetter (1973), who studied the way people found new jobs. Counter-intuitively, he discovered that it was not those closest to you that were the main sources of information about new jobs; it was more likely to be people you hardly knew. This led him to write an article entitled 'The strength of weak ties'. Weak ties are strong in the sense that they are more likely to provide links to new types of information. Strong ties are among people that are close to each other and know each other well. They are therefore more likely to share similar types of information, whereas weak ties are more likely to act as bridges between groups with different expertise and experiences. In the same way, firms that are part of the same industry and distribution system are more likely to have similar types of knowledge and ways of thinking about things.

Granovetter's research was developed further by Ronald Burt (1992), who showed that weak ties play an important role not because they are weak, but because these types of ties are more likely to span structural holes in networks of dispersed types of information. His concept of structural holes focuses on the importance of relations that span otherwise unconnected groups of actors in networks, be they people, firms or other types of groups. Figure 3.3 illustrates the idea of structural holes. The dashed lines indicate weak relations and the solid ones strong relations. In the network depicted there is only one strong link linking the largest sub-network in the network, B, to C, and this bridges a structural hole. The links between subnetworks A and B are also sparse, and this structural hole is spanned by a few weak and strong ties. There are no ties linking A and C directly, which means no relation spans this structural hole and it remains a hole. The position of Robert is very different to James in terms of access he has to people and knowledge in other networks, and this will affect what types of information and knowledge he has and the resources he can potentially gain access to.

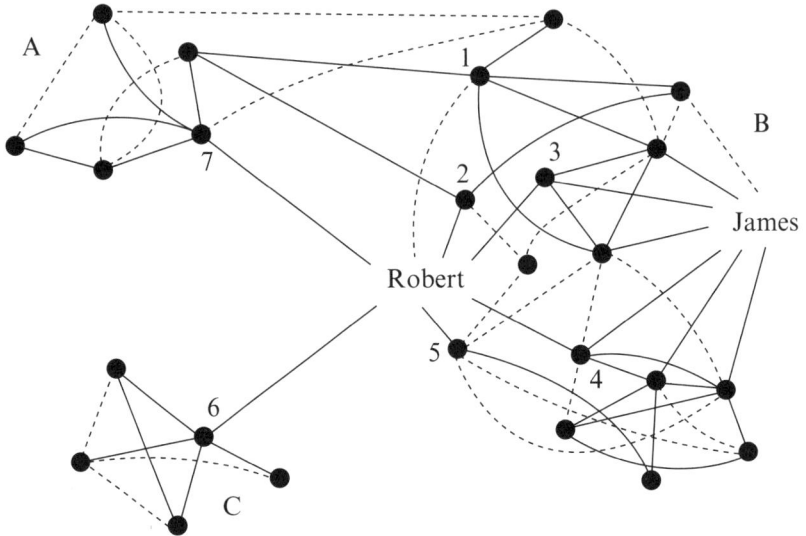

Source: Adapted from Burt (2004, p. 352).

Figure 3.3   Structural holes and weak ties

An example of the way a weak tie spanning a structural hole led to a firm discovering business opportunities in Japan is illustrated in the following description of the process by the founder of the firm:

> we were desperate . . . BioXXX dropped us . . . we had no source of income . . . I thought about a mentor of mine whom I worked with when I was doing my post-doc . . . he's extremely famous in biochemistry and molecular biology in Japan . . . he's a Japanese American . . . he has strong links to Japanese companies . . . so after signing a confidentiality agreement, we showed the technology to him and he said it was really cool and he wanted me to show it to [a Japanese firm] . . . . he was a consultant to . . . Through this contact, I was invited to Japan to make a presentation of [our product], the novel genome sequencing system . . . it took only 30 minutes for them to decide to purchase our invention and the negotiation went on successfully for us. (Chandra et al. 2005)

The foregoing discussion shows how weak ties spanning structural holes can play an important role in bringing together otherwise unconnected information, and contribute to the development of new ideas and the discovery of new types of market opportunities. But strong ties can play an important role in this information dissemination process. This is because there is no reason to believe that ties spanning structural holes necessarily result in the flow of information directly to people and firms with the required prior knowledge, resources and skills to recognise and respond to the potential opportunities. Valuable information may enter a business network anywhere and at any time. But the extent to which it is shared with others depends on the nature of the relations and networks linking firms. The value of new information and contacts is more likely to be recognised and shared with those who are better able to use them if strong cooperative relations exist among relevant people and firms. This is illustrated in the following account of how an electrical firm discovered a new international market opportunity:

> We are quite respected in the industry for high quality products . . . we have served architectural firms in Australia well . . . one of them is Thompson Adsett [a large multinational] . . . they have subsidiaries in overseas countries, including Indonesia . . . they recommended us to the customer and then the customer contacted us directly by phone . . . they came to us and said they wanted to install our nursing call system into their hospital . . . that's how it all began. (Chandra et al. 2005)

It is impossible to know in advance where valuable information lies in a network and what types of productive confrontations and recombinations of knowledge potentially exist. Thus it is difficult to target other types of people and firms to form relations with and business networks to join. Instead, the net has to be cast widely and firms need to be prepared to leverage opportunities as they arise, especially in a complex world of fast-changing technologies where new opportunities come from combining and using diverse types of technologies and disciplines. This is particularly apparent in industries based on leading-edge technologies such as biotechnologies and pharmaceuticals. A study of the business networks of such firms and how they change carried out by Powell (1998) showed how firms in these industries try to develop relations and networks with firms and research organisations spanning a variety of industries and technologies in order to position themselves to stay abreast of potentially relevant developments.

> Rather than seeking to monopolise the returns from innovative activity and forming exclusive partnerships with only a narrow set of organisations, successful firms position themselves as the hubs at the centre of overlapping networks, stimulating rewarding research collaborations among the various organisations to which they are aligned and profiting from having multiple projects. (Powell 1998, p. 230)

The general point here is that the role and position of firms in business networks affect the kinds of knowledge and expertise they develop, due to the activities they perform and the people and firms they interact with. They also shape the flow of information and hence the way a firm's knowledge base develops over time. This affects what a firm can know and do, and therefore the kinds of opportunities and problems they can discover and respond to.

The Burden of Relations and Networks

Relations and networks can impede and distort as well as stimulate the process of innovation. A person's or firm's prior knowledge enables them to see some types of opportunities but not others. The types of opportunities seen for exploiting the three-dimensional fax discussed above illustrate this. Each firm saw only one type of opportunity based on their own knowledge, experience and motivations, and they seemed to recognise this quickly. But they did not see any of the other opportunities. Thus existing knowledge and experience can narrow our vision as well as enhance it in some directions, leading to what some have called 'knowledge corridors' (for example, Saravathy 2003).

This narrowing of vision is reflected in the way radically new ways of doing things often come from outside the mainstream. People and firms already steeped in the current ways of seeing and doing things are likely to be less receptive to ideas that undermine these practices, and are less likely to expose themselves to threatening information of this kind. The history of industrial innovation is replete with stories of firms such as this being a source of major inventions. This includes, for example, the development of xerography by Xerox, which was not part of the existing business copier industry. Established firms in an industry tend to find it difficult to either conceive of or appreciate opportunities provided by innovations, especially if they challenge accepted wisdom and practice in the industry. This effect is reflected in particular in Clayton Christensen's (1997) research on convergent and divergent innovation described earlier.

CONCLUSIONS

The last two chapters have shown us why firms are necessarily embedded in networks of relations of many kinds and how they can enable and constrain a firm's or industry's knowledge, resources, actions and performance. They are potential sources of value in carrying out value-creating activities more efficiently and effectively through the specialisation and division of labour they make possible. They are also the means by which new ideas are discovered and acted on because of the way they shape the creation and diffusion of information and knowledge in business systems. In this way they play a central role in the evolution of business. But they are also a potential burden, a source of bias and distortion, which hampers and interferes with change and development. There is no guarantee that at any time the right combining and recombining of knowledge and resources is taking place – there is no way to know. What we do know is that relations and networks matter. Therefore, how they come into being, how they develop over time, how and why they fail or end, and how to manage interactions in such relations and networks is something we should investigate. These are the topics of the next three chapters; then I consider the implications of our understanding for firms and policy makers.

NOTE

1. This section is in part based on Wiley et al. (2006, pp. 3–5).

4. Business mating: establishing and developing business relations and networks

INTRODUCTION

BOX 4.1   MATCHES MADE IN HEAVEN

It can, apparently, take just three minutes to fall in love with another person. Cavendish Corporate Finance, a British merger-and-acquisitions boutique, hopes that something similar is true in the business world. On October 15th it is holding an 'event' ('conference' would conjure up unsexy images of droning speakers) at the annual meeting in Amsterdam of M&A International, a network of M&A firms, closely modelled on speed dating. The event will enable potential buyers and sellers of companies to get together. Rather than indicating hair colour, educational background or height, suitors tick boxes indicating geographical or industrial desires. Meetings will last only 20 minutes: as with speed dating, the object is merely to see whether there is any chemistry. A bell will be rung when the time is up. 'What people enjoy at conferences are the coffee breaks; this is a lot of coffee breaks,' says Howard Leigh, Cavendish's managing director.

Source: Economist, 7 October 2004.

This chapter is about how firms get together to form different types of business relations, including longer-term 'marriages' or partnerships, as well as more temporary 'affairs' and looser 'friendships'. The term 'business mating' is chosen to refer to the processes involved because the problems and issues involved in developing relations in business are similar in many ways to the way animals and people mate, a subject that has been much studied in biology and social science, starting with Charles Darwin.

As the opening vignette suggests, finding a good partner in life and business is not easy. In this chapter I review some of the main theories and models that have been developed to describe and explain how business relations start and how they develop. In Chapter 5 I examine the kinds of relations they can develop into, the various kinds of relationship attractors towards which relations gravitate. I borrow from theories of mating and relationship development in humans and other animals. The chapter is organised into two main parts. The first focuses on how firms get together in the first place and which types of firms tend to enter into relations with each other. The second examines how relationships develop and change through the interactions taking place over time. This sets the stage for Chapter 5, which examines what business relations can grow up to become, and Chapter 6, which examines the ongoing management of interactions in a relation by those involved, or what I refer to as 'business dancing'.

CHOOSING AND BEING CHOSEN[1]

People are social animals. They survive and prosper in groups through which their needs are met and future generations are produced, protected and socialised. Mating behaviour plays an important role in determining what types of animals, people and firms survive and how their characteristics evolve over time. Darwin focused on the important role of mating behaviour in the evolution of species in his second great book, *The Descent of Man; and Selection in Relation to Sex* (1871), where he introduced the concept of sexual selection. Sexual selection is different from natural selection, which was the subject of his first great book, *On the Origin of Species* (1859). Natural selection focuses on how species develop and adapt to the challenges of their environment in order to survive, where the environment includes both the physical environment and the presence of other species. Sexual selection focuses on how members of a given species adapt to each other in order to reproduce.

Darwin's 'other theory', as it has been called by Richard Dawkins, was at first ignored, and only natural selection was used to explain the evolution of different species characteristics. But now it is realised that sexual selection plays a major role and differences originally attributed to natural selection turn out to be the product of sexual selection. For example, skin colour is usually explained in terms of natural selection with respect to climate, with paler skins evident further from and darker skins closer to the equator. But this does not fit with all of the evidence, as Jared Diamond (1991) has pointed out. Native people with dark skins exist in very temperate climates, e.g. Tasmanian Aborigines, and no American Indians have very dark skins no matter how sunny the climate is. Also, in the Solomon Islands jet-black and lighter-skinned people are to be found living in adjacent regions. These results cannot be explained by the (long) time it takes to evolve skin colour. Instead skin colours are characteristics for which social norms regarding attractiveness have evolved. Those with attractive characteristics are more likely to be chosen as partners, and their genes populate successive generations. This takes much less time than the biological evolution of lighter or darker skin colour to meet environmental conditions.

Theories of business and competition have tended to build on natural selection as opposed to sexual selection theories of evolution. They ignore the importance of business mating behaviour in determining firm survival and evolution in favour of the way firms have to adapt to the challenges posed by their market environment in order to survive. But to survive and adapt to their environment, firms have to develop relations with other types of firms. Just as animals and plants have to mate to preserve their species, so do firms, and this makes theories based on sexual selection relevant to the analysis of business. Who mates with whom and how and why they do so affects the kind of value that is created and delivered to customers, and the way firms develop and evolve over time.

The study of mating behaviour in biology or business is complex because it involves a mutual choice – choosing and being chosen. Much previous writing on partner choice in business focuses on the criteria firms *should* use in assessing the attractiveness of alternative suitors, how work *should* be organised and divided up between them and the type of relation that *should* be established to monitor and control a partner's behaviour. But a firm's degree of discretion in these matters may be quite limited. The problem is often one of getting chosen, not choosing, of finding firms willing to form a relation rather than choosing among a set of possible suitors. This is especially the case when firms are new, have a limited reputation, an unclear understanding of their potential value, and are trying to enter distribution systems and industrial networks with established relations.

Unless it is able to find firms with desired characteristics that also have an interest in what it has to offer, a firm will not be able to form a relation with them. An exchange of values is involved in which each party seeks to meet its needs. But relations involve more than a one-off exchange; they involve the co-production of value over time, which depends on combining the resources and abilities of the firms involved in a productive manner. Therefore the ability to form and develop productive relations depends on the characteristics and resources each firm has to contribute and how they go about interacting with each other. This involves two types of firm fitness: (a) *competitive fitness*, i.e. creating and offering differential advantage to customers; and (b) *relationship fitness*, i.e. developing and sustaining relations with other organisations that contribute to firm survival and growth. Our focus here is on the latter.

RELATIONSHIP FITNESS

Relationship fitness depends on the characteristics of firms that play a role in attracting and securing suitable relationship partners. We can gain some understanding of these characteristics by looking at research that has been done on mating behaviour in other contexts. For example, there has been much research on the characteristics of people who marry each other, or what is termed assortative mating. Married couples resemble each other in many ways (Diamond 1991). They are most similar with respect to religion, ethnic background, race, socioeconomic status, age and political views, with correlations between partners of around 0.9 for these characteristics. Next highest are personality and intelligence, with correlations around 0.4, followed by numerous physical characteristics that are significantly correlated at around 0.2. The latter include features often used to indicate attractiveness, such as height, hair colour, skin and eye colour. But they also include characteristics less obviously associated with attractiveness, including breadth of nose, length of ear lobes, lung volume, size of wrist, and distance between the eyes. Some physical characteristics are even more strongly correlated – such as 0.6 for the length of the middle finger. The same results have been found for people in many different parts of the world, including Europe, America and Africa.

What accounts for these similarities and does it have any relevance to business? Partly the results reflect who you are likely to encounter and have the opportunity to marry, generally those from your own locale and social milieu. Second, they reflect the mutual choice involved, and the fact that marriage involves a form of negotiation in which the two parties agree to choose each other. The more similar a male and female are in terms of political views, religion and personality, the easier it is to reach such an agreement. As a result, married couples are more closely matched in terms of attitudes and personality than dating couples, and the match is closer still for happily married couples. A third reason for these similarities is sexual attraction, which underlies the similarity among various types of physical characteristics, because sexual attractiveness is based to a large extent on physical appearance. Studies show that we tend to marry people who look like ourselves.

Similar types of factors underlie assortative mating in business. First, geographical distance is important in choosing relationship partners, because it is easier to establish and maintain close contact with firms that are not too far away. The importance of this is reflected in the role of domestic industry clusters and industrial networks in developing a country's international competitiveness, such as Silicon Valley and the textile area of Northern Italy. However, the importance of geographical distance as a determinant of marriage and business partners may be declining in an age of rapid travel and communication, and the Internet.

Second, business relations also involve a joint choice, and this is the result of some form of negotiation and courting process. It is easier to form and maintain relations with firms with whom one has a meeting of minds or, in my terms, a productive coupling of schemas, such that both see value in the relation and agree on the ways of doing business. Just as in marriage, the negotiation is easier when both business partners are compatible in terms of their aims and philosophies. As one manager of a small firm remarked, in a study of international business I was involved in, 'the problems and joys of small business are universal', and this influenced the kinds of partners he sought in international markets. Studies show that firms that are similar to and familiar with each other are sought as suppliers and customers, even more so when uncertainty is high. But market conditions may limit choice, leading to businesses with dissimilar and incompatible goals having to do business with each other.

The third factor affecting mate choice is sexual attraction, which may at first seem remote from business. But this lies at the heart of Darwin's concept of sexual selection. Many characteristics of sexual attractiveness evolve because they perform useful biological functions. They convey information about the fitness and match of a partner and hence about the fitness of the offspring that will result. This is why people tend to be attracted to those that look similar to themselves: they are likely to have compatible genes and fitter offspring – offspring that are more likely to survive and reproduce. This in turn increases the prevalence of people with genes for having and appreciating these attractiveness characteristics in future generations. As a consequence, indicators of attractiveness become reinforced and a runaway process can result in which more extreme forms of a characteristic evolve until they interfere with other aspects of fitness. For example, male peacocks are thought to have evolved very long and bright tails through such a process, and it has been suggested that the evolution of the human mind can be explained in these terms (Miller 2001).

What has all this got to do with business? Firms do not produce babies together, but they do produce and co-produce value for each other and for other firms through their interactions and adaptations over time in business relations. Firms have to judge the attractiveness of each other as potential relationship partners in terms of the value that is likely to be co-produced.

The process of evolution of attractiveness characteristics is of course not by sexual selection and inherited characteristics but by cultural transmission, in which firms learn from their experience in relations and by observing and imitating others. Just as in sexual selection, standards of attractiveness develop among firms that influence the types of firms that form relations with each other. Attractiveness characteristics will only develop and survive if they indicate the fitness or potential value of relationship partners, just as they do in the case of sexual selection. Characteristics that do not reflect fitness will eventually die out because firms using them will be less successful, less likely to continue using them and less imitated.

This leads to the question of what kinds of characteristics become fitness indicators among firms. One way of answering this is to examine who mates with whom in the business world. One such study is of a multinational database of international customer–supplier relations in industrial markets developed by the Industrial Marketing and Purchasing (IMP) group of researchers. The research shows that, first, significant correlations existed between a supplier and its international customer in terms of their size, growth rate and degree of internationalisation. In other words, larger firms tended to partner larger firms, growing firms growing firms, more internationalised firms more internationalised firms. Because we are dealing with correlations, we cannot be sure about the direction of causation here. It may be that similar sized firms or firms with similar growth rates or degrees of internationalisation are more likely to meet and form a relationship. Or it may be that the correlations reflect the product of relationships, because firms that work together are likely to grow or not together and have similar or related interests in terms of internationalisation.

To explore further the type of match between partner firms, the research also correlated the sources of a supplier's and its customer's competitiveness, i.e. the supplier's competitiveness in its domestic market and the foreign customer's competitiveness in its own home market, to see if they were linked. The question is, do firms with similar sources of competitiveness tended to form relations in order to reinforce their competitiveness, or do firms with complementary strengths in terms of their sources of competitiveness become partners? Competitiveness was rated on how weak or strong firms compare to relevant competitors in terms of market share, price, quality, delivery capacity, marketing capacity, service, innovativeness, technology, access to supply sources, international experience and adaptations to customer requirements.

When the results for all relations were examined, a mixed pattern of correlations between sources of competitiveness between partner firms was found, suggesting a mixture of similarity and complementarity in competitive resources. But more interesting results emerged when the results for relations that were performing better and worse were compared. This showed that significant differences existed in the way partner resources correlated. In better-performing relations, stronger correlations existed between partner firms for the same source of competitiveness, especially market share, innovation and technology. This suggests that similar firms tend to have better relations. This is probably because firms can negotiate and cooperate better when they have mutual interests and strengths in areas such as quality, innovation and technology. This is similar to the reasons used to account for correlated personality dimensions in married couples.

The important role of complementary strengths is also suggested in the results. For example, in better relations, stronger correlations exist between a supplier's quality competitiveness and its customer's competitiveness in delivery capacity, marketing capacity, service, technology and access to supply sources. These suggest the kinds of skills and resources a customer needs to convert a supplier's higher-quality inputs into competitive market offerings. In addition, a customer's technology strength was strongly correlated with its supplier's strength in terms of innovativeness and access to supply sources. In poorer relations, a supplier's price competition was strongly correlated with its customer's delivery capacity, and negatively correlated with its customer's service strength and access to suppliers. These and other results indicate a different type of relation based on price and quantity, and one in which the supplier is dominant. This type of relation is less profitable. Lastly, for poor relations there was also a strong correlation between the customer's international experience and its supplier's innovativeness, which could indicate the role of the customer as a source of international market information and innovation for the supplier, but not so much a source of direct profits.

Finding and Being Found

A double search process goes on in and between markets as firms both search for and signal to each other indicators of attractiveness. Various types of fitness indicators arise in this search process that help firms identify and evaluate each other as potential partners. Potential fitness indicators include the characteristics that are directly observable, including supplied products and services, the characteristics of sales personnel and other representatives, and a firm's public record of performance. Firm characteristics are communicated through firms actively signalling their potential attractiveness to each other in various ways, including direct sales calls, websites, promotion in the trade press and by participating in trade fairs and other industry-relevant forums where they display their wares. Active search also takes place as firms try to identify and make contact with potential partners, by researching data sources such as directories, websites and trade media, and through advertising for bidders. For example, an export relationship for an Australian telecommunication manufacturer in the Singapore market was identified by a distributor in Singapore, who identified the firm through a directory and learned about its fitness through informal communication networks within the industry in the region.

While such public information gives some indication as to the resources, skills and potential complementarities of other firms, the softer side of relations is much more difficult to see and evaluate. This concerns the ability to work with the other party and their willingness to build a productive relation: how do they behave and interact in relations; are they collaborative or opportunistic; how trustworthy are they? In the main firms learn about these characteristics indirectly, through the experience of relating, or through the reputation firms develop and the experience of trusted others. Research shows that prior relationships have an important influence on future partnerships. New partners are often chosen from among those known from past interactions and relations or introduced via trusted third parties including personal and professional networks of relations. Acting as a conduit to other relations and networks is one of the indirect functions of relations discussed in previous chapters.

From the foregoing discussion we can see that firms need to consider both strategies for finding others as well as strategies for being found. There are many examples of successful relations resulting from chance meetings and unexpected or solicited enquiries from firms that open up new types of opportunities for both parties that were not foreseen. Information is not evenly spread across markets, meaning that firms are limited in what they know and, more importantly, what they don't know and don't know they don't know! Their knowledge comes from their history and experiences, and from the way they are positioned in networks and information channels, as described in Chapter 3. This both enables and constrains what they can see, including potential relationship partners.

Both strong and weak ties with others play an important role in business mating because they affect who finds whom and how they find each other. Weak ties are important because they may act as bridges to new types of information networks and new types of potential partners. For example, a firm with the rights to develop products using a particular kind of seaweed growing wild in the seas around Tasmania was seeking potential partners to develop this resource. At the same time research was being undertaken in Australia, by a university based in Queensland, on behalf of various US firms to identify and examine the potential use of active ingredients found in various sorts of marine life (Chandra 2007). A scientist working on the project knew of the Tasmanian company (a weak tie) and introduced it to a US company with complementary interests in return for a share in the business. This resulted in the development of a productive relation between the Tasmanian and US firm in the development of pharmaceutical products based on the seaweed. Strong ties also play a role because they are the means by which other firms pass on opportunities and introduce potential partners. They may be discovered by others in a firm's existing network and passed on or copied by a firm. For example, an electronics company was able to develop a relation to supply nursing-call systems to a large private hospital in Jakarta (Indonesia) as a result of referrals from a multinational architectural firm that was a satisfied customer (Chandra et al. 2005).

RELATIONSHIP DEVELOPMENT

Choosing and being chosen is only the start of a business relation. As firms interact over time they learn about each other, they alter their behaviour and thinking, their attitudes and beliefs, about each other, they adapt their resources to each other, and personal as well as professional relations, empathies, antipathies and conflicts arise between those involved. A relationship is a type of organisation that takes on a life of its own to some extent; it is a living thing that is continually being and becoming. The interactions and feedbacks taking place create the atmosphere of the relationship, which in turn shapes subsequent actions, interactions and feedback. In this section I consider various models that have been used to characterise and explain the way relations develop over time, and end by proposing an evolutionary perspective on relationship development arising from various types of underlying interacting feedback processes taking place within and between relations.

Stage Models of Business Relations

One way of characterising the development of relations is in terms of a sequence of stages through which a relationship passes on its way to its final state or its dissolution. Two of the most widely cited are those proposed by David Ford (1980) and Bob Dwyer and his co-researchers (Dwyer et al. 1988), and are shown in Table 4.1 and Figure 4.1. David Ford's classification is based on studies of industrial supplier–customer relations in European markets conducted by the IMP group. He divides the co-evolutionary process into five stages based on critical turning points he observes in these case studies. The first stage is before relationship development takes place, and describes the way firms find and evaluate each other and decide to start a business relation. Various types of critical events may trigger the search

Table 4.1 Ford five-stage model of relationships

	1 Pre-relationship stage	2 Early stage	3 Development stage	4 Long-term stage	5 Final stage
	Evaluation of new potential supplier	Negotiation of sample delivery	Contract signed or delivery build-up	After several major purchases or large-scale deliveries	In long-established stable markets
Evaluation initiated by: Particular episode in existing relationship; General evaluation of existing supplier performance; Efforts of non-supplier; Other information sources; Overall policy decision		Experience Low	Increased	High	
Evaluation conditioned by: Experience with previous supplier		Uncertainty High	Reduced	Minimum Development of institutionalisation	Extensive institutionalisation – business based on Industry Codes of Practice
Uncertainty about potential relationship; 'Distance' from potential supplier		Distance High	Reduced	Minimum	
		Commitment Actual: low Perceived: low	Actual: increased Perceived: demonstrated by informal adaptations	Actual: maximum Perceived: reduced	
		Adaptation High investment of management time.	Increasing formal and informal adaptations	Extensive adaptations. Cost savings reduced by institutionalisation	
Commitment Zero		Few cost savings	Cost savings increase		

Source: Ford (1980, p. 342).

97

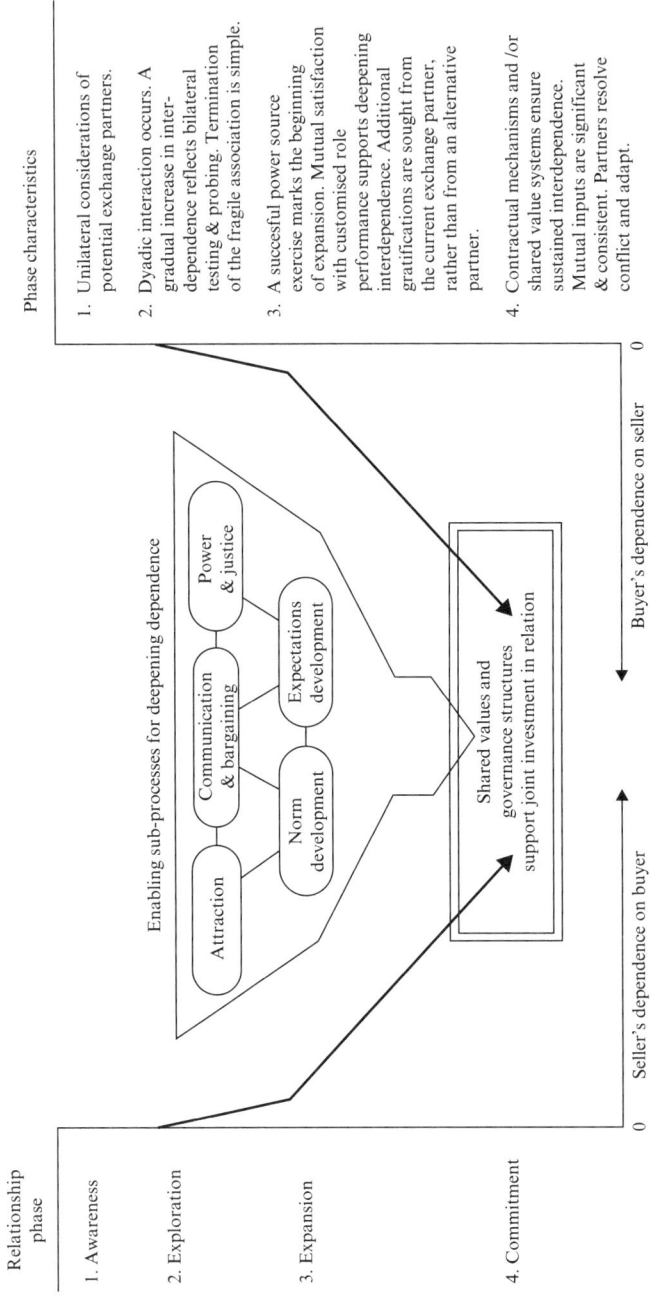

Relationship phase

1. Awareness

2. Exploration

3. Expansion

4. Commitment

Enabling sub-processes for deepening dependence

Attraction — Communication & bargaining — Power & justice

Norm development — Expectations development

Shared values and governance structures support joint investment in relation

0 — Seller's dependence on buyer

0 — Buyer's dependence on seller

Phase characteristics

1. Unilateral considerations of potential exchange partners.

2. Dyadic interaction occurs. A gradual increase in inter-dependence reflects bilateral testing & probing. Termination of the fragile association is simple.

3. A succesful power source exercise marks the beginning of expansion. Mutual satisfaction with customised role performance supports deepening interdependence. Additional gratifications are sought from the current exchange partner, rather than from an alternative partner.

4. Contractual mechanisms and/or shared value systems ensure sustained interdependence. Mutual inputs are significant & consistent & consistent. Partners resolve conflict and adapt.

Source: Dwyer et al. (1988).

Figure 4.1 Sub-processes of the Dwyer et al. relationship model

for a new partner, including experiences in existing relations and the efforts of third parties. The evaluation process is affected by prior relationship experiences and how well potential partners know the other party. This stage accords with my earlier description of the business mating process.

The beginning of the relationship involves speculative and trial interactions through which firms learn about each other. Uncertainty is high and little commitment and adaptation takes place. Depending on the outcomes of these initial interactions, the parties begin to know and understand each other better, which can lead to increased commitment and adaptation. If all goes well, the relationship could mature into an established long-term one in which both parties know each other well, achieve their objectives, the mutual adaptation of activities, resources and schemas is extensive, and actor bonds develop which support and facilitate the relationship. As the relationship continues it may become ever more institutionalised and even taken for granted, which could sow the seeds for neglect, leading to negative experiences and outcomes and the unravelling of the relation depending on the conditions faced. Not all relations will follow this path. At any stage events may conspire to challenge or further reinforce the relationship and the understanding and bonds that have developed. People may shift jobs, firm ownership can change and the performance and experience of firms in their markets may vary. Such crises may prove important tipping points revealing the true nature and commitment of each party to the relation. In addition, changes taking place in connected relations and the efforts of third parties may serve to alter the patterns of actions and interactions taking place with positive or negative effects.

Bob Dwyer and his colleagues propose an alternative model based on theories of personal relations and marriage rather than on studies of particular business relations. They also divide relationship development into five stages, as shown in Figure 4.1. Underlying these stages are various types of ongoing processes that enable the firms to deepen their dependence on each other. These are also shown in Figure 4.1 and include forms of interaction (communication and bargaining), actor bond development (attraction, power, justice, norm development) and schema development (justice and expectations). Out of these processes arises an enhanced level of shared values (schema couplings) and more developed means of coordination (governance modes), which support investment in the relation (resource adaptation and actor commitment). The five stages correspond to a large extent to those described by Ford, except that a dissolution stage is added and no distinction is made similar to Ford's long-term and final stage. Once again all relations are not assumed to go through these same stages or to spend the same time at each stage. Dissolution is possible at any stage but becomes more difficult and costly as the relationship and mutual commitments develop. We shall consider relationship ending in more detail in a section of Chapter 6.

Stage models provide a useful generic perspective on how relations might develop over time, but not all relations develop into long-term highly committed and involved relations. This does not necessarily mean they have failed, because their role and purpose can be quite different. Stage models implicitly assume that relationship development is some pre-given unfolding process in which preceding stages determine subsequent stages and leave little room for the role of management, ambiguity, uncertainty and external events in shaping relationship development.

Other models of relationship development adopt a *teleological approach* in which it is implicitly assumed that a relation is controlled by a firm, which can manage it over time to achieve its purposes. Alternatively, it is assumed that the most efficient structure automatically emerges, as in economic theories of channel and industry structure, including the production and transaction cost theories described in Chapter 3. There is some validity in these types of models. Powerful actors in business relations can have major impacts on the way a relation develops, but market exchange involves interactions among interdependent firms that have some degree of power over each other, no matter how asymmetrical it may be. Less powerful actors are not without strategies to influence relationship development. The search for economically efficient forms of industrial organisation and governance also drives the formation and development of relations. But this is limited by market realities, including: conflicts of interest among firms in terms of what is the most efficient structure; partial, biased and unevenly distributed information and expertise; future uncertainties; the bounded rationality of market actors; the impact of non-economic forces such as the effect of community values, ethical and legal requirements; and the development of personal as well as professional relations among those involved.

AN EVOLUTIONARY MODEL OF RELATIONSHIP DEVELOPMENT

A relationship develops its own history through the patterns of interaction taking place over time. The particular history that develops is a product of many factors, including the prior history of the participants, the aims, objectives and orientations of the parties involved, the sequence of events taking place, the impact of connected relations and events, as well as more general market and environmental conditions.

Figure 4.2 depicts the main processes at work. Once a relationship begins, its development is a co-evolutionary process involving interaction

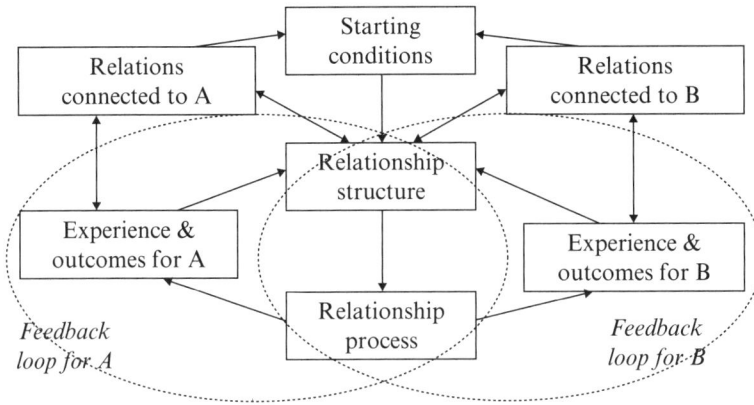

Figure 4.2   Evolutionary model of relationship development

and feedback loops between the structure of a relation at any given time (including at start-up), the interaction processes taking place and the outcomes for each party to the relation. *Relationship structure* comprises the four dimensions introduced earlier: actors, activities, resources and schemas. Each actor engages in various types of *activities* and *interactions* using its *resources* (including knowledge, skills and competences), guided by its goals and theory in use, or *schemas*, and the *bonds* it has with others involved, i.e. its perceptions and feelings towards them. *Starting conditions* refer to the structural conditions that exist when a relationship begins, including the activities, schemas, bonds and resources the parties involved bring to the relation due to prior existence and experience. *Relationship processes* are the ongoing actions and interactions taking place (including cognitive actions), which are the engines of relationship development and evolution. The experience and outcomes of relationship processes result in *feedback effects* in terms of the continual replenishment, modification and co-adaptation of each actor's activities, resources, schemas and bonds. Over time, relationship processes and feedback effects configure and reconfigure various types of *activity links, resource ties, schema couplings* and *actor bonds*, which constitute the relationship structure that exists at any given time. This structure enables and constrains actions and interactions that in turn affect structure, strengthening or weakening it, reproducing or changing it. Relationship structure is continually being made and remade or changed. The overall or macro structure of a relation emerges in a bottom-up self-organising way from the micro processes taking place between and among involved actors, activities, resources and schemas.

Each dimension of structure may be further decomposed into sub-dimensions and processes that have been highlighted in previous research. For example, the types of actor bonds that develop among relationship par-, ticipants, which form the atmosphere of a relationship, include dimensions such as power-dependence, trust, opportunism, understanding, satisfaction and commitment. These are considered further in Chapter 6.

Relations are connected to other relations and transactions; they do not develop in isolation. The processes taking place in connected relations influence each other, enabling and constraining relationship development. Furthermore, the links among processes in connected relations are the source of various types of indirect functions and dysfunctions, as described in previous chapters. These include indirect demand and supply sources, information about markets and technology, referrals and reputation effects.

Starting and Operating Conditions

The starting and operating conditions set the stage and context for relationship development. Among the more important are: the role and purpose of the relation for each participant; the amount and relative dependence of the parties involved; the complementarity and compatibility of the resources of each party; and the more general market and environmental circumstances in which the relationship operates. I consider each in turn.

Relationship tasks: the purpose of the relation for each party
The purpose or function of the relation for each party forms part of their initial schemas, mental model or theory in use, as it is variously called. This includes the expected outcomes from the relation and the role they play in the portfolio of relations of each participant. To generate the expected outcomes tasks have to be performed, products and services have to be designed, produced and delivered to the satisfaction of those involved. These tasks vary from *routine transactions* – involving regularly purchased simple, standardised products and services, using well-established technologies and systems requiring little investment and adaptation – to *complex transactions* – for customised inputs involving the co-development and coordination of innovative technologies, specialist skills and competences and substantial investments. The former include purchases of staples such as paper and office supplies and standardised materials, and the latter the development of new plants and systems with high investment costs and proprietary technologies. There are major differences in the nature and extent of the coordination tasks required in each case, and hence the transaction costs involved. Creating efficient and effective means of interaction

and collaboration is paramount for more complex products, services and technologies, when innovation and adaptation are required, and this poses challenges for the relationship and the way it develops. As I shall show in Chapter 5, different types of relations arise according to the nature and difficulty of the tasks involved, and different types of relationship management styles are required.

For relations to begin, some degree of anticipated mutual fit is required, and this may change over time as a result of what goes on. The functions of the relation for each party need to complement each other to sustain the relation; mismatches will cause relationship partners to drift apart. To illustrate this, consider the different roles a given supplier–customer relationship may play for the supplier and customer.

For the supplier, one way of classifying its customers is in terms of a customer pyramid based on their contribution to sales revenue or profit, as shown in Figure 4.3(a). A few customers contribute a substantial share; these are the most important customers, deserving careful attention, and their loyalty is cherished. Those of lesser value receive proportionally less resources and attention. For the customer its suppliers may be grouped according to the value impact and complexity of the products and services supplied, as shown in Figure 4.3(b). Customers are most concerned about products and services with high-value impact and which are complex. These are potentially important sources of its competitiveness and profitability, and developing good-quality relations with suppliers of such strategically important inputs is appropriate. Less complex but high-impact inputs are more easily sourced and the goal is price reduction, possibly through long-term contracts and reduction of transaction costs through routinising the relation. Low-value impact inputs that are complex require ensuring security of supply, and those that are not complex can be sourced in open markets.

Figure 4.3 shows three types of customer relationship and four types of supplier relationship situations in terms of the motivation to form relationships with the counterpart. But relations involve both suppliers and customers: what happens when different types of motivations encounter each other? There are 3 × 4 or 12 different types of potential relationship situations. Which ones are complementary and mutually reinforcing, leading to the development of strong supplier–customer relations? Which ones lead to a conflict of interests, and what is likely to happen to the relationship between them?

Customers towards the bottom of the customer pyramid will find it difficult to develop close relations with their suppliers, which is fine if the inputs are low-impact value and non-complex. If they are more complex, or have high-value impact, a customer could try to secure supply and

(a) Customer pyramid

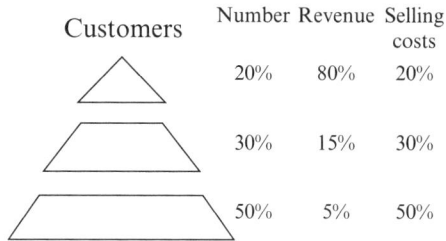

Customers	Number	Revenue	Selling costs
	20%	80%	20%
	30%	15%	30%
	50%	5%	50%

(b) Purchasing portfolio

		Low Complexity	High
Value impact	High	Leverage goal: price reduction	Strategic goal: relationships
	Low	Routine goal: processes	Bottleneck goal: security of supply
		Low	High

Complexity

Source: Figure 4.3b adapted from Kraljic (1983, p. 110).

Figure 4.3 Types of customers and suppliers

reduce costs through long-term contracts with suppliers, because they help reduce the suppliers' selling costs and make the customer more profitable. As a result the customer may be promoted up the hierarchy. The attractiveness of the customer to the supplier is limited unless it can offer additional value in the form of indirect functions such as product and process co-development, market knowledge or reputation and referrals. This may be possible in the case of complex inputs with high-value impact, as the customer will be willing to invest in and contribute such functions.

Another way in which low-value customers can be handled is through intermediaries, who are able to offer scale and scope economies and reduce transaction costs through bulk transactions and reduced contracts. They can also represent the interests of groups of customers to the supplier. For low-impact value inputs this is clearly in the customer's interest, but the problem becomes more difficult for complex products that require specialist inputs. Specialist intermediaries may develop to cater for such situations, as when producers create approved after-sales service suppliers. Another interesting example is of an emergency supplier of electrical components described by Keith Blois (2002). Potential customers maintain contacts with the firm for when an emergency arises, and rely on its ability to find suitable components. The intermediary keeps some stocks and retains links with suppliers world-wide but maintains confidentiality as to which products are supplied to customers. In this way the intermediary provides useful functions for both producers in disposing of excess output and for customers encountering stock-outs of key inputs.

Valued customers are wooed by suppliers who want to retain their custom. This works well for customers sourcing more complex inputs and with higher-value impact. This can be the basis for the formation of strate-gic partnerships. But there are potential conflicts of interest when cus-tomers are interested only in price and the inputs are less complex. Here customers may want to rely on multiple sources and play suppliers off against each other, while each supplier invests in trying to make them loyal to them. As such customers are likely to be attractive to many suppliers, the supplier may have to be content to get part of the action and be prepared to compete with a smaller set of in-suppliers. For example, Japanese man-ufacturers practise sole sourcing of particular inputs to get economies, but reward and retain potential competitors by giving them other business and by helping them learn from winning competitors.

Suppliers may also be able to offer value by sourcing additional inputs on behalf of customers, becoming a systems supplier of complementary inputs, which increases its value to the customer. In other words, they become a type of intermediary by expanding the scope of their activities in ways relevant to their customers.

Relative dependence and power[2]

The purpose of the relationship for each party is closely linked to another type of relationship situation, the relative dependence of the supplier and customer on each other. This is because dependence is a function of the importance of the values provided by each party to the other and how easy they are to replace. The greater the dependence, the greater the power; the balance of power and dependence in a relation affects the way it is likely to develop and how problems and issues are dealt with. Figure 4.4 depicts four types of relationship situations in terms of the power and dependence of firms A and B.

When both firms have little dependence and power, the development of strong relations is not necessary and arm's-length market relations are more likely. But longer-term relations may still develop out of conve-nience and habit, and the opportunity to reduce price and transaction

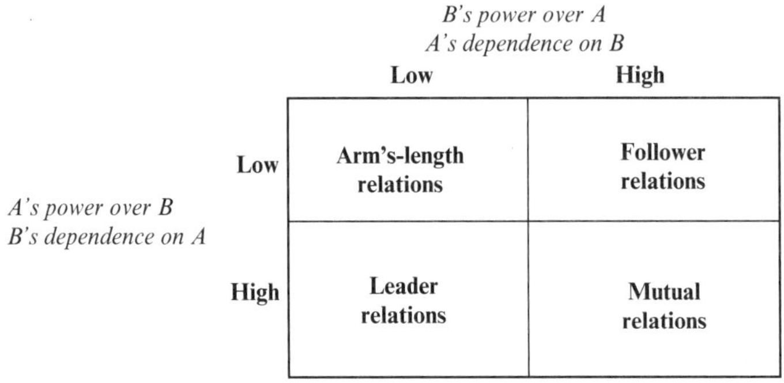

B's power over A
A's dependence on B

		Low	High
A's power over B B's dependence on A	**Low**	Arm's-length relations	Follower relations
	High	Leader relations	Mutual relations

Source: Ritter et al. (2004, p. 178).

Figure 4.4   Balance of power and dependence in a relationship

costs, such as e-procurement systems for routine products and services, e.g. paper and pens. Customers collaborate to set up automated purchase and supply systems with designated suppliers with whom they negotiate long-term agreements. Investing in these systems represents large relationship-specific assets that serve to keep costs down and routinise purchasing.

When power and dependence are asymmetric, one party has the ability to forge the relationship more in its interests. One firm becomes the leader and the other a follower. Franchise systems are examples of relations in which one party has the upper hand, and studies show that conflict can be intense in such systems, in part because activities are designed more in the interests of the franchisor. But such is not always the case. For example, by meeting the needs of the franchisee the franchisor can benefit its own business, and the satisfaction of the franchisee can result in even more control being given to the franchisor. For example, Donald Fites (1996) describes how Caterpillar, a major US earthmoving equipment manufacturer, was able to recover from strong international competition through the development of strong partnerships with its dealers that enabled it to foster better relations and understanding with its end customers.

The weaker party in such relations is not without power, and some degree of dependence exists to form a relationship. Furthermore, the relative value of each party's contribution can change over time, as firms learn to do business with each other, activity routines develop, personal and professional bonds develop and resources become co-aligned. Indirect functions may assume more importance as the weaker party becomes a source of information and advice about developments in related markets, or works with a supplier or customer on product and process improvements. In addition, weaker players can band together to seek better conditions through industry and trade groups and political lobbying.

Conditions of high interdependence create the opportunity both for fireworks and strong collaboration. Each firm is an important stakeholder in the other and each stands to gain or lose from improvements or deficiencies in the other's performance and contribution. An interesting example of this situation is the relationship between Procter and Gamble (P&G), a major supplier of supermarket items, and Wal-Mart, a major retailer in the USA (Kumar 1996). Their relationship is one of mutual dependence, as each needs the other to reach their customers and meet their needs. At one time their relationship was more like war. Wal-Mart sought to achieve the lowest possible prices from its suppliers and P&G tried to find ways to cut costs and charge Wal-Mart extra for whatever it could. This led to minimum levels of cooperation, and personal animosities were high. Both firms were suffering. But a change was brought about through the intervention of a mutual friend of the CEOs of these two companies. As a result of a personal meeting and agreement to change things, a whole sequence of events was put in place to change the atmosphere in the relation. This included building better personal and professional links between the personnel involved at all levels, changing internal relations and practices, even to the extent of removing some recalcitrants, and reinforcing and rewarding more collaborative forms of interaction.

A firm that specialises in bringing about more cooperative relations between firms in business is APRAIS, a UK-based firm with operations around the world. It acts as a kind of business marriage counsellor, especially for advertising agencies and their clients. The firms involved must both want to be involved, which is a good start. APRAIS first takes detailed readings of the existing relation by asking all those involved about each other. It then distils this information and feeds it back to those involved, focusing on areas where problems may exist, and helps search for ways forward, such as realigning incentives and processes. It returns periodically to review developments, to provide feedback and to stimulate further change and, over time, it has had considerable success in moving relations to more collaborative and productive forms.

Complementarity and compatibility of resources

Parties to a relation bring to it various types of resources, including both tangible and intangible elements such as skills, abilities and competences, knowledge and experience, and other relationships. The value produced in a relationship for each party depends on the degree to which these resources complement each other in the performance of required functions, and also on the extent to which they enable the parties to work together effectively.

Complementary resources underlie specialisation among firms, as shown in Chapters 2 and 3. External economies arise from the division of tasks among firms, which are able to perform different assortments of tasks more efficiently, thus benefiting those that outsource those activities to them. The compatibility of relationship partners depends on their planning and decision-making processes, their market and competitive orientations, and the way they value and approach relationships (their relationship schemas). We have already discussed this in terms of the types of firms likely to form relations. In general, like tends to mate with like, and this applies to animals, people and firms. But choice of business relations is generally restricted. Particular assortments of inputs are required that firms cannot provide for themselves given their scale and scope, and resources and market constraints limit the number of different types of specialist firms and intermediaries that can exist. Hence choice may be limited and relations have to be formed with those whom we would otherwise prefer not to deal with. This creates various types of relationship situations that have to be managed somehow. Mismatched partners may learn to live with each other when replacements are hard to find or exit costs are high due to contractual provisions. In one case an accounting firm was retained by a business although an accountant from the firm had raided their trust account and then left the firm. 'They know our business' was the reason given (Young and Denize 1995).

As firms and people get to know each other or personnel change, a relationship can shift its culture from adversarial to collaborative forms or vice versa. A history of the relationship between Volvo and a key supplier reveals that early on, during a critical negotiation, Volvo was trying to get a glimpse of the cost figures being used by the supplier as the basis for its negotiations. In response, the CEO of the supplier showed Volvo the cost figures and from this developed a strong personal bond of trust between the two CEOs. It was only when one of the CEOs died that Volvo eventually took over the supplier (Kinch 1987).

Connected relations
Relationship participants bring with them other relations in which they are already involved, and what happens in them affects and is affected by events in a new relation. Existing and previous relations can play an important role in determining which firms come together in the first place. Connected relations may be more or less interdependent, and both enable and constrain the way each develops. The types of connections are reflected in the functions and dysfunctions that can result from the way activity links, actor

bonds, resource ties and schema couplings in one relation spill over into another. These have been described in Chapter 3 and will not be repeated here. The central issue is that the evolution of a relationship cannot be considered in isolation from other relations to which it is directly and indirectly connected.

Market and environmental conditions
The starting conditions I have so far considered are part of the context in which a relationship functions and affect the kinds of relations that can and do develop. Context also includes the local market and more general environmental conditions. The competitive conditions confronting suppliers and customers in their respective markets, the degree of concentration and the ease of switching affect how dependent each is on the other and hence their relative power. Business customs and practices, industry cultures – or recipes, as they are sometimes called – vary by industry, time and nation, as a result of prior history and local conditions leading to the emergence of different types of relations. For example, some business cultures are more adversarial and litigious, such as the car industry or retail distribution in the USA, whereas others are more cooperative and less inclined to litigation; the number of lawyers per head in the USA is far higher than in other countries, such as Japan. Countries and regions that are more homogeneous, where firms have long histories of trading with each other, or where personal and family connections sustain relations, such as in Scandinavia, China and Japan, are more likely to have developed means of collaboration that are cooperative and less legalistic. Legal systems, particularly trade practices legislation, constrain the types of relations that can develop among firms, as do more general cultural and social norms and values. As a result we observe different types of relations in the same industries around the world, and the formation of effective relations across cultural and national borders is often the most difficult to achieve.

CONCLUSIONS

We now have some idea of the mechanisms at work leading firms to form relations with each other, what I call business mating. We also know about the mechanisms driving relationship development and the factors shaping how these play out over time. The next question to answer is what happens to relations when they grow up or end. The stage models imply some natural progression towards more developed and mature, cooperative relations. But is this necessarily so? Even a casual look around the business world reve that many different types of business relations exist. Are they all or way to the same place? Are some better suited to particular conditions than others? Under what conditions do different types arise and how many different types are there? Which perform better and why, and how do we cope with different types of relations? These issues are the subject of the next two chapters. In Chapter 5 I review the results of studies that have attempted to develop a typology of business relations and consider whether there are superior types of relations in different conditions. In Chapter 6 I consider how firms operate in relations, or 'dance' with each other.

NOTES

1. This section is based on Wilkinson et al. (2005).
2. This section is in part based on Ritter et al. (2004, p. 177–8).

5. Relationship attractors: typologies of business relations

INTRODUCTION

When relations grow up they can become many things, not all of which are foretold in their starting conditions. Each relation develops its own history and takes on its own distinctive personality as it is shaped by historical events, context and contingencies, much like a human personality develops. But a relationship is not the product of one mind and body, but of interacting bodies (firms) and minds that self-organise over time through their actions, interactions and responses, or they part company and the relationship ends. What kinds of relationship attractors are there? What forms of relationship arise in business systems in different circumstances and how stable are they? Which forms function better and in which types of conditions?

RELATIONSHIP METAPHORS: MARRIAGES, FRIENDSHIPS AND AFFAIRS[1]

A metaphor used to characterise business relations is that of marriages versus affairs (for example, Levitt 1986; Dwyer et al. 1988). Marriages are long-term, committed relations in which the parties involved cooperate to achieve their goals, with more or less difficulty along the way, just like real marriages. Affairs, on the other hand, are shorter-term, more exploitative relations, where the other party is used as a means to an end, with little value placed on maintaining the relation. Intermediate forms of relations have also been suggested, resembling friendships and acquaintances.

The marriage metaphor fits naturally as an extension of the idea of business mating discussed in Chapter 4. But the metaphor is limited because it focuses attention more on the reasons for the formation of relations and the types of structural bonds that tie firms together, rather than on the active, ongoing, processes of relating. Relations are co-regulated by the parties involved, co-produced from their interactions and the way they are able to align and coordinate their activities, resources, schemas and bonds. They do not exist unless they are continually re-produced.

Another metaphor is more apt, I believe, at describing the ongoing processes of interacting and interrelating – 'business dancing'. In Chapter 6 I examine how firms interact in business relations in more detail using the dancing metaphor as a generic way of characterising the processes involved. The dancing metaphor is also apt for understanding the different types of business relations that emerge in economic systems because they can be viewed as different types of *dances* that firms co-develop and learn how to dance together as a relation develops over time. To be sure, starting conditions matter (who asked whom to dance and what the opening moves and outcomes were), as well as the conditions and tasks confronting them (the music that is playing and who else is on the dance floor).

There are many types of business dances, performed more or less well by those involved. Some dances involve elaborately coordinated sequences of steps that can be choreographed in advance or emerge from the interaction of the dancers and their knowledge and skills. Other dances involve less complex steps or are more loosely coordinated. Some dances are fast and others slow. Some dances are more adversarial, others more serene. Some dances involve couples, others multiple couples or groups. You cannot marry everyone, but all can take a turn on the dance floor and learn to dance.

Business relating is similar. There are variations in the degree and complexity of coordination required, the nature of the challenges and problems posed by the environment and connected relations, and the speed of change and adaptation required. As a result different business dances emerge, the dancers both lead and follow with greater or lesser skill, and the dance evolves as environment conditions change and the dancers learn more about each other and adapt to each other. Some business dances involve multiple partners, including others directly or indirectly connected, such as suppliers, complementors, distributors and competitors. Firms have to dance with many other types of firm, not all of whom they are able or willing to marry or develop long-term partnerships with. Sometimes it is better to work with existing partners and at other times to change partners. The result is a mix of types of dances or relations in which a firm is simultaneously involved and which affect and are affected by other dances.

A classification of business relations inspired by a dancing metaphor is summarised in Table 5.1. It is a purely speculative exercise in which different types of dances and dancing contexts are used to illustrate and illuminate various dimensions and types of relations. Eight types of relationships are described, with four further differentiated according to whether levels of cooperation and competition are extreme or moderate. These dimensions of relations form part of an empirically based classification of relations to be described in the next section. Each type is portrayed in terms of the type

Table 5.1 The marriages and dances of business relations

Type	Actor bonds	Dance type	Dance mood	Business relation
1a Very low cooperation and competition	Just met or getting divorced	Walking on or off the dance floor	Warm-up or cool-down exercise; not really dancing	Starting or finishing
1b Quite low cooperation and competition	Placid and occasional affair	Line dancing	Coordinated and in unison but not partnering	Arm's-length, indifferent
2a Very low cooperation, high competition	Stormy affair, conflict, quarrel, or proxy marriage, distant	Salsa, lots of screaming and fire	Stepping (perhaps deliberately) on partner's foot, sending false signals when they lead	Poor and declining
2b Quite low cooperation, high competition	Affair or unhappy marriage with no chance of divorce, in counselling	Inept 'New vogue'	Going through the set motions (not very well)	Poor relation in process of change for the better or worse
3a Very high competition, high cooperation	Tempestuous but devoted marriage	Latin medley, (including tango)	Unexpected tempo changes, a crowded dance floor, an expert couple	Good relationship in a challenging environment
3b Quite high competition, high cooperation	Dual-career marriage – joint and conflicting interests	Ballet as well as ballroom, pasadoble	At least as concerned about one's solo parts as the duo's	Good relationship which normalises some opportunism
4a Very low competition, high cooperation	Marriage made in heaven	Waltz, foxtrot or Argentinian tango	Smooth, semi-spontaneous glide, cheek-to-cheek	Highly committed quality relation
4b Quite high cooperation, low competition	Newly-weds or semi-committed	Cha-cha-cha or 'new vogue'	Beginners with talent, (re)-establishing partnerships, simpler steps and/or dance rules	Progressive, developing relation

Source: Adapted from Wilkinson and Young (1994, p. 75).

113

of actor bonds that exist, based on the marriage metaphor, as well as in terms of a type of dance or coordinated action required. The music represents a kind of technology of the dance, which constrains but does not dictate the patterns of movement and dance steps that are appropriate.

The marriage metaphor captures some of the differences between low-cooperation, high-competition relations, which correspond more to affairs, and low-competition, high-cooperation relations, which correspond to marriages. But, in order to depict other types of relations, we need to introduce other dimensions of actor bonds, including the degree of conflict. Thus marriages can be tempestuous (3a) or made in heaven (4a), and affairs can be stormy (2a) or placid (1b). In 4b, semi-committed relations could be an old married couple, who undertake separate but complementary tasks and interact indifferently and/or infrequently, or an arranged marriage, where partnerships have been formed by third parties (such as government or other members of the business network in the case of business firms), or shotgun weddings, where parties have unwillingly contracted to form a relation to ensure survival.

The dance metaphor suggests various forms of interaction among partners that are likely to shape and be shaped by the feelings each has for the other, or what is referred to as actor bonds. The pace of interaction varies from faster to slower dances, such as the salsa in 2a versus the waltz in 4a. Dances are more or less difficult and complex, with a new vogue dance (2b), requiring one lesson to learn, being at one extreme and an intricate ballet or Argentinian tango (4a) requiring years of concentrated training and experience to accomplish well. Dances and relations require more or less physical and psychic contact – compare the tango in 3a with the cha-cha-cha in 4b. And, perhaps most important, dances are characterised by more or less interdependence: from the regimented, machine-like coordination of the line dance in 1b, which requires rules to ensure everyone dances in unison but partners do not really exist and people can join in and leave at any time, to a ballet duet where a failure to catch your partner could result in crippling injury. The quality of the dancing depends also on the skills and experience of the dancers in both a general sense of having a compatible and complementary sense of rhythm, as well as being coordinated, motivated and educated. But it depends also on relationship-specific skills and resources developed over time through a shared history of interaction and joint learning, whereby each can anticipate and respond to what the other is going to do, and the dance couple become a true entity unto themselves.

In dancing, as well as in relationships, history matters. Partners develop partnership-specific skills within the course of relations. Long-term partners such as the Olympic ice dancers Torville and Dean will retain only some of their abilities if they terminate their partnership and form new ones. Within a partnership many patterns of evolution are possible, but these depend to some extent on past history and are thus path-dependent to a certain extent. Over time parties can change the type of dancing they do together and add new dances to their repertoire. Partners move from one dance to another. But skill, based on past experience, also influences the additional dances they may successfully attempt. As they become more expert they can attempt more complex dances. But not all development paths are possible, as the past affects what the parties have in terms of resources, skills and experience to face the future and also how they see and respond to it.

Metaphors are ways of seeing something in terms of something else, of using knowledge from one domain to enlighten another, and business dancing captures some key dimensions of relating and relations. When people dance together they have to move in time to the music and coordinate their actions with each other. Dancing involves active cooperation, not just a type of connection. More importantly, it involves both leading and following, which are important and necessary skills (except when we choose to dance alone).

THREE RELATIONSHIP TYPOLOGIES

While we might be able to categorise dances and rate people in terms of their dancing skills, the same is not the case in business. There is no established typology of business relationships; we can use any or all dimensions of relations, depending on our purpose, to classify them. Various classifications have been offered in the literature, some based on empirical studies and the clustering of observed relations; others are more theory-based. The classification of starting conditions in terms of purpose and relative dependence, as described in Chapter 4, are examples of theory-based schemes. In the following sections I review three empirically derived typologies, each of which reflects different approaches to classifying business relations and relies on different types of relationship data. The first classifies buyer–seller relations according to the mix of cooperation and competition that exists, the second uses clustering methods to identify eight types of industrial purchasing relationships; and the third focuses on supply relations in the car industry in the USA and Japan and classifies relations according to the relative dependence of the parties involved. Each provides a different way of seeing the types of relations that emerge in business. In the final section of the chapter I attempt to reconcile these different typologies using a database of buyer–seller relations I have been involved in developing, which includes the perspectives of buyer and seller firms.

Cooperative and/or Competitive Relations (Wilkinson and Young 1994; Young and Wilkinson 1997)

The first typology results from a database of relations I helped develop over several years as part of the Interfirm Relationships Research Programme (IRRP) at the University of New South Wales. The aim of this project was to gather a detailed picture of business relations in a variety on contexts, using multiple informants including buyer and seller perspectives. Two parallel versions of the questionnaire were developed, one for buyer and one for seller firms in a relationship. We were careful to include relations that performed well and not so well. Hence we first asked respondents to consider examples of relations they were familiar with that they considered to be good, moderately good, not very good and poor working relationships. We then chose one at random to be the focus of the interview.

When we analysed the data, two dimensions were used to classify relations, how cooperative they are and how competitive or adversarial they are. These emerge as separate dimensions rather than opposite ends of one dimension. The cooperative dimension is characterised by a spirit of working together, trust, a concern for the welfare of the other and positive motivation. The competitive dimension reflects self-interested and misleading behaviour and opportunism. We classified relations according to whether they scored high or low on each of these dimensions, resulting in four types of relations. The classification into four types of relations as well as the location and scores on each dimension of particular relations in terms of their degree of cooperativeness and/or competitiveness is shown in Figure 5.1.

First consider relations involving high levels of cooperation. Firms here had stronger commitment to continued trading, personal bonds with each other and greater satisfaction. If they are also competitive, a picture emerged of a relationship under strain, due to asymmetric dependence, power plays and conflict, but held together by bonds built up over time and contractual conditions. Such relations could also be seen as effective, with 66 per cent of the relations in the high cooperation, high conflict being described as good working relationships and only 8 per cent as not good or poor. This suggests that enhanced social and operational functioning due to cooperation can outweigh or overcome many of the problems of higher competition. An example of this type of relation is an advertising agency and a small mining company, which had been highly cooperative and not competitive for a long time, but then the mining company experienced unexpected and rapid growth and became demanding and difficult to work

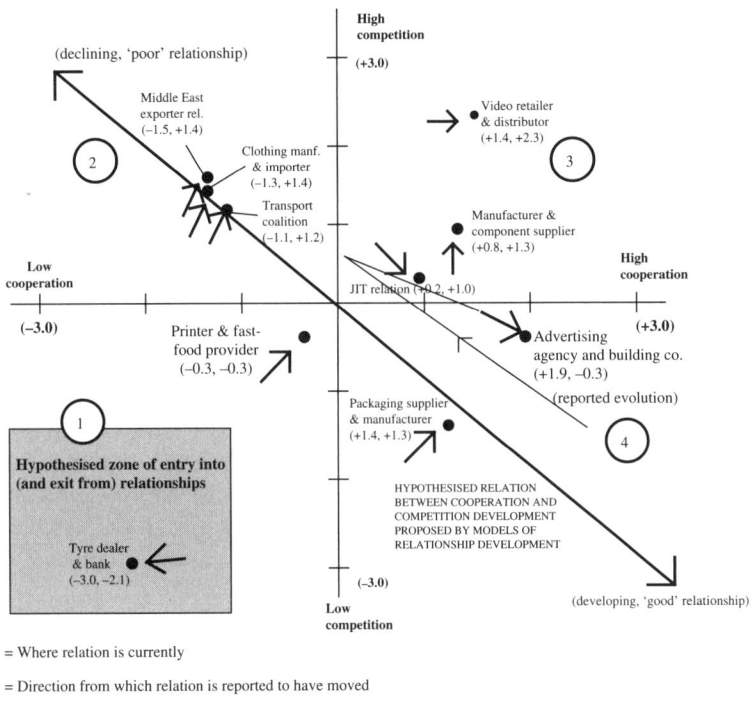

Source: Wilkinson and Young (1994, p. 73).

Figure 5.1   Cooperative and competitive business relations

with. The agency lacked experience in dealing with the problems of large companies and the relation entered a phase of diminished cooperation. But both parties recognised that their long and effective prior association was an asset worth repairing and nurturing.

Competitive or adversarial dimensions may be accepted as a normal part of doing business in some industries. Thus a firm distributing pipes prided themselves on working well with their customers but being loyal to their own interests. They assume their trading partners do likewise and, accordingly, have set up systems and procedures that guard against potential opportunism. This is not perceived to be inappropriate behaviour or conflict-inducing but, rather, sound business practice that has become an accepted part of a stable relation.

Another relation with high cooperation and competition scores is one that is six years old between a distributor of video tapes and a retailer. The firms are highly interdependent and committed, and both are fairly satisfied with the relationship, which has improved over time, with increasing mutual respect and trust. Conflict occurs that can require considerable negotiation to resolve, and the firms report behaving opportunistically on occasion. How can mutual trust and respect develop in this type of atmosphere? This is partly resolved by high levels of mutual dependence and a shared history. They have overcome conflicts and worked together well in the past, during a period of significant change due to the rapid growth of the video market and competition, which resulted in both firms growing rapidly, particularly the retailer, which started franchising outlets. This shadow of the past leads the firms to expect to be able to work together well in the future. In addition, competitors are seen as similar and there are no relationship-specific systems or procedures that tie firms together. In difficult and challenging environments firms have to try harder to successfully interact, which in turn contributes to the higher-than-expected levels of cooperation.

Low-cooperation, high-competition relationships can continue because contractual agreements and exit costs require that they do so. Firms bide their time until conditions permit divorce without great cost. When dependence is low on both sides, cooperation and competition are limited, as there is not much to fight about. Such relations are likely to be forming or dissolving. But such uninvolved, arm's-length relations can be stable and mutually convenient. An example is a fast-food chain and its printer supplying promotional material. The printer is competent and there is a history of successful interactions. The purchaser does not want to establish a loyal, committed relationship. Instead, the printing firm is one of a pool of similarly competent suppliers, used on a quote-for-job basis. Their best efforts could gain them no more than an ongoing share of the available business.

An example of a relationship with low levels of cooperation but high levels of competition is that between an Australian importer and a Fijian clothing manufacturer. The three-year relationship is difficult to coordinate, with much negotiation needed, and formal and informal rules and regulations play an important role. Conflict is intense, especially with respect to financial arrangements and delivery, and is exacerbated by poor communication that arises because of geographical and cultural distance but also because the firms withhold information to gain advantages or to get even. Both parties are very self-interested. They let each other down in pursuit of their own objectives and are more likely to use strong and coercive means of influence, although threats are not effective because the manufacturer is not dependent on the importer. They reflect more the exasperation of the importer than a real negotiation tactic. The relation is not expected to last, although finding a replacement supplier is not straightforward.

There is no clear pattern of development of firms through a sequence of stages, and firms with similar patterns of cooperation and competition may have quite different histories. Most relations are described as moving from the low-cooperation and -competition quadrant to either the high-cooperation, low-competition or low-cooperation, high-competition quadrants. The exception is the printer–fast-food chain relationship, where cooperation and competition increase but the relationship remains in the low-cooperation, low-competition quadrant. High-cooperation and high-competition relationships appear to have developed from either highly cooperative and not competitive relations, or from previous highly competitive and non-cooperative relations. In the former, high levels of competition developed as a result of difficult environmental circumstances. In the latter, high levels of cooperation developed due to the recognition of potential gains and improved management of interdependence, developing effective conflict resolution mechanisms or introducing quality management techniques.

Only in two cases does relationship development appear to follow a life-cycle stages model. The advertising agency relationship became both less cooperative and more competitive for a period of time before reversing itself and becoming more cooperative and less competitive. Also, the relationship involving just-in-time purchasing is described as one with decreasing competition and increasing cooperation over time as the relationship partners worked towards more effective ways of coping with their interdependence.

Purchasing Relations (Cannon and Perreault 1999)

The second classification comes from a nationwide study of purchasing professionals in the USA and their perceptions of relations with their main supplier. The sample covered a range of business and organisational customers from a variety of industries. Relations were classified based on various measures of relationship structure: activity links, i.e. information exchange (the degree of open sharing of useful information) and operational linkages (degree to which systems, procedures and routines have been linked to facilitate operations); actor bond and schema couplings, i.e. co-operative norms (expectations about working together to achieve mutual and individual goals and trust) and legal bonds (binding contractual agreements); resource ties, i.e. relationship-specific adaptations and investments by the buyer and seller; and schema couplings, i.e. cooperative norms (expectations about working together to achieve mutual and individual goals).

A cluster analysis revealed eight types of relations, which are summarised in Figure 5.2 in terms of the type of market and relationship conditions in which they are to be found, i.e. the importance of supply, availability of alternatives, complexity of supply and supply market dynamism.

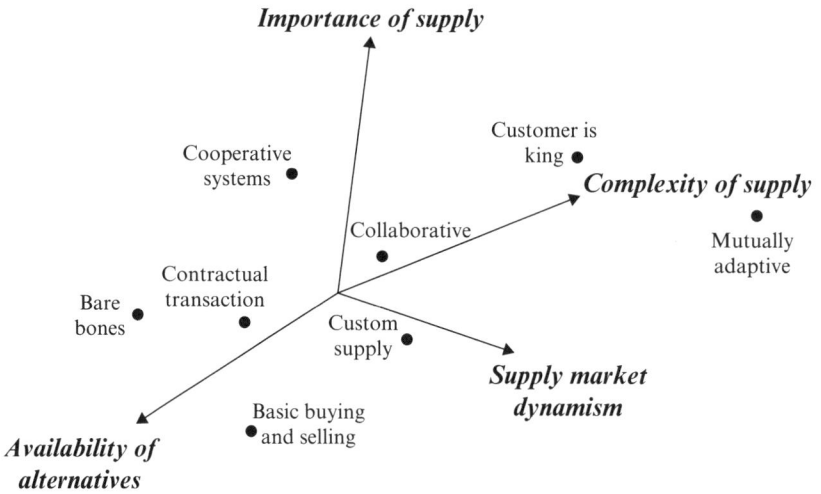

Source: Adapted from Cannon and Perreault (1999, p. 453).

Figure 5.2   Types of supplier relations

Basic buying and selling relations have the least developed operational linkages and adaptations. Legal bonds are not strong and most purchases are from distributors. These are arm's-length market relations that exist when purchases are of simple, low-value, non-strategic inputs, and competition is strong. *Bare-bones relations* are similar with weak legal bonds and little buyer adaptation, but supplier adaptations are greater and there are more developed operational linkages. The market is more stable, and a modest degree of routinised structural linkages has been able to develop. Cooperation and trust are low in both these types of relations.

Strong legal bonds and moderate levels of operational linkages distinguish *contractual relations*. But adaptations, trust and cooperation are low and buyers monitor markets for better offers. These are typically service and government buyers who are required to solicit competitive bids. *Custom supply relations* exist where sellers do not have very high or low scores on any dimensions except in terms of their adaptations to the buyer, hence the name. Buyers report low trust and are not likely to use the supplier as a sole source of supply and monitor the market and their options. A typical example is a supplier of components or equipment in a competitive market. There is little overt collaboration.

Cooperative systems have high levels of operational linkages and cooperation with low levels of legal bonds and buyer adaptations. These relations have the highest levels of trust so they do not require formal legal enforcement mechanisms or the need to rely on market competition to discipline the parties. Fewer risks are involved, as relationship-specific adaptations are low. These relations involve supplying important but not complex inputs, where the parties have worked out a mutually agreeable and probably cost-efficient accommodation that does not require co-development and adaptation.

Collaborative relations have the highest levels of cooperation and high levels of information exchange. Buyer adaptations and operational linkages are not extreme and legal bonds are on the high side. Buyers trust their suppliers and single sourcing arrangements are more likely. These relations sit in the centre of Figure 5.2 and are not challenged to respond to special types of product or market conditions. This kind of partnering might involve long-term contracts with chosen suppliers that support the development of collaboration to some extent, but not high levels of mutually adapted investments.

Mutually adaptive relations, as the name suggests, have high levels of mutual relationship-specific adaptation and investment, and are substantial in terms of dollar value. This is also associated with high levels of operational linkages and information exchange and sole sourcing relations. Yet these relations are not without their problems because reported levels of cooperative norms are only average and buyer trust in the supplier is the lowest of all the relationship types. These relations involve asymmetric dependence, with the buyer more vulnerable because of the investments made and the complexity and dynamism of the market. The supplier's expertise in developing and adapting supply for a customer may be critical, and this underlies the vulnerability and generates an atmosphere that is less conducive to the development of trust.

Lastly, *customer is king relations* also involve asymmetric dependence in the form of relationship-specific resource investments and adaptations by the seller but not the buyer. But other forms of mutual adaptation are apparent. Compared to custom supply relations, for example, they involve high levels of activity links (operational linkages and information exchange), actor bonds and schema couplings (trust, legal bonds and cooperative norms). These are strong and developed forms of relations focused on important, highly complex products and services, where market dynamism is not high so there is time to develop and retain such a relation.

Supplier–Customer Relations in the Car Industry (Bensaou 1999)

The final example comes from a study of car manufacturers and their suppliers carried out in the USA and Japan that included all three US and 11 Japanese car manufacturers. A sample of 447 managers was interviewed, each about one product component and one supplier for which they were responsible. The study was designed to cover a representative sample of products; it was not just focused on strategic relations. Information was collected about many aspects of the relationship, including the product involved, contractual conditions, specific investments, social climate, information exchange and performance. Information about contextual conditions, such as market competition and the nature of the respondent and firm, was also collected.

The study found that in both the USA and Japan car manufacturers are involved in a portfolio of different types of relations in order to obtain the inputs they need. The relations were grouped into four types based on the level of specific investments made by the supplier or buyer because this was strongly linked to the type of relationship that developed. The four cells differ in the characteristics of the product exchanged and its underlying technology, the level of competition in the supplier market, and the capabilities of the suppliers available in the marketplace. The main characteristics of each type are summarised in Figure 5.3.

The Japanese car manufacturers have fewer strategic partnerships than might be expected, 19 per cent compared to 25 per cent in the USA. Both Japanese and US manufacturers make extensive use of market relationships (Japan 31 per cent, USA 25 per cent), which is to be expected given the vast number of components used. The most significant difference was the relative importance of captive supplier relationships in Japan (35 per cent versus 8 per cent) and captive buyer relationships in the USA (42 per cent versus 15 per cent). Market conditions enable the Japanese manufacturers, such as Nissan or Honda, to require their suppliers to locate a plant or warehouse near their plant, provide them with cost data, or send engineers to the final assembly line. These buyers also reduce their dependence by dividing their purchases among a number of locked-in suppliers, even for the same component or technology. The buyer does not invest in specialised assets. In the USA, suppliers avoid becoming too dependent on a buyer and prefer to spread their business among a number of domestic and international customers.

Interestingly, no important differences in performance were found across the four types of relations, indicating that no one type is inherently superior. Instead, different types develop in response to the tasks and conditions involved, and firms have to be able to deal with a portfolio of different types of relations. *Market exchange relations* occur for highly standardised non-complex products with mature technologies and little innovation, when demand is stable or declining and competition is strong among small supplier firms. *Strategic partnerships* arise when high levels of customisation and mutual adaptation are required for expensive, strategically significant

	Supplier investment low	Supplier investment high
Buyer investment low	**Market exchange** • Japan 31%, USA 25% • Highly standardised products; mature, simple technology or well-structured complex manufacturing process; little innovation and rare design changes; little or no customisation; low engineering effort, expertise and capital investment required • Stable or declining demand; highly competitive with many capable, long-established suppliers • Small 'mom and pop' suppliers with no proprietary technology; low switching costs; suppliers have low bargaining power and strong dependence on automotive business	**Captive supplier** • Japan 35%, USA 8% • Technically complex products, based on new technology developed by suppliers; important and frequent innovations; significant engineering effort, expertise and capital investments required • High-growth market; fierce competition with few qualified suppliers; switching between suppliers • Suppliers have important proprietary technology, strong financial capabilities and good R&D skills; low supplier bargaining power, dependence on buyer and automotive
Buyer investment high	**Captive buyer** • Japan 15%, USA 42% • Technically complex product; mature, well-understood technology; little innovation and improvement • Stable demand with limited market growth; concentrated market with few main players; buyers have internal manufacturing capability • Large suppliers with proprietary technology; few strongly established, powerful suppliers; car manufacturers depend on them and their technology and skills	**Strategic partnership** • Japan 19%, USA 25% • Highly customised, technically complex, strategic products; close coordination and adaptation needed; innovation important and frequent design changes; needs engineering expertise and large capital investments • Strong and growing demand; competitive and concentrated market; supplier's turnover due to innovation; buyer has in-house design and testing capability • Large multi-product suppliers with proprietary technology and active in R&D; established skills and capabilities in design, engineering, and manufacturing

Source: Adapted from Bensaou (1999, p. 38).

Figure 5.3 Characteristics of supplier relations with different levels of buyer and seller investments

inputs. Demand is growing and competition is intense and concentrated. Innovation and technological development also play an important role and buyers switch to access suppliers with valuable proprietary technology and R&D skills.

Captive buyer relations arise in situations where components are technically complex but the technology is mature and innovation is not important. Also, demand is stable and there are few established suppliers with strong bargaining power on whom buyers are dependent. Lastly, *captive supplier relations* involve technically complex components based on new technology developed by the supplier and innovation plays a key role. Heavy capital investment is required and it is also likely to be a high-growth market with fierce competition among few suppliers who have the relevant expertise, resources and proprietary technology. Suppliers are very dependent on the customer and industry.

Even though there is no systematic difference in performance across the four types of relations, there is variation within a type, suggesting that some are better managed by the parties involved than others of the same type. I consider different ways of managing in relations in Chapter 6.

SUPPLIER VERSUS CUSTOMER PERCEPTIONS OF BUSINESS RELATIONS[2]

In this section I attempt to reconcile the different relationship typologies described and compare the way suppliers and customers view business relations. I consider whether both sides of a business relation can and do see it in the same way and, if they do not, what this means for the development and survival of the relation. The data I draw on here come from the second stage of the Interfirm Relations Research Program at the University of New South Wales. IRRP2 involved a further development and refinement of the research instrument used to gather relationship information from firms and, once again, comprised a mix of interviews with buyer and seller firms. Each interview focused on only one relation and these were selected so as to be spread across relations that were regarded by the respondents as very good, moderately good, poor or very poor working relations. Multiple respondents were interviewed and an attempt was made to interview people from the buyer and seller firm, but this was usually not possible. Altogether IRRP2 added 345 relations to the database and these are the basis for the results described here. They are evenly split between buyer and seller perspectives.

Cluster analysis was used to identify different types of business relations in terms of six dimensions of the atmosphere, or relational bonds, of business relations. The dimensions used were based on those identified in previous research as important: power/dependence; cooperativeness; trust; competitiveness and/or opportunism; understanding; closeness/distance. These dimensions are discussed in more detail in Chapter 6. Other dimensions of the relation, including the kinds of interactions taking place, the characteristics of the firms, products and services involved and the environment in which it operates, were used to develop a picture of each type of relation.

I first consider the types of relations emerging when we combine buyer and seller perceptions of relations. This allows us to see if relations group into buyer versus seller perceived types or whether more generic types emerge that can be seen through the eyes of either the buyer or seller in a relation. A word of caution here: the IRRP2 database does not contain paired buyer and seller perceptions of the same relation; instead it comprises samples of relations described by either buyers or sellers. Our analysis identified five generic types of relations that could be described by buyers or sellers, although some were more likely to be described by sellers or buyers because they are more or less likely to find themselves in such relationship situations. But of course all relations, by definition, have a buyer and seller. After I have described the five generic types I report the results of separate cluster analyses undertaken for buyers and sellers. This was done to see if more subtle variations on the generic relationship themes exist from a buyer's or seller's perspective. Finally, I compare the relationship types identified using IRRP2 with the three typologies already described in this chapter.

Generic Relationship Types

Five types of relations were identified in the total sample. *Disgruntled followers* comprise 19 per cent of relations. These are very competitive or opportunistic relations in which the firm of the person interviewed, usually the supplier, is dominated (that is, in terms of both dependence and degree of influence) by their business counterpart. The weaker firm tends to be smaller and very dependent on the counterpart, with 28 per cent of its sales or purchases, on average, going through the relation. Individual transactions tend to be large and occur relatively frequently, using a highly standardised ordering procedure. Despite high levels of opportunism and poorer future prospects for the relation reported by the respondent, these relationships are among the most enduring of all relationship types, having lasted on average 13 years. This may be due to the lack of suitable alternatives because, despite only moderate satisfaction, firms endure such opportunistic atmospheres, remain together for extended periods of time and in most cases the relation is still expanding.

Manipulative leaders are the most common type (27 per cent) and appear to be the counterpart of disgruntled followers. They are also competitive and opportunististic, with one firm dominant, but in this case it is the interviewee's firm. These relations are a more mixed bunch of buyer and seller reported types, with the dominant party the larger firm and most often this is the seller. These relations are much more diverse than disgruntled followers in terms of the frequency of trading, the size of transaction, degree of standardisation, degree of substitutability and complexity of the products traded. The prospects are seen as good for both parties in the relation, perhaps reflecting the interviewee's firm's belief in its ability to benefit their partner organisation. Interestingly, these relations rate the lowest in terms of performance, suggesting that the dominant player may persist due to their ability to dictate what goes on.

Benevolent independent relationships make up 17 per cent of the sample. These rate very low on opportunism, and the firms involved are not very dependent on each other and are roughly equal in size. Communication is infrequent and the products/services traded may be readily substituted as the alternatives are seen to be as good. The average duration of these relations is seven years. Both parties are believed to have very good future prospects, with only *close relationships* (see below) being seen as having better. The relation is rated the most satisfactory on average of all relations, and this is reflected also in perceptions of benevolence, low levels of conflict and the relation being coordinated without the use of any strong influence tactics and with minimal reliance on formal coordination methods such as contracts or legislation. This relation appears to be a successful, mutually beneficial one involving products, services and partners that are necessary but not critical to a firm's business.

Arm's-length relationships comprise 14 per cent of the sample. They have low ratings on any indicator of relationalism, are opportunistic, with unbalanced, though not very strong, power. These relations have lasted on average five years, the shortest of all types. Transactions are typically small and infrequent, and substitutes are readily available. Satisfaction, performance and future prospects for each party are rated the lowest of all types, with the respondent firm being perceived as more successful or the 'winner' in the relation. Performance has changed little since the beginning and, unsurprisingly, alternative relation partners are seen as superior. Coordination is highly formalised, relying on contracts and infrequent communication, and strong influence tactics are used by both parties, which is indicative of the high levels of bargaining and conflict in these relations. These relations resemble adversarial buying and selling relationships in which a lack of any significant close ties creates an environment of conflict and dissatisfaction. Each party is able to influence the other to some extent, which is perhaps enough to stop them switching to more attractive partners, at least in the short term.

The final type is *close relations*, which comprise 25 per cent of the sample. They have very high scores on all measures of relationalism, including cooperativeness, trust, commitment, understanding, closeness, interdependence and benevolence (i.e. non-opportunism). They are also among the longer lasting, with an average reported duration of 11 years. These relations are not balanced but asymmetric in terms of dependence and power, with the interviewee's firm typically being larger than its counterpart and more important to it than it is to them. Frequent and large transactions occur for difficult-to-substitute products or services, and these are carried out through standardised ordering procedures. Close relations also rate highest in terms of satisfaction, future prospects for the relation partner and relation, in part because there are few viable alternatives available. They have improved over time. Coordination takes place using formal coordination processes and frequent communication, without the use of strong influence tactics. Bargaining is unlikely and conflict is the lowest of any types.

Buyers' versus Sellers' Perspectives

The five generic types do not separate according to whether the respondent firm is a seller or buyer; the clusters comprise a mix. This suggests that it is the form of the relation that is affecting what each sees, rather than there being different types of relations from sellers' and buyers' perspectives. In order to investigate this we analysed buyer and seller respondents in the sample separately. Similar types identified for the total sample were found, as expected, but additional subtypes emerged.

Relationship types for seller respondents
The first type is characterised by asymmetrical influence, but lower levels of total dependence compared to other seller relations. What dependence exists favours the seller. These characteristics are similar to manipulative leader relations, with the respondent's firm (in this case the seller) seeing itself as the dominant party and 28 of the 31 were so classified in the total sample. Seller 1 relations appear to be much more independent than manipulative leader types in the total sample, suggesting a slightly different perceived form. The second type is relational, non-opportunistic and interdependent, and like close relationships in the total sample (31 of the 33). This suggests that close relations are perceived in much the same way by both parties. Type 3 has the lowest levels of relational orientation and high levels of opportunism. Dependence is high and favours the seller. However,

even though the seller is less dependent, buyers exercise more influence. Although sellers are more powerful, buyers may have a greater motivation to try to influence their counterpart in order to get their requirements considered more seriously. These attributes make this type very similar to arm's-length relationships (19 of the 22). Type 4 has distinctively benevolent and independent characteristics, and has the highest ratings on relationalism, similar to benevolent independent relations (23 of the 26), although the relationalism scores are significantly stronger. Type 5 is opportunistic, and dependence is very asymmetric, with the seller much more dependent on the buyer, similar to disgruntled followers (14 of the 19). But they have significantly lower reported influence asymmetries, which could be because disgruntled followers are more commonly buyers, where influence asymmetries may be more extreme. Hence sellers in such relations are more likely to report suitable alternatives to their relationship partner being available, to be larger and to place lower importance on the counterpart's business. The last type is highly opportunistic and interdependent, with dependence heavily favouring the seller; they are mostly manipulative leader relations (28 of 37).

These results show that, for sellers, manipulative leaders comprise two subtypes 1 and 6. A comparison shows that, while both have high levels of dependence, asymmetric influence and opportunism, their average scores are different. Sellers perceive two types of manipulative leader relations, one being more relational, interdependent and yet more manipulative, and the other less relational, independent and, although still manipulative, significantly less so. In terms of other relationship characteristics, type 6 are seen as performing better, more satisfactorily, and communication is seen as more frequent.

Relation types for buyer respondents

Buyer type 1 is highly relational, non-opportunistic and interdependent, with marked dependence and influence asymmetries. In terms of the first three characteristics, they resemble close relationships but the high levels of buyer dominance are more like manipulative leader relations and this type comprises a mix of manipulative leader, benevolent independent and close relations, with more than half being close relations. This suggests that these types can appear to be similar from a buyer's perspective. But this is not always so, because manipulative leader and benevolent independent relations are also represented in other types of buyer relations. Type 2 is not relational in orientation, is opportunistic and, like type 1, has high levels of dependence and influence asymmetries favouring the buyer. The first three characteristics match arm's-length relations but high dependence and influence asymmetries make them like manipulative leader relations and they do comprise an equal mix of both types. I examine their difference more closely in a moment. Type 3 is highly opportunistic, interdependent and, unlike 1 and 2, has strong dependence and influence asymmetries favouring the seller. These match disgruntled followers, with 41 of the 48 so classified. Type 4 is non-opportunistic, independent and has strong influence asymmetries favouring the seller, which makes it similar to benevolent independent relations (23 of the 28). One difference is influence asymmetries, which are higher than in the total sample.

The buyer relationship clusters do not show a clear match with those for the total sample. In particular, type 1 is a mix of three types, type 2 a mix of two, and manipulative leader relationships and benevolent independent relations are split between two types. To investigate this further, more detailed comparisons were made. The three subtypes in type 1 appear to buyers as variants of a single relation. Even though their degree of absolute interdependence varies, all are rated as relational and have asymmetric patterns of influence and, to a lesser degree, asymmetric dependence.

Manipulative leader relationships are highly opportunistic and benevolent independent relations are independent, in sharp contrast to the characteristics of close relationships. But, from a buyer's perspective, both manipulative leader and benevolent independent relationships comprise two distinct subtypes. The manipulative leader relations in type 1 are less opportunistic and more relational than in type 2. Benevolent independent relationships in type 1 are significantly more relational, and have dependence and influence asymmetries more like manipulative leader relations than those in type 4 (i.e. the buyer firm is dominant). Hence these subtypes are more similar to close relationships for buyers.

The arm's-length and manipulative leader relations in type 2 take on distinctive characteristics. Although both are non-relational and opportunistic, the arm's-length relations in type 2 are significantly less relational than the manipulative leader relations, and more opportunistic. In addition, their patterns of influence are different, with buyers (i.e. the respondents) in manipulative leader relations influencing the seller much more than the reverse. In contrast, such influence asymmetries are far less marked in arm's-length relations and, what little influence is being exerted, is more by the seller than the buyer.

A COMPARISON OF RELATIONSHIP TYPOLOGIES

In this section I compare the relations just described using the IRRP2 database with those described earlier in the chapter. This reveals some of the limitations and distortions occurring, and provides further clarification.

The mapping of the five generic types in terms of Young and Wilkinson's (Y&W) framework, shown in Figure 5.4, reveals several problems of classification. First, distinctions forced by the 2 × 2 classification lead to potential misclassifications, such as grouping together manipulative leader and disgruntled follower relations and dividing benevolent indepen- dent relations between the arm's-length or committed, mature quadrants. Second, subtypes are missed in the committed, mature and adversarial quadrants. Third, to increase the separation and contrast among the quadrants, Y&W removed relations scoring close to the mean on each dimension. The effect of this is to remove a substantial proportion of manipulative leader, disgruntled follower and benevolent independent rela- tions – these mid-range types are not detected.

None of the five generic types is located in the Y&W arm's-length quad- rant; instead generic arm's-length relations exist in a more adversarial guise in the adversarial relations quadrant. This may be because relations in the arm's-length quadrant are just starting or finishing, rather than reflecting particular types of relationship attractors, i.e. what the relations will become when they grow up or cease. Y&W's committed, mature relations have only moderate levels of interdependence, which is unexpected. This may occur because some benevolent independent relations fall into this quadrant, and this will tend to reduce average levels of interdependence in the quadrant.

In spite of these problems there is still a good fit between the two typolo- gies, especially for generic relation types clearly located in a quadrant. For example, normatively opportunistic relations are much like disgruntled fol- lower relations. This gives us some confidence in the validity of the taxon- omy and shows us how our methodologies affect what kinds of relations we are and are not able to detect and characterise well.

The comparison with Cannon and Perreault's (C&P) eight types of rela- tions is more difficult as these were developed based on various measures of the behaviour taking place in a relation, rather than dimensions of rela- tionship atmosphere. So, in order to compare them, the characteristic relationship atmosphere of each of the eight types was used. These are sum- marised in Table 5.2 in terms of three main dimensions: cooperativeness/ trust; absolute interdependence, reflected in the total level of relationship- specific adaptations and investments; and relative dependence, as reflected in the amount of relationship-specific adaptations of the respondent's firm compared to the relationship partner (called here Firm X).

Although C&P identify eight types of relationship behaviour, only five distinct types of atmosphere exist in their sample, which indicates that a particular type of relationship atmosphere can be associated with more than one pattern of behaviour. For example, two distinct patterns of

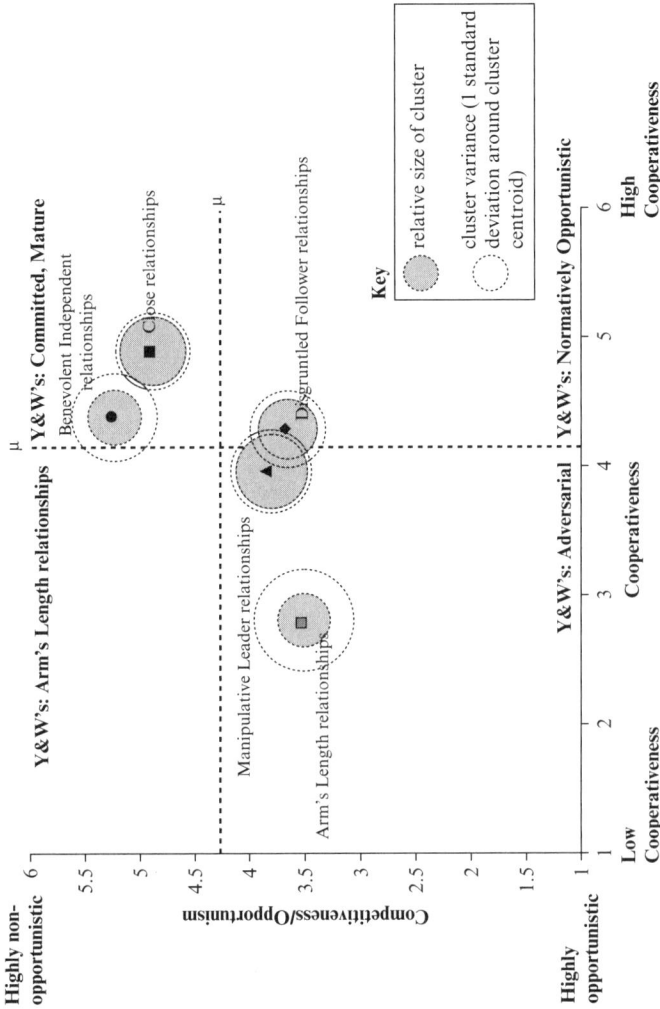

Note: Circle sizes denote relative sizes of clusters.

Source: Wong (2006, p. 81).

Figure 5.4 Mapping the five generic relations in Y&W's typology

Table 5.2   Atmospheric characteristics of C&P's (1999) relationships

C&P's relationship type	Cooperativeness/ trust	Absolute interdependence	Relative dependence
Basic buying and selling	H	L	R≈X (L)
Bare bones	L	L	R>X (M)
Contractual transaction	L	L	R>X (M)
Custom supply	M	H	R>X (H)
Cooperative systems	H	L	R>X (H)
Collaborative	H	M	R≈X (L)
Mutually adaptive	M	H	R≈X (L)
Customer is king	H	H	R>X (H)

Source: Adapted from Wong (2006, p. 83).

behaviour are linked to the generic relation type benevolent independent relations. One is basic buying and selling, which involves lower levels of operational linkages and legal bonds and simple, routine exchange. The second is cooperative systems, where high levels of operational linkages and low usage of legal bonds are typical. Arm's-length relations can exhibit two distinct types of behaviour – bare bones, with very routine trade, and contractual transactions, when strong legal ties are used to compensate for low levels of cooperation. Finally, three patterns of behaviour are linked to the generic type close relationships, i.e. collaborative, mutually adaptive and customer is king. Collaborative behaviour is highly cooperative and involves sharing proprietary information. Mutually adaptive behaviour, as the name suggests, involves high levels of mutual adaptations.

The positioning in Bensaou's framework of the five generic relation types is shown in Figure 5.5. Forcing a 2 × 2 classification on the relations hides distinctions among them. First, arm's-length and manipulative leader relations are close but fall into different quadrants. Second, two quite distinct types exist in the market exchange quadrant – benevolent independent and arm's-length relations, which should not be aggregated. To describe a 'typical' relation in the market exchange quadrant is therefore misleading, as it comprises at least two subtypes and averaging them describes a non-relation that falls between two relationship 'stalls'. In technical terms the distribution of relation types in this quadrant is at least bimodal. Key differences include how good the relationship partner's competitors are (many good ones available in the case of arm's-length but not

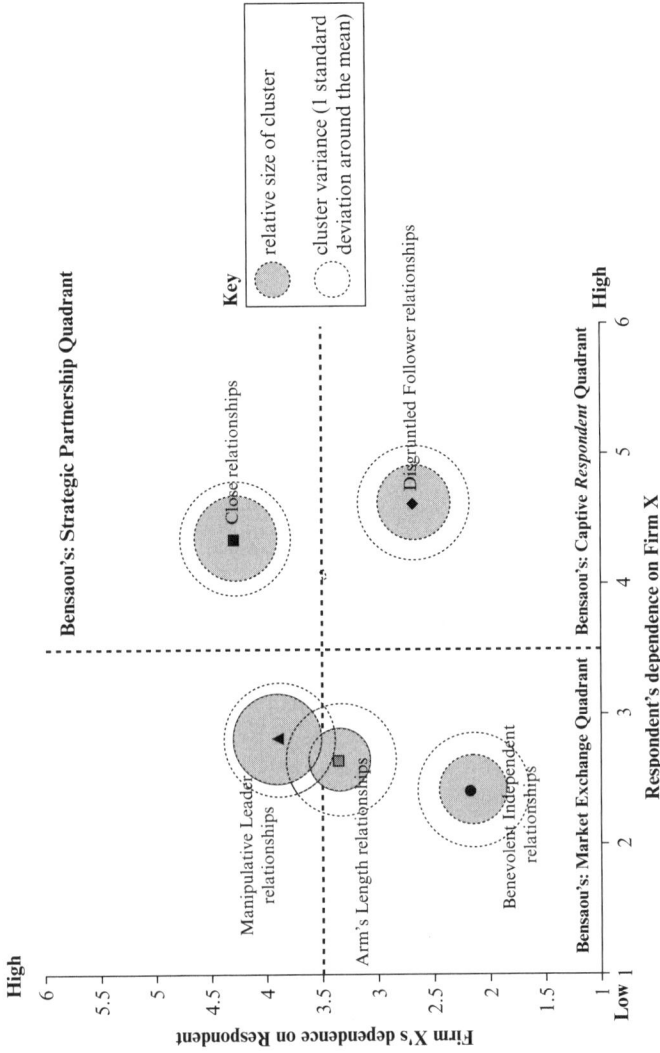

Note: Circle sizes denote relative sizes of clusters.

Source: Wong (2006, p. 79).

Figure 5.5 Co-mapping Bensaou's and IRRP2 typologies

so for benevolent independents) and the relationship atmosphere (more positive and cooperative for benevolent independents and more complex supplies).

The foregoing comparisons show that each typology offers insight into the nature of interfirm relations that can develop in business. They are broadly compatible and complementary, but the ones based on clustering methods, i.e. IRRP2 and C&P, provide a richer picture and are able to identify additional types and subtypes that are obscured by imposing a rigid 2 × 2 classification scheme.

THE EMERGENCE OF DIFFERENT TYPES OF RELATIONS IN MORE AND LESS STABLE ENVIRONMENTS

It is all very well to understand the different types of relations that can and do exist in business, but when do different types emerge and which are the best types to aim for in particular circumstances? Is there a 'best' form of relation, one that always performs better, or is it a case of horses for courses? The relations that exist and persist are a product of their history and the environment in which they operate, including other relations they are connected to in their networks, as was described in Chapter 4. A key aspect of the environment is how difficult, complex and turbulent it is, as this affects the kinds of problems, opportunities and issues to be dealt with. I go into this issue in more detail in Chapter 7, where I examine the management challenges posed by relations, but here I consider how complexity and turbulence affect the kinds of relations that come to exist. This is done by undertaking a cluster analysis of relations in the IRRP2 database for relations operating in more and less turbulent environments.

The results show (see Figure 5.6) that, in more unstable environments, there are more ways for relationships to exist than in more placid contexts. This suggests that, when challenged, relations are forced to adapt into subtypes suited to different environments. It is not that entirely different types of relationships emerge; it is more like variations on the themes indicated by the five generic types.

By comparing the types of relations identified in more and less stable environments we gain insight into the effects of market stability on each of the generic relationship types. Of course, I cannot make strong claims here as we do not follow the way particular relations have developed; all we have is the results of a survey of key informants about various aspects of relations they are familiar with, including their history. Such descriptions are suspect in that what we remember can be selective and rationalised based

Stable environment relationship types   **Unstable environment relationship types**

DF unstable A
- Relational (0.45)*
- Opportunistic (−1.26)**
- Interdependent (0.56)
- Dependence R<X (1.10)
- Slight influence R<X (0.17)***

Disgruntled follower
- Slightly unrelational (−0.18)
- Opportunistic (−0.65)
- Interdependent (0.42)
- Dependence R<X (1.43)
- Influence R<X (0.99)

DF unstable B
- Slightly relational (0.25)
- Slightly non-opportunistic (0.01)***
- Slightly interdependent (0.16)
- Dependence R<X (0.98)
- Slight influence R<X (1.32)

ML unstable A
- Unrelational (−0.78)*
- Slightly opportunistic (−0.03)
- Independent (−1.33) ***
- Dependence R<X (−0.50)
- Influence R<X (−1.80)

Manipulative leader
- Unrelational (−0.31)
- Opportunistic (−0.46)
- Slightly interdependent (0.03)
- Dependence R>X (−0.56)
- Influence R>X (−0.82)

ML unstable B
- Slightly unrelational (−0.20)
- Opportunistic (−0.37)
- Interdependent (0.32)
- Dependence R>X (−0.91)*
- Influence R>X (−1.04)

Benevolent independent 1
- Relational (0.68)
- Benevolent (1.40)
- Independent (−0.41) ***
- Dependence R<X (−0.27)
- Slight Influence R<X (−0.09)

BI unstable
- Relational (0.73)
- Benevolent (1.08)
- Independent (−1.23)
- Slight dependence R>X (−0.02)
- Slight influence R<X (0.14)

Benevolent independent 2
- Relational (0.24)**
- Benevolent (0.64) *
- Independent (−1.54)
- Dependence R<X (0.34)*
- Influence R<X (0.42)

AL unstable A
- Unrelational (−1.77)
- Slightly benevolent (0.19)***
- Independent (−0.38)
- Dependence R>X (−0.44)
- Influence R<X (0.83)

Arm's-length
- Unrelational (−1.60)
- Opportunistic (−0.69)
- Independent (−0.38)
- Slight dependence R>X (−0.16)
- Influence R<X (0.53)

AL unstable B
- Unrelational (−1.64)
- Opportunistic (−1.80)***
- Independent (−0.73)
- Dependence R>X (−1.24)**
- Influence R<X (0.47)

Close
- Relational (0.89)
- Benevolent (0.85)
- Interdependent (0.81)
- Slight dependence R<X (0.04)
- Influence R>X (−0.30)

C unstable
- Relational (0.91)
- Benevolent (0.66)
- Interdependent (0.92)
- Slight dependence R>X (−0.01)
- Influence R>X (−0.32)

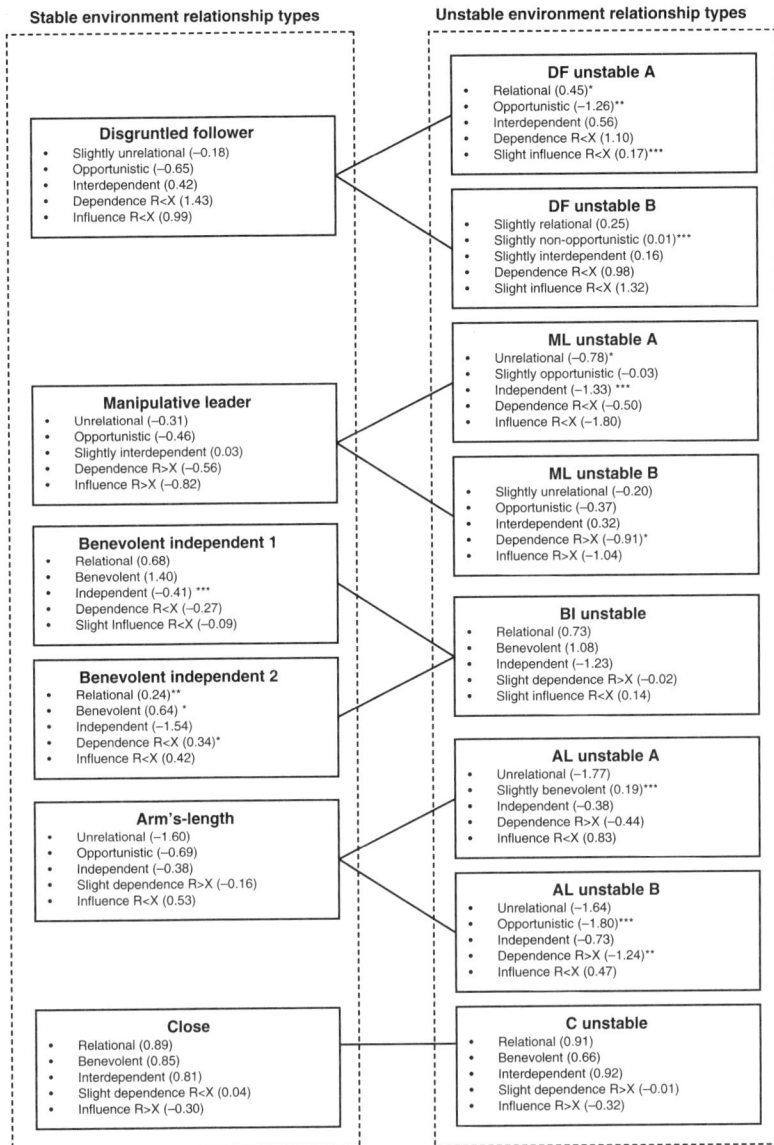

Note: Mean scores in parentheses; * indicate significant differences.

Source: Adapted from Wong (2006, p. 87).

Figure 5.6   Types of relations existing in stable and unstable environments and their possible developmental links

on the current state of a relation and our role and experience in it. I am currently involved in research tracking the history of many business relations but there are no results to report yet. Hence I can only speculate about the patterns of development leading to different types of relations.

Two types of disgruntled followers emerge from the analysis in unstable environments, suggesting that, when they are challenged by market instabilities there are two ways forward. One way is to become more relational and balanced in terms of relative influence but to remain opportunistic. The other way is to become less opportunistic while remaining a follower. Manipulative leaders also have two subtypes in unstable environments – either less relational and more independent, or remaining essentially the same except that the respondent's firm has even more power. The first subtype appears to be less effective, with less optimistic business trends and future prospects for the counterpart. Managers in the dominant role here, it seems, should strive for even more dominance in order to handle such relations effectively in turbulent environments – at least that is their view.

Benevolent independents exist in two ways in stable environments but in only one way in unstable environments. One stable type is similar to the unstable form of the relation but with lower levels of independence. The other is less relational and benevolent, with more asymmetrical dependence. As I have already argued, the two benevolent independent relations in stable environments may be transitionary forms of close and arm's-length relationships, which are more viable in placid environments. As they have not yet fully developed into true close or arm's-length relational forms, these two subtypes can be forced by exposure to market instability into a more distinctly benevolent independent type.

Arm's-length relations exist in two ways in unstable environments. One has a more benevolent outlook, suggesting that a way of operating in unstable environments is to believe more in one another – to hold hands against adversity. The other form of arm's-length is more opportunistic, with the power of the respondent's firm being a possible contributory factor. Powerful firms are more able to shift problems of instability onto the weaker, a strategy that has been noted in studies of Japanese supplier networks. This also helps explain why the second type appears to be less effective, with lower levels of improvement for Firm X. Lastly, close relations exist in much the same way in stable and unstable contexts, which implies that, of all relationship types, they may be an effective and stable form regardless of the turbulence of the environment. This supports other research indicating that these types of collaborative relationships are effective and able to deal with environmental change (Doney and Cannon 1997; Ganesan 1994).

PUTTING THE TWO SIDES OF RELATIONS TOGETHER

A business relation, or indeed any type of personal relation, involves at least two interconnected and interrelated parties – it takes two to tango! But the research studies described only look at a relation through the eyes of those involved – the buyer and the seller. When we examine the types of relations existing for sellers and buyers separately we are able to identify distinct types of clusters. From the sellers' perspective they closely resemble the five generic types identified in the total sample, except that manipulative leader relations appear as two subtypes, with one more relational, interdependent and manipulative than the other. From the buyers' perspective, a different set of relations exists, including subtypes of manipulative leader and benevolent independent relations. In addition, some of the differences between subtypes are greater than any differences with other generic types. These results suggest that buyers are either describing a distinctly different set of relationship types than sellers, or that they are viewing the same generic types of relations differently.

We cannot pair buyers and sellers in relation types, as the data come from only one side in each case. But the relationship types identified do indicate potential pairings, which are summarised in Figure 5.7. The matching of pairs was done by comparing scores on complementary questions, such as how the seller rated the buyer compared to how buyers rated themselves on the same dimensions. Simple comparisons of average scores were used to identify matched pairs. Two obvious pairings are the benevolent independents, as perceived by both buyers and sellers, and manipulative leaders–disgruntled follower relations. In the first pair both sellers and buyers perceive the same type of relation; in the second the parties describe their respective roles in the same generic asymmetric relation in which the seller is most often dominant.

A variant of benevolent independents for buyers matches a manipulative leader subtype seen from the seller's perspective. The only difference is in the reported level of opportunism, which could be explained by the weaker party in such relations (the buyer) choosing to believe the relationship is more benevolent than it actually is. This is a way of coping with its inability to effect change in the more opportunistic dominant member (i.e. the seller). In a similar way, disgruntled followers, as perceived by sellers, are moderately relational, while their possible buyer counterpart might be one that perceives the relation as less relational and more arm's-length. Due to high dependence on the buyer, sellers may prefer to see the relation as more relational than it really is.

The same seller also fits as the potential counterpart of the manipulative leaders seen by buyers. The pairing differs only in terms of reported levels

Seller firm perceived relationship types   **Buyer firm perceived relationship types**

Matches
Exceptions
noted

Benevolent independent
- Relational (0.64)
- Benevolent (0.78)
- Independent (−1.29)
- Dependence R<X (0.23)
- Slight Influence R>X (−0.02)

Benevolent independent B(a)
- Relational (1.01)
- Benevolent (1.28)
- Independent (−0.71)
- Dependence R>X (−0.64)
- Slight Influence R>X (−0.13)

Benevolent independent B(b)
- Slightly unrelational (−0.05)
- Benevolent (1.11)
- Independent (−1.17)
- Dependence R<X (0.35)
- Influence R<X (0.76)

Opportunism

Manipulative leader S(a)
- Unrelational (−0.48)
- Opportunistic (−0.29)
- Independent (−0.66)
- Dependence R>X (−0.53)
- Influence R>X (−1.09)

Manipulative leader B(a)
- Relational (0.39)
- Slightly benevolent (0.07)
- Slightly independent (−0.04)
- Dependence R>X (−0.77)
- Influence R>X (−0.93)

Manipulative leader S(b)
- Slightly unrelational (−0.08)
- Opportunistic (−0.73)
- Interdependent (0.59)
- Dependence R>X (−0.91)
- Influence R>X (−0.51)

Opportunism

Relational

Manipulative leader B(b)
- Unrelational (−0.74)
- Opportunistic (−0.41)
- Slightly independent (−0.20)
- Dependence R>X (−0.69)
- Influence R>X (−0.73)

Disgruntled follower
- Relational (0.38)
- Opportunistic (−0.96)
- Slightly interdependent (0.03)
- Dependence R<X (1.58)
- Slight influence R<X (0.13)

Dependence

Disgruntled follower
- Slightly relational (0.05)
- Opportunistic (−0.50)
- Interdependent (0.45)
- Dependence R<X (1.16)
- Influence R<X (1.15)

Relational

Arm's-length
- Unrelational (−1.62)
- Opportunistic (−0.43)
- Independent (−0.47)
- Dependence R>X (−0.38)
- Influence R<X (0.81)

Arm's-length
- Unrelational (−1.76)
- Opportunistic (−0.94)
- Independent (−0.26)
- Dependence R>X (−0.60)
- Slight Influence R<X (0.16)

Close
- Relational (1.03)
- Benevolent (0.85)
- Interdependent (0.94)
- Slight dependence R>X (0.12)
- Influence R>X (−0.32)

Influence

Close
- Relational (0.74)
- Benevolent (0.75)
- Interdependent (0.83)
- Slight dependence R>X (−0.09)
- Influence R>X (−0.40)

▬▬▬ Strongly matched pairs (No substantial differences)   ▬▬▬ Moderately matched pairs (One substantial difference)

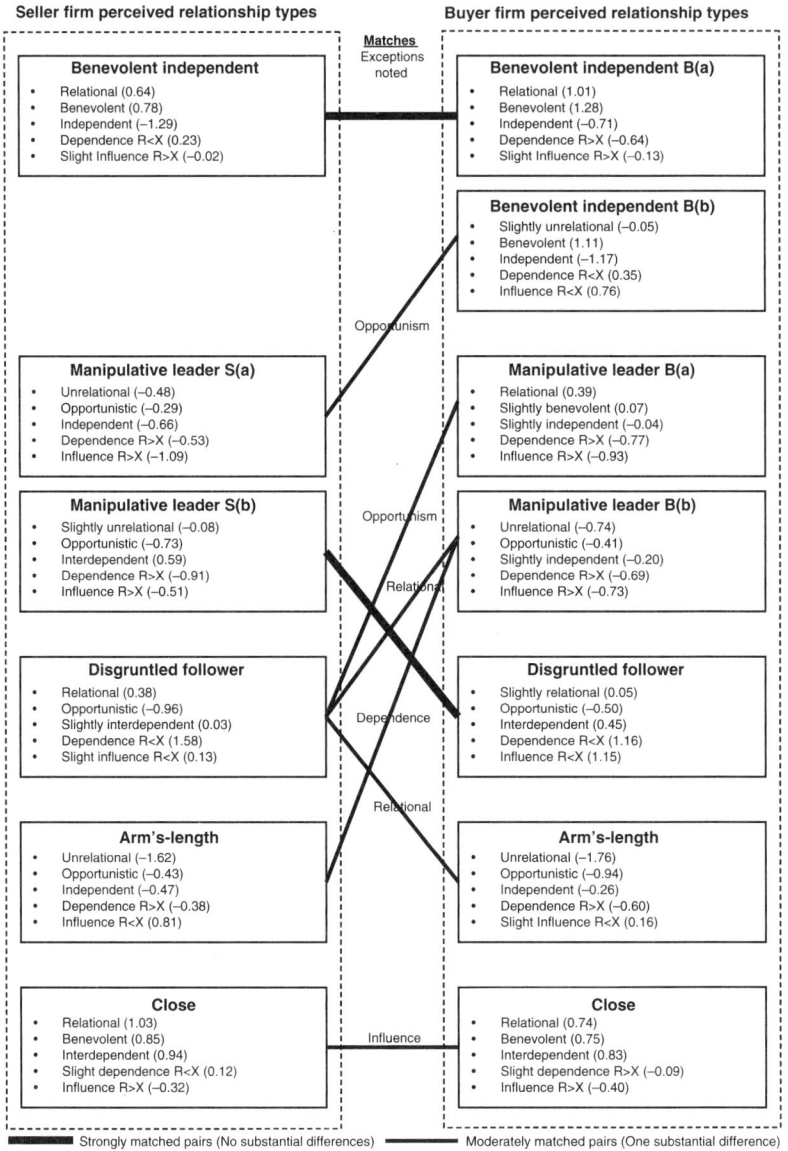

Source: Adapted from Wong (2006, p. 91).

Figure 5.7   Matched pairs of buyer and seller relational types

of opportunism, with the dominant buyer seeing the relationship as neither benevolent nor opportunistic, but the dependent seller sees it as highly opportunistic. Such differing perspectives could be due to the seller's scepticism due to the buyer's greater power, or the dominant buyer mistakenly believing the relationship is less opportunistic because they are in charge. Power corrupts, so the saying goes, and research on the effects of power on the power-holder by David Kipnis (1976) and others shows that those able to exert substantial power tend to downplay the contributions of those subject to their influence. The pairing of disgruntled followers with manipulative leaders B(b) is suggested because the two perspectives differ only on relationalism. The dominant buyer sees the relation as less relational, whereas the weaker seller may prefer to see it as relational, as a way of coping with their more vulnerable position.

Another possible counterpart for buyers' manipulative leaders are sellers' arm's-length relations. The only difference is that both see themselves as less dependent, which is a more comfortable thought to have! Finally, close relations are similar for buyers and sellers, although both parties claim to be more influential, which, again, is a self-serving type of schema.

CONCLUSIONS

Relationship classification schemes of the type described in this chapter can help managers appreciate the diversity of relationships that can exist, which ones may be best suited to different situations, and how coordination and management within different types of relations varies. What has been shown is that one size does not fit all: different kinds of relations arise in various contexts in order to cope with the problems and opportunities that arise. No one relation appears to be the best or most likely to evolve, and a simple stage model of relationship development and evolution is inadequate. Many relationship histories are possible, and history matters in terms of the challenges faced or not, which in turn shapes what each party knows and does not know about the other. In this way resources, understandings, bonds and schemas are co-constructed and laid down that affect the way the relation and parties involved can and do respond; and so the future is enabled and constrained.

Much popular business literature advocates the development of close, long-term relations as the best form of business relationship. We have seen that a more nuanced view is appropriate. Close relations can be highly satisfying and perform well but so can other types of relations. Benevolent independent relations have equally high levels of performance and satisfaction, and disgruntled follower relations are amongst the highest performers. This reinforces C&P's (1999) and Bensaou's (1999) findings that not all relations need necessarily develop into close, long-term relations to be effective. Instead, parties may be equally happy to continue in independent yet efficient partnerships concerning easily replaced products and services, such as benevolent independent relations or, for disgruntled followers, they may find that being the weaker may have its advantages. It is sometimes effective to let the other party deal with the problems and decide what to do, so long as they are not actively working against your firm's interests. This is compatible with prior research showing that high levels of power attributed to a supplier are linked to high levels of satisfaction (Wilkinson 1981).

Relations are not managed by one party; they are co-managed, co-developed and co-regulated, and what happens is co-produced, even if one party does play a dominant role. And even if a firm's lot is to be the weaker member in a relation, the problem of relationship management does not disappear. Managing interactions with those on whom one depends is relevant whether you are the leader or the follower, and is perhaps most challenging and yet most potentially productive when both parties make equal, yet different, complementary contributions to the way the relation operates and performs. It is to these issues I turn in Chapter 6.

NOTES

1. This section is based on Wilkinson and Young (1994, pp. 74–8).
2. The final sections of the chapter are based on research carried out by Charles Wong for his B.Com. Honours thesis in the School of Marketing at UNSW in 2006, working under my supervision. They are partly reported in Wong (2006) and Wilkinson et al. (2007, pp. 3–8).

6. Business dancing: managing and being managed in business relations and networks

---

A cat had made acquaintance with a mouse, and had spoken so much of the great love and friendship she felt for her, that at last the Mouse consented to live in the same house with her, and to go shares in the housekeeping. 'But we must provide for the winter or else we shall suffer hunger,' said the Cat. 'You, little Mouse, cannot venture everywhere in case you run at last into a trap.' This good counsel was followed, and a little pot of fat was bought. But they did not know where to put it. At length, after long consultation, the Cat said, 'I know of no place where it could be better put than in the church. No one will trouble to take it away from there. We will hide it in a corner, and we won't touch it till we are in want.' So the little pot was placed in safety; but it was not long before the Cat had a great longing for it, and said to the Mouse, 'I wanted to tell you, little Mouse, that my cousin has a little son, white with brown spots, and she wants me to be godmother to it. Let me go out to-day, and you take care of the house alone.' 'Yes, go certainly,' replied the Mouse, 'and when you eat anything good, think of me; I should very much like a drop of the red christening wine.'

But it was all untrue. The Cat had no cousin, and had not been asked to be godmother. She went straight to the church, slunk to the little pot of fat, began to lick it, and licked the top off. Then she took a walk on the roofs of the town, looked at the view, stretched herself out in the sun, and licked her lips whenever she thought of the little pot of fat. As soon as it was evening she went home again. 'Ah, here you are again!' said the Mouse; 'you must certainly have had an enjoyable day.' 'It went off very well,' answered the Cat. 'What was the child's name?' asked the Mouse. 'Top-off,' said the

Cat quite coolly. 'Top-off!' echoed the Mouse, 'it is indeed a wonderful and curious name. Is it in your family?' 'What is there odd about it?' said the Cat. 'It is not worse than Crumb-thief, as your godchild is called.'

Not long after this another great longing came over the Cat. She said to the Mouse, 'You must again be kind enough to look after the house alone, for I have been asked a second time to stand godmother, and as this child has a white ring round its neck, I cannot refuse.' The kind Mouse agreed, but the Cat slunk under the town wall to the church, and ate up half of the pot of fat. 'Nothing tastes better,' said she, 'than what one eats by oneself,' and she was very much pleased with her day's work. When she came home the Mouse asked, 'What was this child called?' 'Half-gone,' answered the Cat. 'Half-gone, what a name! I have never heard it in my life.'

Soon the Cat's mouth began to water once more after her licking business. 'All good things come in threes,' she said to the Mouse; 'I have again to stand godmother. The child is quite black, and has very white paws, but not a single white hair on its body. This only happens once in two years, so you will let me go out?' 'Top-off! Half-gone!' repeated the Mouse, 'they are such curious names; they make me very thoughtful.' 'Oh, you sit at home in your dark grey coat and your long tail,' said the Cat, 'and you get fanciful. That comes of not going out in the day.' The Mouse had a good cleaning out while the Cat was gone, and made the house tidy; but the greedy Cat ate the fat every bit up. 'When it is all gone one can be at rest,' she said to herself, and at night she came home sleek and satisfied. The Mouse asked at once after the third child's name. 'It won't please you any better,' said the Cat, 'he was called All-gone.' 'All-gone!' repeated the Mouse. 'I do not believe that name has been printed any more than the others. All-gone! What can it mean?' She shook her head, curled herself up, and went to sleep.

From this time on no one asked the Cat to stand godmother; but when the winter came and there was nothing to be got outside, the Mouse remembered their provision and said, 'Come, Cat, we will go to our pot of fat which we have stored away; it will taste very good.' 'Yes, indeed,' answered the Cat; 'it will taste as good to you as if you stretched your thin tongue out of the window.' They started off, and when they reached it they found the pot in its place, but quite empty! 'Ah,' said the Mouse, 'now I know what has happened! It has all come out! You are a true friend to me! You have eaten it all when you stood godmother; first the top off, then half of it gone, then . . .'

'Will you be quiet!' screamed the Cat. 'Another word and I will eat you up.' 'All-gone' was already on the poor Mouse's tongue, and scarcely was it out than the Cat made a spring at her, seized and swallowed her.

Verily, that is the way of the world.

Source: Jacob and Wilhelm Grimm, 'Katze und Maus in Gesellschaft', *Kinder- und Hausmärchen* (*Children's and Household Tales – Grimms' Fairy Tales*), no. 2.

Once partners are chosen, the dancing begins, and so it is in business. Dancing can be good and bad for either or both, as the grim Grimms' fairy-tale story opening the chapter reminds us. In this chapter I consider different approaches to managing business relations and networks, ending relationships and the interaction and evolution of different relationship management styles in market systems. I discuss two main approaches to relationship management, the power–conflict view and the trust–commitment view. This is followed by a discussion of how, when and why relationship partners part company and what the effects are on other relations, including future interactions with a previous relationship partner. As we shall see, this takes us back to the issue of relationship start-up because, as relations end, they set the stage for other relations to emerge. The final section considers the way different approaches to managing relations interact with each other within and across relations and networks, and how relationship management styles develop and evolve in market systems producing ecologies of different types of relationships that coexist.

MANAGING IN ESTABLISHED RELATIONS AND NETWORKS

> Keep your friends close but your enemies closer.
>   (Michael Coreleone, *The Godfather*)

We now have some idea about the different types of business relations firms can be involved in and why and how they develop in different conditions. In this section I consider the alternative ways firms can and do manage their interactions in ongoing relations of different types. This is about managing *in* relations and networks, not about the management *of* relations and networks, in the sense of how firms may try to shape the kinds of relationship portfolios they are involved in and their network positions. I begin by returning to two studies of business relations described in Chapter 5, the IRRP2 study and Bensaou's study of supplier–customer relations in the car industry in Japan and the USA, and examine how high and low-performing relations of each type are managed by those involved. This leads to the identification of two broad relationship management perspectives: the power–conflict view and the trust–commitment view.

PERFORMANCE AND MANAGEMENT IN DIFFERENT TYPES OF BUSINESS RELATIONS

The IRRP2 database and the relations Bensaou studied in the car industry can be used to identify how relations that perform better are managed compared to those that perform worse. For the IRRP2 database we linked differences in performance measures to characteristics of relationship coordination, and the results suggest that there is not one best way of co-ordinating relations (Wong 2006). Disgruntled follower relations are typified by opportunism and being dominated in the relation by the counterpart. Here both satisfaction and performance are directly linked to greater use of formal coordination processes. This may reflect the means of domination but also that formal methods, such as reliance on industry standards, may reduce the potential extent of negative opportunistic behaviour because they are specified outside the relation as conditions of trade. In addition to this, satisfaction is linked to frequency of communication and lower levels of conflict, while enhanced performance was associated with greater use of weak influence methods and less use of strong tactics by the other firm.

As for disgruntled followers, satisfaction in manipulative leader relations is greater the less conflict present, which suggests that, even though one party is dominant, conflict may still weaken the relationship. Performance is worse when both the level of bargaining and use of strong influence tactics by the weaker party are more likely. The results indicate that dominant parties might do well to encourage use of weak influence tactics where possible and utilise formal means of reducing the extent of bargaining in such relationships.

Satisfaction in benevolent independent relationships is linked mainly to conflict, indicating the sensitivity of these relations to the degenerating of benevolence. Performance is also better when strong influence tactics are less used, which could be the cause or consequence of poor performance. For arm's-length relations, the respondent firm's use of strong influence tactics is linked to lower satisfaction. These relationships use such tactics the most, and the results could be a signal not to overuse them. As we are dealing with correlations here, it could be that dissatisfaction is more a driver of the use of such tactics than they are the cause of dissatisfaction.

Both are possible. No significant predictors of performance in arm's-length relations were found.

No significant predictors of satisfaction were found for close relationships, probably because satisfaction tends to be high in all of them. However, for performance, the use of strong influence tactics was significant. Interestingly, greater use by the respondent is linked to better performance, while greater use by the other party is linked to lower peformance – maybe because the respondent's firm is being bossed around in ways not to its liking. But this is not much of an issue, as close relations rate the highest on performance.

A similar type of analysis was carried out by Bensaou in his study of relations between car manufacturers and their suppliers. They did not differ in terms of their average performance but, if high- and low-performing relations are compared, significant differences emerge in the way the parties involved manage their interactions and in the relationship structure that has been co-produced. No information is available about the history of these relations but, in general, poor performance arises as a result of mismatched relational design or a poorly managed but appropriate design for the relationship. Mismatched relational design stems primarily from incompatibilities in the relationship schemas of the parties involved. These schemas are reflected in the types of activity links and resource ties desired, and are influenced by, as well as influence, the nature of the actor bonds that exist. For example, firms that have not developed a trusting, cooperative relationship atmosphere cannot commit to the same degree of relationship-specific investments, co-ordinated action and adaptations, and this limits the benefits flowing from the relationship to each party and affects the transaction costs involved.

The characteristics of high-performing relations of each of the four types are summarised in Figure 6.1. Clearly, different relationship management styles are effective depending on the relationship type. But there are some common themes such as the impact of product technology and market structure. Relationships involving components with similar degrees of maturity in their underlying technology, in their degree of complexity and the extent of concentration in the supplier market, tend to be managed in similar ways. Product technology and complexity affect the nature and extent of the coordination tasks facing the supplier and customer, and how novel the problems are. For mature technologies, even those with complex products, prior experience and industry knowledge are extensive, suppliers' and buyers' requirements are well known, and effective methods of coordination and adaptation have been worked out (captive buyer relations), or they are routinised (market exchange relations). But for newer technologies, where innovation and design change are constant and rapid, it is not possible to adopt pre-established effective methods of coordination and adaptation. Instead, more intense interaction, communication and

	Supplier investment low	Supplier investment high
Buyer investment low	**Market exchange** • Highly routine and structured operational coordination and monitoring • Limited communication except at contract negotiation • Limited time spent with supplier staff • Positive atmosphere, supplier has good reputation and is fairly treated • No real collaboration • No early supplier involvement in design	**Captive supplier** • Greater burden on supplier • Complex coordinating task • Little communication, few visits, mostly by supplier to buyer • Limited time allocated to supplier • High mutual trust • Limited collaboration, left up to supplier
Buyer investment high	**Captive buyer** • Structured task, highly predictable • Extensive and continuous exchange of detailed and important information, frequent and regular visits to each other • Large amount of time spent with supplier • Tense atmosphere, lack of mutual trust, supplier's reputation not necessarily good • Strong effort by buyer toward cooperation • No early supplier involvement in design	**Strategic partnership** • Highly ill-defined and structured task, frequent unexpected events • Extensive, frequent and deep communication, regular visits and personnel exchange (e.g. guest engineers) • Large amount of time spent with supplier's staff • High mutual trust and commitment to relationship, strong sense of buyer fairness, supplier has excellent reputation • Extensive collaboration • Early supplier involvement in design

Source: Adapted from Bensaou (1999, p. 39).

Figure 6.1 Characteristics of high-performing relations in different contexts

commitment are required, and this can come from the development of mutual trust when both parties have heavy investments in the relation (partnership relations) or when one party is clearly dominant and can expect the other to cooperate fully (captive supplier relations).

Two Schools of Thought[1]

As has been shown, many different types of relations can and do exist with and between firms in business markets. They arise under different conditions and require different styles of interaction to co-regulate them efficiently. I say co-regulate rather than manage to re-emphasise the point that relationships are not managed by one party in the relation, even if one is dominant. Relations involve interaction among parties that are interdependent, and contribute to the management of the relation by the way they manage their actions and interactions in it.

Two main schools of thought may be distinguished regarding relationship management. One takes the perspective of one party in the relation and how to control the relation in its own interests. The focus of attention is the means of control or power in the relation: how to get it and how to use it. Conflict in relations is also of central concern because this is seen as a potential source of sub-optimisation for the focal party. The problem is how to recognise and diagnose sources and manifestations of conflict in relations and how to deal with them effectively. This school of thought may be referred to as the power–conflict view of relationship management. In marketing, this school of thought is particularly associated with the study of firm relations in distribution channels and in customer relationship management theories. Starting with an important book edited by Louis Stern in 1969, attention in distribution channels research began to focus on the analysis of what were called the behavioural dimensions of distribution channels. The concepts and methods drew heavily on ideas from social psychology, sociology, politics and management. While other dimensions of relations were included in the 1969 book and in subsequent research, such as role theory, norms, satisfaction and communication, most attention focused on power and conflict and their consequences. The power–conflict school was not limited to the study of distribution channels. The central ideas are reflected also in one of the leading strategy books:

> Spread purchases . . . in such a way as to improve the firm's bargaining position. The business given to each supplier must be large enough to cause the supplier concern over losing it . . . Purchasing everything from one supplier may yield that supplier too much of an opportunity to exercise power or build switching costs . . . A purchaser would seek to create as much supplier dependence on its business as possible and reap the maximum volume discounts without exposing

itself to too great a risk of falling prey to switching costs . . . Create a threat of backward integration. (Porter 1980, pp. 123–4)

Or, as one manager observed, 'The conventional wisdom is that business is war, cooperation is for wimps, and winning is everything. Boundaries must therefore be firmly established and defended, communication restricted' (James 1994, p. 61).

The adversarial, zero-sum nature of the relationship game, i.e. when I win you lose, also characterises Oliver Williamson's development of the theory of transaction costs. Firms attempt to forge contracts or governance structures to protect themselves against the opportunism of others, especially when relationship-specific assets are at stake and uncertainty and risks are high. Dependence on others is, in this view, inherently dangerous and to be avoided, reduced or protected by various means. There is obviously truth in these ideas, but they are not the complete story. As we have seen, some firms are able to develop successful, mutually compatible relations in which each commits specific resources and is dependent on the other. In such situations each is highly vulnerable to opportunism from the other party. Just as in personal relations, the one you love can hurt you the most, but they also can bring you the most joy.

An alternative perspective on relations and how they can and should be managed emerged in the 1970s in research on interfirm relations carried out in Europe by the Industrial Marketing and Purchasing (IMP) group. They made a comprehensive study of the important international and domestic relations industrial producers and suppliers had with each other. This led them to realise that most business took place through the operation of long-term buyer–seller relations. The main problems confronting firms were not to attract new customers or find new suppliers, but to sustain and manage relations with key suppliers and customers that had been in existence for many years. These relations accounted for most of their business. Moreover, these relations were not characterised by continual power plays and conflict. Both parties could be active in the relation, not just the seller and, in many, personal and professional relations had developed among staff at different levels of the business that played an important role in the functioning of the relation. In addition, firms had made substantial commitments and adaptations to each other.

These findings did not fit neatly with the power-conflict view of relations and the traditional focus in marketing on manipulating a firm's marketing mix to best target and attract customers. The development of long-term, cooperative relations involving mutual trust between buyers and sellers was simply not considered. This led the IMP group to propose an interaction model of business marketing, in which the interactions between buyers and sellers over time created a relationship atmosphere and mutual adaptations and commitments that allowed the relation to function effectively. Not all relations were of this type but firms usually had a number of significant such relations, through which key resources and knowledge were accessed and co-developed. This model was later extended to include the connections between relations or the network view of business markets, which underlies the whole of this book – because I am an IMPer!

Parallel developments were taking place elsewhere in the study of business markets and distribution channels, which increased the attention given to relations and their development and to dimensions other than power and conflict, including trust, commitment, pledges, fairness, satisfaction, relational norms and cooperation. Developments were also taking place in consumer markets with the advent of relationship marketing and customer lifetime valuation, which led firms to focus more on keeping versus getting customers and on various types of loyalty programmes.

A view emerged that the study of conflict and power may have inadvertently focused attention on the study of sick rather than healthy relations (for example, Morgan and Hunt 1994; Young and Wilkinson 1989). Indeed, researchers searched for situations in which conflict and power plays were more obvious, leading to many studies of franchisee and franchisor relations, and relations associated with the car industry. A focus instead on healthy relations led to the emergence of a trust–commitment model of marketing relationships. Here the main drivers of relationship development and performance were trust, the ability to rely on the other party to act honestly and fairly, and to take your interests into account, and commitment, the investment of psychological and material resources in the relation. Various factors affected the extent to which these could be developed in a relationship, including shared values, communication, perceived benefits, switching costs and lack of opportunism. And various outcomes flowed from the development of these two interrelated dimensions, including acquiescence to the other's wishes, functional forms of conflict, cooperation, loyalty and reduced uncertainty.

The main characteristics and differences between the the power–conflict and trust–commitment views of relationship management are shown in Table 6.1.

FOUR KEY DIMENSIONS OF RELATIONSHIPS AND RELATIONSHIP MANAGEMENT

The two main approaches to relationship management focus attention on four dimensions of relations, about which much has been written. All

Table 6.1   Power–conflict versus trust–commitment views of relationship management

	The power game	The trust game
Modus operandi	Create fear	Create trust
Guiding principle	Pursue self-interest	Pursue what's fair
Negotiating strategy	Avoid dependence by playing multiple partners off against each other	Create interdependence by limiting the number of partnerships
	Retain flexibility for self but lock in partners by raising their switching costs	Both parties signal commitment through specialised investments, which lock them in
Communication	Primarily unilateral	Bilateral
Influence	Through coercion	Through expertise
Contracts	'Closed', or formal, detailed, and short-term	'Open', or informal and long-term
	Use competitive bidding frequently	Check market prices occasionally
Conflict management	Reduce conflict potential through detailed contracts	Reduce conflict potential by selecting partners with similar values and by increasing mutual understanding
	Resolve conflicts through the legal system	Resolve conflicts through procedures such as mediation or arbitration

Source: Kumar (1996, p. 105).

relations involve these four dimensions and relationship development is largely a product of the way they change and affect each other over time. Here I introduce some of the main characteristics of each. The main argument is that these dimensions are all forms and conditions of relationship communication and interaction, whether by word, deed or gesture, that are co-regulated by those involved. Communication and interaction have feedback effects on the relation that shape the development of activity links, actor bonds, resource ties and schemas couplings. Power and influence focus on the potential and actual effects of interaction on each party's actions and responses. Conflict focuses on incompatibilities among the intended and actual interactions of those involved and how they are dealt with. Trusting and being trusted focus on how people and firms come to depend on others to act and interact in predictable, honest and caring ways, adjusting their own behaviour accordingly. Commitment involves psychological, behavioural and resource investments in relationship interaction.

All interaction involves these dimensions in one way or another in an intricate dynamic dance. Anticipated or actual action incompatibilities (conflict) leads to interaction that has both intended and unintended effects (influence) on those involved. Such interaction is conditioned by prior experience reflected in the degree of trust among the parties involved and their commitment. The experience and outcomes of interaction reduces, resolves, redirects or exacerbates conflict and reinforces or changes perceptions and positions of power, trust and commitment.

Power and Influence

A firm's power is its ability to affect the behaviour of others and rests ultimately on the dependence of others on it. The more others are dependent on it, the more power it has over them. Control is sometimes used to represent an extreme form of power, as when a firm can specify what another will do, or it is used as another name for power. Dependence in turn may be traced to the resources a firm directly and indirectly controls, its power base, that others value, and the potency of a resource in creating power depends on demand and supply conditions, or what may be summarised in terms of its value, inimitability, rarity and non-substitutability (VIRN). The more valuable it is to others, the less easily imitated, the greater its scarcity, and the less easily substituted it is, the greater the power resulting. A firm's power base includes tangible and intangible elements including economic resources, skills and competences, knowledge, relations and positional resources. Perceptions matter as well as the resources a firm actually controls, and a commonly used classification is French and Raven's (1959) five perceived bases of power developed in social psychology. These are *reward and coercive power* based on a firm's ability to promise and provide benefits or to threaten and punish others. In business economic rewards and punishments can play important roles, as in the promise of or threat of withholding business from another, and promises and threats concerning price, credit and resource support. Sometimes the term power is equated only with coercive power, but I use the term more broadly.

Expert power is based on the knowledge and expertise of a firm that enables it to provide or withhold potentially valuable information and advice. *Legitimate power* is based on formal legal rights and privileges in the form of patents, licences, franchise agreements and other types of

152 Business relating business

contractual provisions, as well as less formal authority in the form of business and industry customs and practices that grant firms power in some areas, such as price or technology leadership. Last is *referent power*, which is based on a firm's personal bonds and identification with another firm which could stem from prior relationship history and reputation.

Power is the potential to affect others; how it is used is another matter, the realm of influence and influence tactics. Research shows that people and firms use all manner of influence tactics in attempts to get their way that are not easily classified in terms of the bases of power. For example, people and firms with strong reward and coercive power can use simple requests, hints, threats, promises, rewards and punishments. All influence tactics are forms of communication, by word, deed or gesture, designed to affect another's behaviour. There have been two main approaches to classifying influence tactics: one is more theory-driven, involving logical deductive classifications of tactics; the other is more empirically driven, based on studies and reports of how people try to get their way. I shall briefly review the main contributions of each approach.[2]

Theory-based classifications have focused attention on the impacts a firm can have on various aspects of the planning and decisions of others, including the objectives set, the planning premises, the alternatives considered and how they are evaluated, chosen and implemented. Some of the useful distinctions resulting from this type of analysis are between coercive and non-coercive tactics, begrudging and non-begrudging, positive and negative sanctions, contingent and non-contingent, and direct and indirect means of influence.

Coercive means of influence are associated with threats and punishments that make others worse off if they do not comply. These can include economic costs as well as threats to withhold information and promised rewards, to damage another's reputation, or to take legal action. These tactics are associated with adversarial forms of interaction in business relations. Non-coercive means are those involving promises and rewards, including economic and non-economic forms and various types of assistance and cooperation. Such means are more associated with collaborative relations. Begrudging and non-begrudging means of influence parallel the distinction between coercive and non-coercive but emphasise the reactions of the target rather than the actions of the influencer (Hunt and Nevin 1974). Begrudging compliance is when the target ends up doing something against its will, whereas non-begrudging forms of influence lead the target to change its will, alter its mind about what is best to do. The distinction between positive and negative sanctions is similar to that between non-coercive and coercive tactics, i.e. making the target of influence better off if they comply or worse off if they don't. These can include economic rewards and punishments. Positive sanctions result in a different relationship dynamic encouraging further compliance, whereas negative sanctions can be a source of antagonism and further resistance.

The distinction between contingent and non-contingent tactics refers to whether the rewards or benefits offered depend on the target's subsequent behaviour. Thus promises, rewards, threats and punishments of any kind are contingent means of influence because what happens is contingent on the target's behaviour.

So far I have focused on direct means of influence, as when firm A tries to directly influence firm B's behaviour. Indirect means of influence involve changing the environment of B so as to constrain or direct their behaviour. This can be done by A influencing others that in turn influence B's behaviour, as when firms appeal directly to end consumers in attempts to pull products through distribution systems. It can also involve the suppression, redirection and obfuscation of issues that are of interest to the target, as in negotiations, rather than direct persuasion.

The costs and benefits of different types of influence are also of interest, as it is hardly in the interests of a firm to gain compliance when the costs of doing so outweigh the gains. Costs and benefits are direct and indirect. Rewards and punishments are an obvious source of direct costs, as are the time, effort and resources used in negotiating with the target and monitoring their behaviour. These are examples of transaction costs. The use of authority or threats is less costly as they involve no extra costs if the target complies, as is compliance based on respect and admiration or following another's advice. Self-fulfilling contractual provisions that establish incentives for the target to comply and to demonstrate compliance are less costly to administer, though they are likely to be more costly to negotiate up front. Time-consuming negotiations, monitoring costs, the costs of dealing with the target resistance, and switching costs add to the costs of influence.

Indirect costs come in the form of effects on the focal relation and on connected relations over time. Resistance and begrudging compliance can have adverse effects on the target's attitude and commitment to the relationship, damaging relationship bonds and leading to more problems in the future. This can have spillover effects in other relations as it affects a firm's reputation, the response of other relationship partners and its ability to find new partners.

Influence tactics play a central role in the dynamics and feedback cycles of a relation, as the parties involved seek to influence each other and resist the influence of others, succeed or fail and learn about each other. The use of positive and negative sanctions can, over time, drain a firm's resources and reduce its power, as economic resources and market position and reputation become eroded, as threats are no longer taken seriously or as ever more rewards are expected and demanded by relationship counterparts. Alternatively, a positive feedback cycle may arise, as when rewards and advice result in target firms benefiting from complying, which in turn leads them to revise their plans and attitudes in ways that reinforce the new patterns of behaviour and enhance the power of the influencer. For example, the relationship between P&G and Wal-Mart changed from a cycle of threats, adversarial bargaining, recriminations and revenge tactics to one of greater collaboration, interaction and integration of activities that reduced costs to each and produced more rewards, thereby strengthening the relationship.

The second approach to classifying and studying influence tactics is based on empirical studies of the way people and firms try to get their way. This has revealed a more complex assortment of tactics that does not easily fit within the neat logico-deductive categories and that also focuses attention on how the use of power in different ways not only affects the target but also the one doing the influencing. These studies began in the 1970s and 1980s, and have resulted in the identification of an array of tactics used in different situations.

A common distinction emerging from people's and managers' reports of how they try to get their way is that between strong, weak and rational tactics. Strong tactics are those involving both positive and negative sanctions, including various types of threats and promises, including legal sanctions. A key characteristic is that, if the target complies, the influencer is likely to attribute this to its influence. It will believe it caused the behaviour. Weak tactics involve simple requests for compliance, pleading, drawing attention to past favours and ingratiation. Here the target's compliance is more up to the target than the direct result of the influence tactics. Rational tactics involve all means of persuasion including arguments, provision of information, using experts, appeals to precedent, norms and values etc. These are designed to affect one or more aspects of the target's decision-making process.

An important result related to this classification is the way the use of strong means of influence can affect the influencer's perceptions of the target. This is revealed in controlled experiments in which the target's performance on a given task is controlled to be the same but some influencers are given stronger tactics of influence. Influencers given the stronger means of influence rate performance as worse, even though it is identical. This is explained in terms of the cause of behaviour being attributed more to the influence tactics used by those given strong tactics. As a result some of the value of the target's behaviour is not due to them but to the influencer, and hence the target's performance is downgraded. Similar results have been found in other studies of influence, including interfirm influence. The implications for relationship management are important, for they indicate how a vicious cycle of strong and potentially coercive influence feeding off and damaging performance can develop. As firms use strong and controlling means of influence they will tend to attribute more of any success to their own intervention rather than to that of the target, which may undervalue the target's contribution and reinforce the use of strong tactics. Over time such a cycle can undermine a relationship and be difficult to jump out of. The links between use of strong tactics and performance and satisfaction described above are indications of this, as are the different perceptions of buyers and sellers in a relation.

Apart from the distinction between strong, weak and rational tactics, which seem to pop up in one way or another in every study, more domain-specific tactics have been identified in different influence settings. The most general classification scheme is the Profiles of Organisational Influence Strategies developed from research on the use of influence among co-workers, bosses and subordinates in firms by Kipnis et al. (1980). This is summarised in Table 6.2. While developed in terms of intra-firm tactics of influence, the same scheme has been applied to interfirm influence (for example, Rao and Schmidt 1998). The different types of tactics have different attributes in terms of their likely use in different situations, including the power and position of the influencer and target, and the type of influence problem, and in terms of their costs of use and likely success. To date there have been few studies that have systematically examined the processes by which different influence tactics are chosen and their consequences. The focus has been more on documenting when different types of tactics are used.

Friendliness and ingratiation depend on personal relations and sensitivity, and are used more to gain personal favours when your power base is weak. Overuse can be damaging and lead people to suspect your motives. *Bargaining* involves negotiation and exchange of benefits that are valued differently by the parties involved and include future reciprocation which creates obligations. Both economic and social obligations become involved and in some cultures, such as China, interfirm relations have been characterised as forms of obligational contracting in which each firm seeks to give and receive favours that are balanced over time (Redding 1990). *Reason* refers to rational argument, information, evidence and expertise, and is used particularly in initiating change. *Assertiveness* is a two-edged sword, useful when you know you are right and as it overcomes target resistance, but it can lead to target ill will. It is often used as a back-up strategy when the target is reluctant to accept your ideas and may be used in combination with other strategies such as reason.

Appeals to higher authority rely on the formal chain of command and are more applicable within firms. But they can play a part in interfirm influence,

Table 6.2   Profiles of Organisational Influence Strategies (POIS)

	Examples	Power base
Friendliness or ingratiation	• Causing target to think well of you • Create a favourable impression	• Personality, interpersonal skills • Sensitivity to moods of others
Bargaining	• Negotiation and the exchange of benefits or favours • Use social norms of obligation and reciprocity • Offer additional concessions	• What you can trade in terms of time, effort, skills and resources controlled
Reason	• Relying on data and information to support your requests • Use of facts and logical argument	• Knowledge and expertise • Ability to communicate
Assertiveness or pressure	• Using a forceful manner • Demands, setting deadlines, expression of strong emotions • Give impression you are in charge and expect compliance • Emotional displays of temper	• Personality and emotional resources, acting ability
Higher authority or legitimating	• Appeal *formally* to higher authority • Ask higher authority *informally* to deal with your request or speak to target on your behalf	• Formal chains of command
Coalition	• Mobilise others to assist	• Relations with others in the organisation and externally
Sanctions	• Backing up requests with official policies, legal rules and contracts, peer pressure, rewards or withholding of same, punishments	• Economic, legal and social resources

Source: Adapted from Kipnis and Schmidt (1982).

as when appeals are made to higher authority in another firm or to other legitimate authorities. This is more a back-up strategy used to overcome resistance and can undermine the relation with the target if overused. *Coalition* strategies make use of the power of numbers and are complex and time-consuming to implement. They depend on a person or firm's position in a network and the nature and quality of relations connected to the focal relation. Overuse can damage the relation with the target to the extent that perceptions of a conspiracy arise. Within firms, *sanctions* are primarily used by bosses to influence subordinates; between firms these shade into dimensions of negotiation and bargaining. Issues arise such as the potential loss of credibility when promises are not met or threats not carried out.

Later research by Gary Yukl (2001) and others has refined and extended this set of tactics. Two further types of influence strategies have been added: *inspirational appeal* and *consultation*. The former concerns requests or proposals that arouse enthusiasm by appealing to a target's values, ideals and aspirations, or increasing their confidence in being able to do the task. Consultation refers to seeking the target's participation in planning a strategy, activity or change for which the target's support is desired.

The preceding analysis presents power and influence in a rather one-directional manner, as A trying to get B to do something they would not otherwise do. But influence acts involve interaction in which both parties affect what goes on and the results achieved. Anticipations of likely response from the other party affect tactic choice, and tactics invite different levels and types of resistance and countermoves. Lack of success and/or resistance from a target may lead to the use of stronger means of influence and engender further resistance, producing an escalation of tension and conflict in the relation. Over time, firms in a relation learn how to deal with each other and patterns of influence and response become part of the ongoing patterns of interaction taking place.

Conflict

The logic of market relations requires that the parties involved achieve mutual and improved satisfaction through working together rather than alone; coordinating and interrelating complementary skills, knowledge and resources, with each contributing inputs and gaining outputs. But the process of bringing people and firms together, and coordinating their efforts over time, is not without its problems, due to potential conflicts of interests and opinions leading to disagreements and disputes of various kinds. These problems have their upside and downside. Transaction cost analysis focuses attention on the problems and costs involved in achieving and maintaining coordinated action, including negotiating agreements, monitoring performance and settling disputes, and we have seen in Chapter 2 how such costs can outweigh the benefits of outsourcing activities to others.

Transaction benefits or relationship functions, as discussed in Chapters 2 and 3, focus on the upside of relations and interactions. Another way of saying this is *productive friction*, a term coined by John Hagel III and John Seeley Brown (2005). Conflict, here, is seen as a source of learning, stimulation, creativity and innovation. By confronting problems and interacting with others with different perspectives and competences, new knowledge can be created, new types of solutions identified and relations can be strengthened and improved. Whether conflicts and disagreements are productive or destructive for the relation and the parties involved depends on the nature and extent of the conflicts that arise and how they are managed, which in turn depend on other dimensions of relationship atmosphere such as power and influence processes, trust and commitment.

It is useful to distinguish between the sources, manifestations and management of conflict. The sources of conflict stem from incompatibilities between the parties involved such that doing what one wants to do interferes with what the other wants to do. These incompatibilities stem from five main sources: competing goals, resource scarcity, discrepant perceptions and domain definitions and power plays (Rosenberg and Stern 1970). These sources become manifest in various types of disagreements and disputes between the parties that are more or less intense. The outcomes of these depend on how the conflict is dealt with by the parties involved.

Competing goals are an inherent part of market transactions and relations as each party tries to increase its benefits or reduce its costs. This leads to disagreements over price and margins, and other contractual provisions. Firms face problems and issues related to their market and network positions that do not necessarily coincide happily with those of their relationship counterparts. The efficient scale and timing of some activities may not coincide across a relation, as when car manufacturers strive to maintain large-scale consistent production runs and end up in conflict with car retailers who face seasonal demand patterns and the need to handle and resell trade-ins for many sales. Firms have *limited time and resources* and have to trade off the benefits and costs of devoting more time and resources to some customers and suppliers compared to others, and their priorities may not match. Goal incompatibilities, as well as different experiences and communication networks, can lead to *different perceptions* about products and markets and what to do, leading to additional disputes. For example, disputes often arise between manufacturers and supermarkets about the mix of products to be included in different categories and the space allocated to each. Firms may also disagree as to who is responsible for performing different tasks and the role and importance of each.

Assertiveness

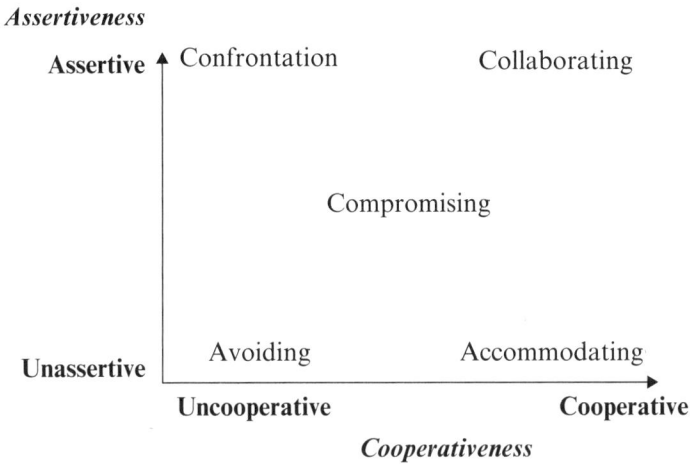

Assertive ▲ Confrontation   Collaborating

                     Compromising

Unassertive   Avoiding   Accommodating

          Uncooperative   **Cooperative**

                Cooperativeness

Source: Adapted from Thomas (1992, p. 266).

Figure 6.2   Five types of conflict management

Lastly, power and influence can be sources of conflict as well as means of dealing with them. First, firms compete to control, i.e. to have power over, the relationship and its direction. Second, the way power is exercised, the influence tactics used, can be a source of resentment and begrudging yielding of control, creating the grounds for further conflict. Or influence may occur in a way that leads to willing cooperation, improved understanding and the granting of more power and influence.

The main strategies for managing conflict are depicted in Figure 6.2. These are distinguished in terms of the extent to which the needs of each party in the relation are taken into account. *Assertiveness* refers to the extent to which one's own interests are considered and *cooperativeness* refers to the extent to which the others' interests are considered. *Confrontation* involves a win–lose type of interaction in which the more powerful party wins. This could involve the use of strong and assertive influence tactics. *Accommodating* is the complement of confrontation and involves acceding to the wants of others. This may not be a weak tactic but part of a longer-term exchange of favours, or an ingratiation tactic designed to gain more power later. *Avoidance* may involve switching partners or both parties ignoring or suppressing an issue of little importance to either. *Compromise* is the essence of negotiation and reaching a mutually agreeable position based on give and take by both parties. *Collaboration* involves the search for win–win solutions that may involve mutual adaptations and innovation.

Trust

Trust is a topic that has received much attention in recent years but, surprisingly, was largely ignored by researchers in management and marketing until the late 1980s. Trust involves relying on another party to act in an expected way and caring about you. This can come about in various ways, and people disagree about whether to call all of them trust. For example, one influential classification of trust is based on a study of Japanese and British buyer–seller relations in the car industry (Sako 1992). Mari Sako distinguishes between *contractual trust*, based on the expectation that each party will adhere to the promises made in the contract, *competence trust* based on beliefs and expectations a firm is able to perform its role adequately, and *goodwill trust*, based on mutual expectations of commitment to each other.

Underlying these categories are two basic dimensions reflected in the distinction between *cognitive or calculative trust* and *emotional or affective trust*. The former rests on a logical, rational, calculus of advantage, as when a firm might expect another to cooperate with it because of the costs and benefits to the other compared to alternatives. The ability of the other party to carry out the necessary activities is part of this assessment and may be referred to as competence trust. But is this really trust? It is just a calculation of costs and benefits. This contrasts with emotional or affective trust, which comprises two main components: benevolence, a belief that a person or firm has a genuine concern for your welfare, not just self-interest, and will not act opportunistically; and credibility, that a person or firm communicates in an open and honest way. This type of trust is associated more with personal than business relations, but it also plays a role in business because what gets sorted out in markets is not just economic exchange but human cooperative relations (Fligstein 2001). Through the personal and professional interactions taking place, managers and boundary personnel, such as sales and purchasing officers and service personnel, develop personal affinities, antagonisms, admiration and respect that lead to different forms and degree of trust and distrust. Personal emotions such as trust, together with cognitive elements, allow human cooperative relations in business to be developed, sustained and enjoyed.

The role and importance of personal relations in business is particularly evident in some cultures that are more homogeneous (e.g. Japan and Scandinavia), in cultures with strong trading cultures (e.g. Arab and Chinese cultures) and in developing countries, where there is an absence of established business infrastructure to support and protect private enterprise, markets and contracts. Studies of business relations in Scandinavia and Japan have demonstrated the role and importance of long-term relations between firms that underpin much business. These are born out of a long history of trading between people with strong personal affinities, similarities and loyalties that carry over into international business operations and trade.

Personal, family and regional ties play an important role in Chinese society and business, as reflected in concepts of *guanxi* and obligational contracting (Wilkinson and Yeoh 2005). *Guanxi*, or personal networks rooted in family, home town, school or workplace ties, facilitate referrals and introductions and favours are stored, remembered and returned when appropriate. It functions like an insurance system, ensuring the reliability and reputation of others, and creates indebtedness in terms of social obligations or *renqing*. This is a form of social capital that plays a key role in the success of overseas Chinese business empires. But these types of networks are not peculiar to Chinese and Eastern business. Research on business relations in the West have emphasised the important role played by personal and social relations, and *guanxi* has been compared to the 'old-boy network'. However, personal networks are more likely to be seen as problematic than advantageous in the West, as reflected in comments about 'nepotism', 'pork-barrel politics' or 'jobs for the boys'.

In developing countries with underdeveloped business infrastructures and legal systems, who you are rather than what you are matters more in forming business relations. This is because, without easy access to contractual enforcement mechanisms and well-developed financial systems, personal relations of trust and reputations of honest and fair dealing have to play a more important role. In Western cultures business relations may start based more on economic logic, and personal bonds may develop subsequently, reinforcing the relation. In Eastern cultures and less developed countries personal relations can be the starting point and the foundation for the formation of business relations. As countries develop, become more involved in international trade and take on more of the trappings of Western market systems, the role and importance of such personal bonds become less critical. One of the key problems confronting international business is how to establish and develop productive relations with counterparts spanning different cultures and customs of business.

Trust between people in business develops over time through the experience and outcomes of interactions over time (Huang and Wilkinson 2006). The exploratory first steps of a relation involve little risk and simple forms of trust based on mutual interest and respect for each other's competence. They do not require strong emotional bonds but they set the stage for further developments involving stronger emotions, more sophisticated assessments and higher-risk strategies. As the relation develops and the mutual benefits of long-term cooperation become clear, personal bonds can arise as well as a concern for each other's welfare and interests, which helps sustain the relation. This also creates opportunities for additional types of indirect relationship functions to emerge. An alternative scenario is that early disappointments damage the development of emotions associated with trust, leading to indifference or distrust.

Research on trust has gained momentum in recent times with increased attention being given to relationship, partnering and collaboration in business. It has also become an important focus of attention in online trading systems. This is because the advent of the Internet and the ability to connect people and firms rapidly around the world creates problems of trust and reliability. It is easy to set up a website offering products and services and to send out millions of emails to people all over the world promoting your services. The Internet cuts across national borders and legal systems, which makes it difficult to police. In order to handle these problems various institutions and methods have been devised to help establish the credibility and trustworthiness of online traders and trading systems. These include the development of trust brokers, firms that have established reputations based on bricks-and-mortar business, setting themselves up as intermediaries who vet and recommend particular suppliers and services, and the use of personal comments and feedback from satisfied and dissatisfied customers as a way of determining the reputation and trustworthiness of products, services and traders. For example, E-Bay and Amazon provide means for personal feedback and commentary that helps others evaluate the value and risks associated with online trading. The problem is not solved, however, as who is to vet the commentators?

Commitment

Committing something involves directing it to some use or place and not to other uses and places. Commitment is a form of investment in a relation – an allocation of effort, attention, affection and resources to interactions with some people and firms and not others. Such investments restrict or reduce what can be committed to other relations. Resources and effort committed to one relation are not available for others; attention time is limited and you cannot love or like everyone to the same extent. Such commitments are forms of sunk costs that have no value or limited value in other relations. We encountered one example of this in Chapter 2 with the concept of relationship-specific assets. These are investments in people, machines, processes, and ideas dedicated and adapted to a relation.

Commitment leads to dependence and power, to the extent that investments in a relation are specific and cannot be switched easily to other relations. If a firm commits all its purchases to one supplier, it is more dependent on that supplier and vulnerable to opportunistic behaviour on their part. Similarly, the learning and adaptations that take place over the life of a relation make the parties involved more dependent on each other, and affection for another leads to vulnerability and dependence. The greater the commitment to another firm, the greater the dependence on it and the greater the power of the other firm. Commitment comes in various forms, including economic, psychological, social and cultural dimensions, each creating different types of dependence which in turn affect the scope, strength and type of power resulting and even how it can be used (Sharma et al. 2006).

The concept of commitment is linked to that of *obligation*. I first realised this when a questionnaire we were using to study interfirm relations was translated into Chinese. When it was back-translated the questions used to measure commitment emerged as forms of obligation. As I have commented already, obligational contracting is a feature of Chinese business relations, as well as trade relations in other cultures, due to the importance of *guanxi* and the granting and receiving of favours. If a favour has been given it is rather like dipping into the bank account with the other party, and repaying the favour represents a 'payment' or contribution to the account, which helps keep it in balance over time. Obligation is not the same as commitment for it focuses on the consequences of *not doing* something of value for another person or firm, whereas commitment focuses on what *is done* to the other in the form of directing resources, attention, affection and effort. Both commitment and obligation function to sustain and develop relations, and they are both a cause and consequence of trust. Trust in another is in a sense a kind of commitment, to depend on another's words and deeds and expect them not to act in ways that deliberately advantage you. The greater the trust, the greater the commitment or investment in the relation that is possible, and the degree of investment combined with the experience of interactions and outcomes in the relation serve to reinforce or change trust.

A distinction can be made between behavioural and attitudinal or psychological commitment (Sharma et al. 2006). *Behavioural commitment* involves overt investments in the form of effort, activities and resources. Psychological or *attitudinal commitment* refers to the extent to which the relation with another is directly or indirectly valued and the importance of the role played by the relationship in a firm's plans or schemas. These two dimensions are interrelated, in that attitudinal commitment drives behavioural commitment, which reinforces or not attitudinal commitment, depending on the direct and indirect experience of interactions and the outcomes arising. Obligation is a form of attitudinal commitment which stems from social norms arising in the institutions of society, including social norms and legal systems.

A range of motivations underlies commitment and obligation, including economic, psychological, social and cultural and even biological, if we believe research on the biological bases of trusting and affection. Economic motivations include access to the resources and expertise of others through relations and the potential to reduce transaction costs and risk through the development of relationships. Non-economic motives include the intrinsic value of interacting with others due to personal bonds and affinities, social obligations and norms of reciprocity. These motivations lead to the identification of various subtypes of commitment which may be linked to different bases of power, such as those enumerated by French and Raven (1959).

Affective commitment stems from respect, affection, emotional attachment and social bonding with a partner. This leads to a desire to develop and strengthen a relationship with another person or firm due to familiarity, friendship, personal confidence and respect built up through interpersonal interaction and trade. Affective motives create intrinsic transaction benefits that add value to a relation, helping to maintain it and making it more resistant to rival offers. Such commitment leads to forms of referent power and informal sources of authority or legitimate power, and may contribute to the perceived expertise of the other party. *Obligation-based commitment* arises from a sense of moral duty and responsibility towards others, a sense of ought, that creates legitimate power for the other party. This may be a product of past favours and norms of reciprocity, as in obligational contracting observed in Chinese business relations, or result from more general industry and cultural norms, such as collectivist norms and nationalism that favour local firms over foreign. A firm committed out of economic motives could readily break a business relationship, whereas a firm committed out of obligation and affect would be less able to do so.

Calculative or cognitive commitment is based on a rational calculation of the rewards and costs of continuing a relationship versus switching. Switching costs create what can be called *negative or locked-in commitment*, a begrudging form that creates forms of reward, coercive and legitimate power in the relationship. Firms can threaten legal action based on contractual provision, threaten to not use or promise to use relationship-specific investments such as customised products and processes. *Positive or value-based commitment* is also cognitive but here there is a calculation of positive economic benefits from continuation, not a fear of loss from switching. Table 6.3 summarises the various forms of commitment in terms of whether they depend on economic or non-economic costs and benefits, and whether the focus is on the value produced in the relation or the costs of switching.

Table 6.3   Forms of commitment

	Economic	Non-economic
Value of the relation	Cognitive or calculative positive commitment	Affective commitment
Switching costs	Cognitive or calculative negative or locked in commitment	Obligational commitment

A mix of bases of commitment will be relevant in any relation and will change over time as a relationship develops. In this process there will be both more to lose and the value or not of the relation will have been demonstrated. The bases of commitment also depend on industry and cultural contexts, such as the nature and role of formal contracts and the costs and ease of their enforcement. For example, a study of business relations in a collectivist culture found that the stability of business is paramount and dissolving a business relationship is socially risky (Kim and Oh 2002). A firm's reputation and its potential attractiveness as a relationship partner will depend on many factors, including the resources and skills it has, its existing relations and network position (something I discuss in more detail in Chapter 7) as well as the direct experience of those that deal with it and how this is communicated to others.

Can you buy a business relationship (Anderson et al. 2001)? The answer to this question depends to a large extent on the strength and kind of commitment involved. For example, if an industrial customer is highly committed to a particular supplier or distributor, what happens if the supplier is taken over? How likely is the customer to stay with the supplier? Much depends on the type of commitment to the supplier and the nature of any relationship to the firm taking over the supplier. If affective and obligation commitment dominate, the customer is more likely to leave if the relevant personnel and culture of the supplier change as a result of the takeover. But if the commitment is more calculative and based on economic value and/or switching costs, the takeover is less likely to affect the relationship, so long as the products and services provided do not change. The extent to which customers and other members of a firm's relationship portfolio are committed or loyal to a specific firm and its personnel, or to the kind of products or services provided, can have a significant effect on the valuation of a target firm – specifically, the valuation of its goodwill. The evaluation of goodwill in professional practices, such as legal, consulting, accounting and medical partnerships, is one area where this problem features in the finance literature and led one judge to distinguish between three types of clients – cats, rats and dogs. 'The cat prefers the old home to the person, the dog represents that part of the client who follows the person rather than the place, and the rat follows neither and drinks elsewhere' (Lonergan 1998, p. 368). In my terms, the cat has cognitive commitment, both positive and locked in, the dog has some form of affective commitment but probably not obligation commitment, and the rat is an uncommitted opportunist. The reputation and relational capital of the firm taking over another obviously matters as well, and this can help increase or reduce the commitment of existing relationship partners.

THE EVOLUTION OF RELATIONSHIP ECOLOGIES

As we have seen, many types of relations and patterns of interaction are to be found in business, even within one firm's portfolio of relations. There is no way of managing interactions with other firms that is inherently superior: it depends on starting and operating conditions. One firm cannot impose a form of relationship management on another; it takes two to tango and two (at least) to produce a relationship. A power-conflict approach by one party cannot live successfully for long with a commitment-trust approach by the other party. The former would be able to take advantage of the latter by making promises it did not intend to keep and by acting opportunistically. Either the relationship ends and new types of relations form and/or the parties have to change their behaviour, becoming mutually adversarial, mutually cooperative, arm's-length or dominated by one side. We have seen examples of all these in Chapter 5.

The development and evolution of relations is not confined to what goes on in one relation in isolation. Relations are connected both directly and indirectly to each other. What goes on in one relation spills over into others as the experience and reputation of trading partners lead firms to change the way they deal with each other, and they learn to search for new types of partners to deal with. Changing connected relations is one way of responding to problems and issues in relations, such as asymmetric and coercive power. This is typified by what has happened in the auto-parts supply industry in the USA in recent times. Suppliers have to deal with a small number of very large multinational car makers, who wield enormous buying power and whose purchasing departments have a history of squeezing their suppliers' profit margins. Captive suppliers, as revealed in Bensaou's analysis of car industry business relations considered earlier, are at the mercy of their buyers. To combat this situation, suppliers have tried to redress the balance of power in various ways, by altering the value, inimitability, rarity and non-substitutability of their resources.

To limit the suppliers' purchasing power they have tried to reduce their dependence on the car industry by diversifying into other industries, and they have tried to increase their own bargaining power with car makers by changing their relations with competitors, complementors and their own suppliers. These strategies have met with various degrees of success, as revealed in a recent industry analysis (Mercer et al. 2004). Mergers and acquisitions have led to some consolidation in the supply industry, including the elimination of the smallest firms and the emergence of some large, diversified suppliers, such as ArvinMeritor, Dana Corporation and Lear. Firms have moved into complementary products to become complete subsystem or module suppliers, such as seat makers moving into carpet supply or spring suppliers also supplying shock absorbers. However, suppliers remain very small compared to their customers, and the value and substitutability of the assortments they supply is limited. Purchasing departments were still able to pick apart the assortments offered to reduce prices for individual components.

A more successful strategy is for suppliers to focus on vertical linkages between suppliers at different stages of the value chain. This creates additional value that is less substitutable and less easily imitated. For example, if a car maker buys two kinds of brake systems through different departments, selling both brake systems provides little extra leverage, but if a first-tier supplier of automotive interiors specifies the second-tier suppliers of consoles, diversifying into console production is more valuable than adding extra interior products. The economies of doing this depend on scale and scope efficiencies, as discussed in Chapter 2, and the ability to create additional value through the development of productive relations with second-tier suppliers leading to product and process improvements. The development of relationship and process resources is much more difficult to duplicate or reverse-engineer. Another strategy for adding value and reducing dependence in the car industry is that used by second-tier suppliers, who have focused on key components of larger systems and broadened their customer base to suppliers in other industries. Examples include producers of washer nozzles used in windscreen-wiper systems, specialised balance shafts that prevent engine vibrations, and electric sensors.

Changes in environmental conditions also have profound effects on the types of firms and relations that develop and survive. They can undermine the logic of existing relations while reinforcing others, threaten the survival of some firms while benefiting others, introduce new types of firms and people into an industry with different values, schemas, experience and networks, all of which can have knock-on effects throughout the network. Examples include: the opening up of markets to new types of competitors with different relationship schemas and networks; changes in technology that alter the activities that have to be performed, their complementarity and similarity, and efficient operating scales; changes in demand and supply conditions that alter the balance of power and the economics of insourcing and outsourcing; and changes in rules and regulations that force the break-up of firms, prevent mergers and acquisitions, or outlaw certain types of business relations.

Business relations and networks are in a constant state of being and becoming. They are not rigid, static entities but living systems that are constantly being reproduced and reinforced, or undermined and changed, through ongoing processes of action and interaction. In any given period the residues of the past are present in the kinds of firms that exist, how they perceive and respond to each other, and the bonds and ties that exist between them. This shapes action and interaction that at the same time feed back to affect the ongoing success of firms and relations – how they are perceived, and the bonds and ties that exist. There are many possible evolutionary paths that relations and networks can follow, all based on the workings of the underlying mechanisms and principles I have discussed. But there are so many factors at work, combining in different ways and in different sequences to affect what happens, that it is impossible to predict the future, which remains fundamentally uncertain and unknowable to those involved, and to policy makers. How firms and policy makers attempt to deal with these uncertainties is the subject of Chapters 7 and 8.

Advances have been made in recent years in understanding and modelling the dynamics and evolution of complex adaptive systems such as business relations and networks. These theories and methods are associated with the science of complexity and networks. They allow us to understand how and why different kinds of relations and networks are likely to emerge, the key factors and tipping points that are important in their development, and the kind of role that managers and policy makers can and cannot play in affecting what happens.

An interesting example of the application of these methods is in modelling the evolution of cooperative versus non-cooperative relations. The emergence of cooperation among selfish animals, people and firms has puzzled researchers in biology, economics and business. The problem is most easily seen in terms of the classic case of the *prisoner's dilemma*. In a market context we may describe this in terms of two firms that could co-operate by trading with each other, each giving up something in exchange for something of greater value. If each keeps their side of the bargain, both gain from the trade. But there is a risk that each will renege on the deal by trying to keep the product or service provided by the other and not paying them, or by collecting payment from the other and not providing the

Firm B

		Cooperate	Defect
	Cooperate	+3,+3	–2,+5
Firm A	**Defect**	+5,–2	+2,+2

Figure 6.3   Prisoner's dilemma payoff matrix

product or service in exchange. This is the non-cooperative or defect strategy which, if successful, leads to a greater gain for the defector and a loss for the other. If both defect, neither gains as much as they could by the trade. Figure 6.3 shows one possible set of payoffs for the two firms. If both cooperate, the payoff is 3 units of net profit for each. If both defect, they keep what they would have traded, which to each of them is valued at 2 units. If one defects and the other cooperates, the defector gains 5 units of value provided by the other but avoids the cost of providing something in exchange, and the cooperator incurs the cost of providing its contribution (−2 units) but gets nothing in exchange.

What is the best strategy for each firm? Consider Firm A: what is its best strategy if B cooperates? It is to defect and gain + 5, which is better than the net gain of + 3 if it cooperates as well. If B defects, what is A's best strategy? Again it is to defect to avoid the 'sucker's payoff' of −2 and settle for keeping what it already has, i.e. + 2. The same incentives apply to Firm B, so the logical outcome is for both to defect and for no trade to occur. But we know trade occurs all the time, so what brings this about? Most importantly, market exchange is not a one-shot deal; people want to trade with each other again and with others, and what happens, or doesn't happen, in one transaction will affect subsequent transactions with the same firm. In addition, firms learn about each other's behaviour indirectly, through observation and communication among them; the reputation of a defector will be tarnished as a result. This makes it more difficult for them to find other firms to trade with in the future. The development of trust and commitment in relations, and of a firm's reputation more generally, are examples of these learning processes at work. Lastly, legal systems and other types of institutions develop to allow firms to enforce contracts, although this can be a costly and time-consuming process that is only used in extreme cases.

When firms need to continue trade to meet their needs, the prisoner's dilemma problem becomes an *iterated prisoner's dilemma* (IPD), and this changes everything. In order to make the problem even more realistic we can allow firms to choose whom they want to trade with, i.e. choice and refusal of trading partners, and to allow communication among firms. These kinds of problems admit of no simple solution because a firm's behaviour in the short run will affect its success in the future, in terms of whom it can trade with and whether other firms are likely to cooperate or defect when trading with it. Outcomes also depend on the mix of types of firms around to trade with, who is part of your network or group, the types of strategies they use and how these change over time, and how easy or difficult is it to find out how other firms are likely to behave. These types of problems are the subject of game theory in economics and business, a major research area leading to the award of a number of Nobel prizes. A formal mathematical analysis of these types of problem is not relevant here. What is relevant is that the development of computer modelling techniques allows us to study how strategies and trade relation networks evolve among people and firms under different conditions, and in particular how cooperative strategies emerge.

One of the first models of the emergence of cooperation to gain widespread attention is that developed by Robert Axelrod (1984), a political scientist, and his colleagues. In a series of tournaments based on the iterated prisoner's dilemma he investigated the success of different strategies over time. Strategies could be more or less sophisticated, such as defecting or cooperating all the time, randomly choosing whether to cooperate or defect, and strategies that involved teasing out what the other player's strategy is and then using this knowledge to advantage. The basic structure of the game was that players in the tournament played each other a number of times, after which the results for each player were computed. Based on the results, the number of firms playing different strategies increased or decreased depending on how successful they were. The idea is that more successful strategies are more likely to survive and be copied. The revised population of players then played each other and the new results were assessed. This led to further modification of the population of players in terms of the strategies they played and so on. Over time the mix of strategies in the population changed and one type of strategy did particularly well, 'tit for tat' (Axelrod 1997). This is a deceptively simple strategy of cooperating on the first play of the game with any partner and then copying what the other player did in the previous play. Subsequent analysis revealed why this strategy did so well compared to others. First, it is 'nice', in the sense that it cooperates initially and will continue to cooperate if the other player cooperates. But it cannot be exploited very much and will respond if provoked, such that a defection

	1	2	3	
	8	Player A	4	
	7	6	5	

Figure 6.4   The eight neighbours of Player A on a square grid

will be met with subsequent defection. It is also forgiving because if the other party starts to cooperate, it will reciprocate. Lastly, it is a simple strategy and easy for others to recognise and adapt to.

Axelrod was also able to show how groups of cooperators can emerge and survive among other firms that are defectors. Each player is positioned on a checkerboard-type grid with eight neighbours, as shown in Figure 6.4 for player A. The grid wraps around on itself at the top, bottom and sides to avoid edge effects. Firms play iterated prisoner's dilemma games with their eight neighbours only, and after a number of plays outcomes are assessed. Players can then change their strategy to copy the best-performing one of their neighbours. Thus a defector may learn from its neighbour that tit for tat works better. Over time clusters of players emerge on the grid playing different types of strategies, including groups of co-operators, who sustain themselves by cooperating with each other, despite many other firms defecting. This outcome suggests how groups of cooperators can become established as they reinforce each other's behaviour in the face of defection from others. For this to happen, firms have to be able to recognise those they have dealt with before, as happens in a neighbourhood. The 'neighbourhoods' of business would comprise groups of firms in a network or region that trade with each other more regularly.

Subsequent research has extended these results. It has been shown that tit for tat, or strategies resembling it, such as tit for two tats, can evolve and survive in various situations, and can resist invasion by non-cooperative strategies. Mistakes and misunderstandings about each player's strategy can be important. For example, if both players are using tit for tat, and one misinterprets a cooperation as a defection and defects the next time, the players could get into a situation of repeated defection as each responds to the defection of the other. Of course, further mistakes could re-establish cooperation. The structure of the payoffs also matters. The prisoner's dilemma is only one type of game and different kinds of problem arise in other game conditions, with tit-for-tat-type strategies not necessarily being the best. This is important because trading conditions and the payoffs to firms change over time as they adapt to each other and environmental conditions change. What might be a good strategy in one situation may not work as well when conditions change. I take up some of these issues in the following chapters as they relate to the development of relationship and network strategies for firms and policy makers.

A particularly interesting finding is that it may be important and even inevitable that some nasty strategies remain in the population of players. This is because, once a population dominated by cooperators is established, it provides the environment for naïve cooperators to develop and survive. This can happen over time as firms become used to trading with each other and stop taking any precautions. Then, when a firm is taken over by a non-cooperator from another industry or network, or managers change, introducing a more adversarial culture, some firms become vulnerable. But if there is always some chance of encountering nasty as well as nice trading partners, there is less danger of firms drifting towards more vulnerable patterns of action and interaction.

To sum up, we can see that research shows how, over time, stable networks of cooperative actors can emerge that resist invasion from non-cooperators. In other words, nice guys can win! But the nature of cooperation that survives is not a naïve form of cooperation but one that is prepared to adapt to the strategies of others – one that allows it to benefit from interacting with cooperators and that is not taken advantage of by non-cooperators. I will have more to say about this type of research and modelling, and the role it can play in guiding the development of relationship and network strategies and policies, in the following chapters.

RELATIONSHIP TERMINATION

We now come to the final stage of a relationship's life – its death. But do relations die? In this section I want to argue that to a large extent the energy created in a relation, especially in the form of resources and knowledge co-created, in the personal and professional bonds and schema couplings developed, live on and are conserved in many ways. They reappear in other forms in other relations, as people, ideas and knowledge move around. This leads to the principle of the *conservation of relationship energy*, paralleling the first law of thermodynamics, which is about the conservation of energy in physics. The transfer and transformation of relationship energy into other forms of relations leads us back to the way relations start.

The termination or dissolution stage of business relations has been given less attention than other aspects of relationship development and management (at least until quite recently), yet it can have important consequences for those involved. Relations can fail and firms can withdraw from relations at any stage of their development, but when this happens after the parties involved have made substantial commitments and adaptations, such as Ford's long-term stage or Dwyer et al.'s commitment stage, there is much to lose in the form of relationship-specific assets, which have limited value elsewhere, potential legal costs, recriminations and reputation effects.

Dissolution tends to be associated with failure; the final outcome of a vicious cycle of declining satisfaction, commitment and performance, and increasing conflict. But this is not always the case. As we shall see, firms may part amicably, with the intention or possibility of coming together again in the future. Relationship termination may be part of a planned strategy, as firms move into new markets and respond to changing market circumstances. In some industries short-term relationships may be mutually desired because rapidly changing technologies and market conditions make it difficult to know whom to partner with, and firms do not want to become locked into relations with the wrong kinds of partner. In Silicon Valley, for example, rapidly changing patterns of short-term partnerships are evidently, so I am told, more the norm than long-term relations because of the fast-evolving nature of the computer and software industry.

It is not always clear when relationships end. Ceasing to trade is a reasonable criterion to use, but studies show various patterns of trading and non-trading over time, with some firms moving their business among a limited set of partners – a kind of polygamous loyalty. Are these relations continually being broken and restarted, or is this another type of relation with a different rhythm of interaction? Even when trading stops completely, other forms of interaction may continue, such as information exchange and other types of social and business interaction. Residues of the past remain in the form of resources created and used, including the knowledge and skills learned, mutual understanding and the positive and negative social and personal bonds that have been created. These ideas, resources and bonds can affect how a firm operates in other relations and the kinds of relations it can and will establish in the future.

Business relating business

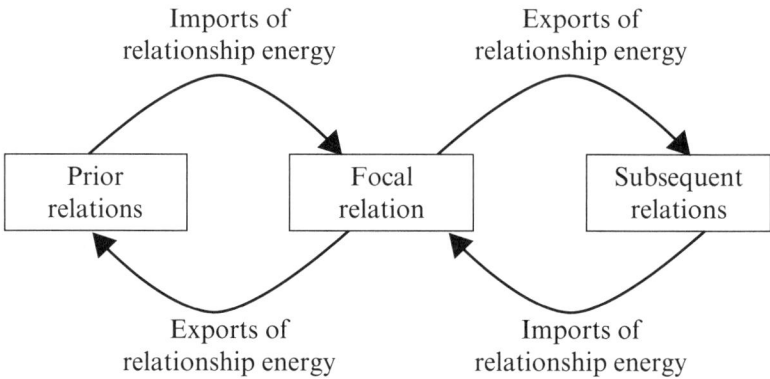

Figure 6.5   Exporting and importing relationship energy

Social and personal bonds established over time can play a major role in some types of trading relations, particularly those involving high levels of personal service such as consulting, advertising, market research and law firms. For example, a study of auditor–client relationships found that individual attachments affect the likelihood of clients switching, and a study of relations between firms and their accountants showed that social bonds can be strong enough to stop clients switching even when firms were shown to be guilty of gross incompetence (Seabright et al. 1992; Young and Denize 1995). In project marketing, maintaining extensive contacts among likely subcontractors and principals is an important part of developing a firm's competitiveness, and these contacts manifest themselves in trading relations only when a particular consortium bids successfully for a contract.

Figure 6.5 shows the connections between relations in terms of the exports and imports of relationship energy. Positive imports of congenial and trusting social bonds may help to establish the focal relationship more quickly and move it towards a more advanced stage of development. The mutual trust, goodwill, personal regard and commitment to people in the relationship partner, as well as the knowledge and cooperative habits built up in other relations, provide the foundation on which to build the new relation. Alternatively, negative imports of conflictual and non-trusting relations may adversely affect the establishment and development of a new relationship. There may be feedback effects among relations, for example, when experience in one relation reinforces or undermines the bonds with and reputation of others.

Case studies can be used to illustrate the way relationship energy is exported and imported. These come from research conducted by the IMP group. As part of a Swedish study, a selection of relations involving

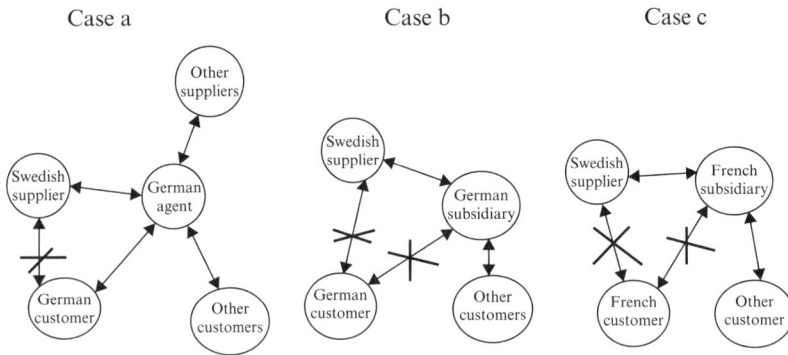

Note: X = ended relationship.

Figure 6.6   Cases of relationship dissolution

different types of industrial products was studied over time. The first interviews, with both sides of the relation, were carried out in the late 1980s and
subsequent interviews took place about five years later. Of the 11 studied,
three had ceased trading with each other at the time of the subsequent
interview. How these relations ended and what happened afterwards shows
the transfer of relationship energy among relations.

A Case of Reduced Trust

Case A is about a relationship between a Swedish supplier of industrial
equipment and associated know-how and its German customer. The relationship began in 1987 when the German firm purchased half a million
dollars' worth of new equipment. The supplier operates worldwide, with
sales varying from half a million to 10 million dollars, depending on
whether they supply new equipment or rebuild existing equipment. The
technology of the three main competitors is similar. About five or six orders
are handled per year, mostly involving new customers and countries, and
the durable nature of the specialised equipment means that inter-purchase
times can be several years. It is not worth the supplier maintaining a sales
operation in each country, and selling directly from Sweden is problematic,
so they use independent agents to gain new customers.

The agent in Germany has been used since 1986 and it played an important role in initiating the business relationship. The agent is a subsidiary of a
Swedish company belonging to another industrial group to that of the supplier. The agent sells nine different types of equipment on behalf of a number
of suppliers to customers in one industry. In 1994 it had seven or eight

customers in Germany, including some continuing relations and one-off sales. The agent commented that personal and social relations are common in the industry, which was described as being like a small family: 'you always meet the same people and many of them [come] from the same school'. The agent's main task is to assist the supplier during the sales phase, which may take one to two years for one order. During this phase contacts between all parties can be intense, with the supplier visiting the customer several times, and they get to know each other well. The customer sometimes contacts the supplier directly but, mostly, contacts are via the agent. The agent imports relationship energy from the contacts and networks maintained with potential customers in gaining customers for the Swedish supplier and, through successful servicing of customers, further develops these relations.

The supplier designs the product and makes the offer to a potential customer. The agent is not always involved in meetings concerning technical details. The supplier sets prices and takes care of invoicing, and the agent assists when the customer is not paying on time. The agent is not involved in the installation phase, but afterwards keeps in touch with the customer and reports any problems. If problems arise, a specialist from the supplier is usually needed. The supplier's salesman described the relationship with the customer as follows (although he spoke Swedish!): 'Athough we call our sales projects, what we really have are customer relationships. This is so because a plant where the equipment is included is never finished. It lives its own life and develops in different ways.'

After the first order in 1987, the customer made other minor purchases. In 1989 the customer planned to rebuild the equipment in its plant and, because the supplier saw this customer as an important bridge for expansion in Germany, it was prepared to make considerable concessions to keep the business. The customer was important for the agent as it accounted for 10 per cent of its sales and bought a range of products. The customer, on the other hand, did not see the supplier as an important counterpart. At this time, three people from the supplier were involved in the business relationship, two from the agent, and four from the customer. The supplier and customer met once or twice per year, usually without representatives from the agent, the agent met with the customer about five times a year and with the supplier about once per year.

The agent was an important conduit for business information from the customer, and a social link. Personal relations between the supplier and customer were not great, in part due to language and cultural differences. The customer had stronger and more personal relations with the agent, who played an important role in smoothing out misunderstandings with the supplier. The agent also believed that good personal relations existed with both the customer and the supplier.

The supplier visited the customer several times with proposals for rebuilding the customer's equipment. In 1991, the customer was taken over by another Swedish company. At one time the customer cancelled the project but later asked for another proposal. But in the summer of 1993 the customer rebuilt the equipment on its own. The supplier was disappointed that it was not contacted before the customer decided to do this and given a chance to lower its price. It felt that the customer was using its ideas in rebuilding the equipment, but it could not do anything. A complicating factor was that, at the time, the customer was under severe economic pressure, due to overcapacity in the industry and low prices.

The supplier believes that the customer will buy equipment from them in the future, 'now that we have built up a relationship with them'. But it intends to be more careful about handing over technical information, because experience has taught it to have less trust in the customer. For the agent, the customer continues to be one of its main accounts, with sales people visiting the customer about once a month and there is phone contact about twice a week. The supplier does not have any contact with the customer. The agent continued to work for the supplier in Germany, although, during 1994, it was working mostly on behalf of other suppliers.

In this case the existing agent–customer relation, involving several products and frequent personal contacts, together with the agent–supplier relation, was the vehicle for establishing the supplier–customer link. Relationship energy was imported from these other relations and developed in the focal relation. The ending of the relation did not lead to relationship energy in the form of the social bonds disappearing, as these were already being maintained in other relations between the agent and the customer. Also, links between the agent and the supplier were maintained with regard to serving other customers. So here relationship energy was conserved, and even developed through use in the focal relation.

The Case of the Vanishing Firm

The second case involves the relation between a Swedish industrial tool maker and its German customer that began in 1965. The supplier used a distributor in Germany to take care of all contacts with German customers until 1989, when it established its own sales subsidiary. This changed the relationship with the customer and, from 1989 to 1990, a new product was developed collaboratively with the sales subsidiary and the customer. The customer is government-owned, buying various types of tools from the supplier, changing over time and from project to project. Some tools are standard, whereas others have to be adapted to suit specific requirements.

The supplier was established in the mid-nineteenth century and makes tools used in several industries. It has subsidiaries or associated companies in all major markets and is one of the leading companies in its field, with a wider range of products than its competitors. In the late 1980s, of its 15 main competitors, five were operating in Germany. Before establishing its subsidiary in Germany, the supplier saw its distributor as its customer, with no involvement in the market beyond that. As a result, after it established its own subsidiary, problems arose because it did not have any routines established for selling, marketing or pricing the products in Germany. Several people work in the sales subsidiary and all the sales people are technicians, able to modify the tools to suit the customer. A service person also visits customers when problems occur. Sales people regularly visit important customer job sites to see that the tools meet requirements and to work on developing new tools with them. This means they get to know each other well and strong personal relations can develop.

Direct contact between the supplier and customer started when the sales subsidiary was established. At that time the customer was seen as important because it accounted for about 10 per cent of total sales in Germany and because it was useful for technological development and product-technology ideas. The supplier believed it very unlikely that the customer would stop buying from them and, if it did, it would have serious consequences for them. Two people were involved in the business relationship from the supplier, one from the sales subsidiary, and three from the customer. The supplier met with the customer twice a year and the sales subsidiary met them much more frequently.

In 1988/9 the customer reduced its purchases dramatically and it remained that way for several years. The relationship ended in 1992 when the German government, which owned the customer, decided to close it down. This was due to high production costs in Germany and increased competition from imports. Only two firms remained in the industry in Germany. The relationship energy was redistributed to other relations by the supplier buying the licence to manufacture a product they had co-developed with the customer. In addition, many people from the customer moved to new companies and a number of these continued to deal with the Swedish supplier in their new roles.

In this case relationship energy has been created through continual trading and contact since the mid-1960s, first through a distributor and then, more directly, through a sales subsidiary. Joint product development has taken place, which indicates a mature relation involving commitment and trust and, in the first interviews, there was a common expectation of continued trading. Changes in the market situation of the customer led it to be closed down, and relationship energy was transferred through the licensing of a co-developed product and through the social bonds and contacts reappearing in other customer relationships for the same supplier. Many of the customer's ex-employees continued to work in the same industry, some of them in firms that were customers of the focal supplier. This is quite natural, since the focal supplier was one of the leading companies in its field and there are few competitors. Thus, even though the focal business relationship ceased to exist, the supplier and the sales subsidiary continued to do business with individuals from the ex-customer, who brought with them some of the social bonds created in the focal relation. Of course, as the customers are new, the role of the sales subsidiary may be different from that in the focal business relationship.

The Case of the Sleeping Relationship

The final case concerns a Swedish supplier of industrial components and its French customer. Deliveries were first made in 1978, and one reason for the establishment of the relation was a friendship between a salesman in the Swedish supplier's French sales subsidiary and a person from the purchasing department of the French firm. The Swedish supplier was established in the mid-nineteenth century and makes standard components for large original equipment manufacturers (OEMs) and sub-suppliers to OEMs. The customer relationship of concern here is with a sub-supplier, who also makes components similar to the Swedish supplier's. Market conditions changed over the period studied, with sub-suppliers becoming far more important as OEMs began to buy products incorporating the relevant component from them rather than buying direct. Also, there was intensive price competition among OEMs in the late 1980s due to the entry of new firms and excess capacity, which led to an eventual shake-out of component manufacturers, and the Swedish supplier's component business was sold to an international group in the early 1990s. The change of ownership did not affect the type of products manufactured or the markets in which they are sold.

The product is easy to transport and store, and up to 80 per cent is delivered directly to customers by the supplier, with delivery times being reduced from one to two months in 1988 to a matter of weeks in 1990/1, and to days in 1995. Technical issues became more important over the period whereas negotiations in the earlier years were more focused on delivery times and prices. The French sales subsidiary took care of most negotiations, although the supplier could become involved.

In 1988 the supplier and sales subsidiary expected a rapid increase in sales to the customer, and that profitability would be rather good. The supplier saw the relationship with the customer as important because it enhanced its image in France, as well as being a bridge for further expansion. Four people from the supplier were involved in the relationship, two from the subsidiary, and seven from the customer. The supplier and the customer met about twice a year, with someone from the sales subsidiary always present. The managing director of the supplier and the person from the customer who started the relationship had met a couple of times. The sales subsidiary and customer met about six times per year, and both the supplier and the sales subsidiary were involved in giving technical assistance to the customer. About 12 deliveries were made each year to the customer.

In the early 1990s the customer stopped buying from the supplier because the customer's product was radically changed. Although it was of the same type, the modified product was aimed at a customer segment that did not need the same level of quality as before, so it could source from lower-quality suppliers. The purchaser who initiated the business relationship had by then retired. However, he continued to work as a consultant on purchasing matters for another company in France, and the Swedish supplier has established a relation with this firm.

In this case the knock-on effects of competition and changes in the sub-supplier's (i.e. customer's) target customers, with associated production technology shifts, weakened the link with the supplier company. There is no obvious other deterioration in the relation, despite the subsidiary being taken over a number of times during the period, and the relation could be restarted if market conditions changed. The heart of the relationship energy here seems to be in the social bonds between the salesman in the Swedish supplier's French sales subsidiary and the French customer's purchaser. Energy from this social relationship initiated and sustained the relationship, and further nurtured these bonds, such that the purchasing agent later facilitated the development of other relations.

We should not make too much of these three cases, but they show that relationship dissolution is not necessarily a process of disengagement due to dissatisfaction; it can be due to external circumstances weakening the logic of the relation. Relationship energy, particularly in the form of personal contacts, bonds and goodwill, is imported into a relationship and helps start it up; it is also used and developed in the relationship and passed on. The cases show that relationship dissolution is not a clear-cut issue.

The cases also highlight the importance of two stages of relationship building not considered much in other stage models (see Chapter 3). First, there is a stage before the relationship begins in the form of existing and prior *supporting or competing relations*, whose relationship energy may spill over into a focal relation in either a positive or negative way. Second, there is a stage after dissolution, disengagement or suspension of trading, which may be called *relationship aftermath*, in which relationship energy is transferred, conserved and/or transformed. Bonds and adaptations in resources and activities made through long-term relationships create opportunities or problems in developing subsequent relations. It is rather like two pieces of a jigsaw puzzle that have been adapted to each other and, when they separate, they need to look for matching pieces with which to form similar links. In short, relationship history matters in shaping future relationship history.

The cases suggest ways in which firms can better utilise relationship energy. Firms can conduct *relationship audits* of previous and existing relationships to reveal hidden resources of knowledge, contacts, goodwill and personal trust that may be of benefit to the firm in developing subsequent relationships. They also help a firm to make sense of changes in relations in industrial networks that result from personnel moving around. Universities and other institutions develop alumni associations in order to retain and make use of relations with previous students. In a similar way firms could conduct their own 'alumni audit', keeping track of where key personnel in their own firm and relationship partner come from and move on to, and whom they get on with best.

Prior relationship and network experience is an important criterion to use in evaluating new personnel. Advertising agencies, law firms and consultants are particularly sensitive to the business-generating potential of new recruits moving from other agencies or from potential customer organisations. People moving from important positions in government are also prized by firms who deal regularly with governments as customers and/or regulators. The US military–industrial complex is noted for these types of move, as documented, for example, in James Fallows's 1982 exposé of the industry. Another illustration is in the development of cross-cultural relations. As shown in the entries over the years in the Multicultural Marketing Awards in Australia, firms are able to make use of the cultural diversity and language skills of their workforce to reach out to new types of markets at home and abroad. Personal and professional contacts and networks, as well as knowledge, cultural sensitivity and communication skills, can play an important role in establishing and maintaining key relations.

The case studies provide lessons on how to go about relationship termination. The problem is how to disengage while retaining any relationship energy built up for potential future use in this or other relations. Different strategies are called for depending on the type of relation and the nature of the energy created. Arm's-length trading relations have no real relationship energy and only continue if there are repeat orders. Those that are more long-term need more care in order to identify the key holders of relationship energy. While trading may cease, other forms of personnel interaction may continue, and even be encouraged, through personal initiatives, social events, round-table discussions and regular follow-up communication. The future benefits of preserving such relationship energy cannot always be foreseen through some kind of rational calculus of advantage. Unanticipated opportunities or problems occur from the residues of previous relations, introductions can be made, knowledge gained, and trading can recommence.

Another issue is that of managing relationship succession, when key personnel involved in a relationship move on to other firms, retire or die. One strategy is deliberately to rotate boundary personnel such as sales people and account managers among accounts and regions to avoid over-dependence on particular personnel and to guard against cosy deals being made. But this can adversely affect the development of relationship energy, depending on the nature and complexity of the relationship and the degree of mutual adaptation required. An alternative strategy is to recognise that, in industrial markets, many people are often involved in developing and sustaining a business relationship, not only sales and purchasing, but general management, engineers and technicians. To the extent the relationship energy resides in multiple personal relationships, some redundancy and buffer against unforeseen problems of personnel change can be accommodated more easily. Diplomats are moved from country to country and face the problem of passing on important contacts to their replacements. Some consistency in relations can be maintained through the more permanent local staff employed, but passing on personal relations and contacts built up over years is not easy, and much depends on the motivations and incentives of those involved.

CONCLUSIONS

This chapter concludes our discussion of the way business relations develop: how they are established, who tends to 'mate' with whom, the factors affecting the development of relations and the forms they can take, and how they end (or not). Relationship ending is as much a beginning as an ending because out of the ashes or joy of a relation come other relations. Relations really never stop; they continue and transform themselves over time in the way activities are performed, resources are adapted, bonds develop among people, in the way they affect people and firms' relationship schemas and in the other relations they spawn and infect.

In Chapters 7 and 8 I consider what all this means for the individual firm and manager trying to find their way in this crowded and ever-changing network of relations and players, and for policy makers trying to control and regulate business. As we shall see, there are strong parallels between the two as both are active participants in the very systems they seek to inhabit, develop, exploit, explore, control, police, regulate and direct.

NOTES

1. This section and the remainder of the chapter is based in part on Wilkinson (2001).
2. The discussion here draws in part on Cameron and Wilkinson (1997), Dixon and Wilkinson (1986), Huang and Wilkinson (2006), Kipnis et al. (1980), Wilkinson (1973, 1974a, 1974b, 1979, 1981) and Wilkinson and Kipnis (1978), among others.

7. Strategies for firms in business relations and networks: the extended enterprise and soft-assembled strategies[1]

INTRODUCTION

The foregoing chapters have examined the kinds of relations and networks that firms are involved in, the kinds of issues confronting firms in developing and managing in these relations and networks, why relations and networks exist, the functions they perform, the forms they can take and the way they develop and evolve. In this chapter we return to the issue of management *in* relations and networks, and examine how firms can and should go about developing and managing their interactions with others in different types of environments in order to achieve desirable outcomes. In Chapter 8 we consider the implications of relations and networks for policy makers: how they can and should go about monitoring, regulating, policing, controlling, directing and fostering business relations and networks so that they contribute to the performance and sustainability of a nation's business system and its development and evolution.

Existing theories of management focus on the individual firm as the primary unit of analysis. Managers sense and analyse their environment, and formulate and implement plans of action and response through which they survive and prosper or not. The determinants of a firm's ability to survive and prosper are explained in terms of their resources, competences and orientations relative to competitors that allow them to identify, occupy and defend viable niches in markets. This focus tends to assume that the firm is in control of its destiny and the fittest firms survive.

There is obvious truth in these theories but they ignore the fundamental problems arising from the interdependent nature of business enterprise. A firm is not an island, an isolated unit of action. Firms, as we have seen, are embedded in networks of relations spanning industries and nations through which their behaviour and performance are directly and indirectly connected to those of other firms and organisations. This results in unavoidable interdependences that create complexities and uncertainty for management, as well as opportunities and strengths. The interdependent nature of business is becoming ever more obvious and significant as revolutions in the speed and cost of travel and communication, the globalisation of markets and the complex and interrelated nature of technologies reshape network and market boundaries, and permit and require firms to reach out to distant places, industries and technologies in order to gain access to key resources, knowledge and inputs, and to find and serve customers.

The problem of interdependence is minimised by assuming that a focal firm initiates and manages, i.e. controls, relations and networks. This is reflected in concepts of marketing channel captains or commanders and network leaders, and theories about the management *of* relations and networks. But this avoids the main problems posed by relations and networks: they are co-developed, co-regulated and co-managed, and firms are simultaneously involved in many relations, both directly and indirectly, that influence each other and firm performance in various ways. No one firm is in charge and the management problem is one of managing *in* existing relations and networks, not management *of* them. The verb to manage, in English, has two meanings: to control and direct others, as in manage a firm or unit; and to cope, as in managing to get through the day without creating too much of a mess. It is the second meaning of the term that is more suited to the idea of managing when it comes to business relations and networks, and indeed for any type of social relation.

THE EXTENDED ENTERPRISE

In this and the next chapter I portray firms as components of larger, complex adaptive systems of relations and networks involving other firms and organisations. These networks of relations form what we might think of as a distributed group body and mind that is able to do more, see more and think more than any of the individual actors that comprise it. I like to think of it as a form of extended phenotype or enterprise, something like a social insect colony, in which the parts exist by means of and serve the whole as they go about attending to their local issues and problems. What happens is not simply the result of the talents and resources of the individual actors and how well or not they solve the particular problems they confront; what happens depends fundamentally and inexorably on the way the parts of the system are interconnected and how their behaviour influences others, both directly and indirectly, over time and place. This larger system of relations and networks, of which individual firms are a part, produces the outcomes we see – the valued products and services we buy and consume, the new resources, goods, services and processes we invent, adapt and employ, and the problems, threats, opportunities and delights we encounter along the way.

The role of individual firm management is to contribute to the development, reproduction, operation and evolution of the group mind and body of which they are a part, so as to promote their own survival as a viable member of a group. But they may not succeed, and that may not be a bad thing for the larger system.

As we have seen in earlier chapters, relations and networks can play many roles in helping or hindering a firm's performance and development. They are the means by which firms access and co-develop key resources, skills and knowledge, and the means by which value is developed and delivered to intermediate and final customers. They are the means by which the collaborative advantage underlying firms' competitive advantage in domestic and international markets is created and sustained. But the establishment of collaborative advantage is not a one-way process: the same relations and networks are also the means by which other firms gain collaborative advantage.

By working with and through others, a firm is able to think more things, see more things and do more things; it is able to recognise, understand and respond to opportunities and problems that it otherwise could not. On the other hand, its extended enterprise can damage and limit a firm's capacity to see, do and think, narrowing its access to information, resources and technology. The overall result depends on the way a firm manages its interactions with others, both directly and indirectly, and the way they manage their interactions with it. Each firm strives to position itself to gain and sustain advantage from the relations and networks in which it is engaged. Giving advantage is part of gaining advantage.

THE CAUSAL TEXTURE OF ORGANISATIONAL ENVIRONMENTS

The role and significance of relations and networks in contributing to a firm's performance depends on the types of problems and opportunities it confronts and how well it can cope with them without the help of others. When markets are uniform, stable and well known, and resources and relevant technologies can be understood and controlled by a single firm, the firm may be able to rely more on its own efforts and resources. This was the situation in some industries in the past, such as automobiles and some food products, in which highly vertically integrated firms arose, e.g. General Motors and Nestlé. The operations of these firms stretched from raw materials supply to finished products through to distribution to the final customer. But, increasingly, this is not possible, as the world has become more complex, dynamic and interconnected. In most cases it is impossible now for a single firm to cope with all the activities involved in converting raw materials into meaningful products and services because they span different industries, markets, technologies and countries, and are subject to different degrees and types of uncertainty and change. This means that firms have to rely more on the activities and contributions of others to whom they are directly and indirectly connected.

We may distinguish between firm environments in various ways. Marketing and management texts tend to focus on the nature and content of specific features of the environment, such as the economic or legal framework, overall market demand and supply conditions, or socioeconomic conditions. These are important considerations that affect the way relationship and network strategies are developed and adapted in particular industries or nations, but here I am concerned with differences that are more fundamental than this. I am concerned with the inherent complexity, dynamics and systemic properties of a firm's environment that affect the kinds of strategic problems or issues it confronts, or what has been called the *causal texture of the organisational environment*, as first proposed by Fred Emery and Eric Trist (1965).

The causal texture of the environment focuses attention on the types of interactions taking place between and within a firm and the environment in which it operates. Figure 7.1 shows the basic framework, with four types of interactions: within the focal firm or system (L_{11}), within the environment (L_{22}), system to environment links (L_{12}) and environment to system

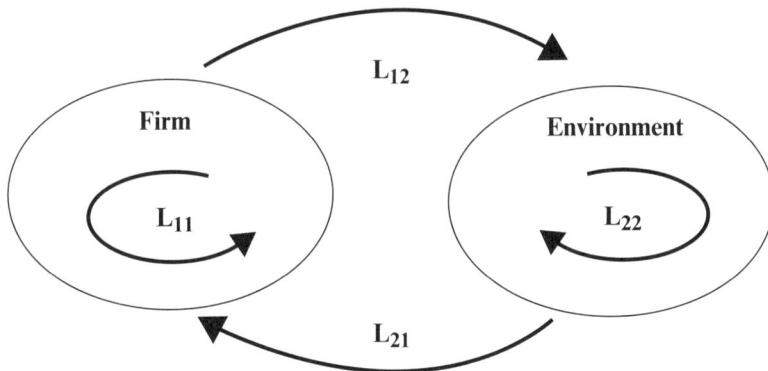

Source: Adapted from Emery (1999, p. 8).

Figure 7.1 Firm and environment

links (L_{21}). The problem of adaptation for a firm is not so much to the ever-varying specific pattern of stimuli encountered, the content of its environment, but to the underlying structural or systemic properties of the environment that produces these stimuli – for example, are they a product of random variation or complex interacting systems? The problem is that of matching the properties of the system with that of the environment, i.e. of aligning L_{11} with L_{22}, which takes place through the processes of learning about environmental changes (L_{21}), and adaptive planning and response (L_{12}).

Emery (1977) identified four types of environments in terms of the complexity and uncertainty of the problems they pose for firms operating in them. The differences are related to the role and importance of each of the four types of interactions shown in Figure 7.1. The main features of each type are summarized in Table 7.1.

Any environment comprises a mixture of these four types because environments exist within environments (Emery 1999). Firms operate in many environments at the same time; these vary in their complexity and uncertainty, including those associated with the markets from which it sources various inputs, the markets in which it sells its outputs and the locations in which it carries out its operations. Even in the same market environment a mixture of types of problems arises, varying in their complexity

Table 7.1   Four types of environments

Environment	Characteristic problems
1. Random placid	Survival depends on the firm's own resources (L_{11}) and luck
2. Clustered placid	Survival depends on the firm's own resources (L_{11}) and its ability to reach out into the environment for what it wants and avoid dangers (L_{12})
3. Disturbed reactive	Survival depends on the firm's own resources (L_{11}), its ability to reach out into the environment for what it wants and avoid dangers (L_{12}), and its response to the intentions and capabilities of competing others (L_{21})
4. Turbulent	Survival depends on the firm's own resources (L_{11}), its ability to reach out into the environment for what it wants and avoid dangers (L_{12}), its response to the intentions and capabilities of competing others (L_{21}), and coming to grips with the complexity and systemic properties of the environment (L_{22})

Source: Adapted from Emery (1977, p. 10).

and relevant uncertainty. In addition, the causal texture of a particular environment is not fixed. It can change over time as the firm and environment develop and co-evolve, resulting in shifts in the characteristic types of problems arising. In the following sections I discuss each of Emery and Trist's four basic types of environment, starting with the least complex.

Type 1: Random Placid Environments

A random placid environment is a market space of opportunities that is randomly scattered and does not change in response to a firm's activities. A firm resembles a small fish in a big pond in which it cannot know what will turn up next, when or from where. In this situation there is no optimal location or market position or strategy to follow, as any market position or strategy is equally likely to be beneficial or not, and discovering one opportunity or problem gives no guidance as to the nature of other opportunities or problems. Here, no strategy is better than the best tactic, and random behaviour, such as tossing a coin to decide the next move, is just as good as any other move. As Emery (1977, p. 6) describes it, 'The guiding principle is "catch as catch can" and the characteristic forms of behaviour will necessarily be exploratory and trial and error; vacillating from one hunch to another, even switching to contradictory hunches rather than being persevering or parsimonious.' Learning in such an environment is impossible as any patterns detected are illusions and give no guide for future action. Speculating on the stock market is much like this, as Nassim Taleb's delightful book *Fooled by Randomness* (2005) shows us.

The focus of adaptation here is the focal firm itself, as all that matters is its resources, reflected in L_{11}, and luck (Emery 1977). The environment is similar to what Knight (1921) refers to as risk, or randomness with knowable probabilities, rather than uncertainty, which is randomness with unknowable probabilities. Given the random nature of the environment, larger firms, or those that have more resources to sample a larger part of the environment, will tend to have payoffs closer to the mean value of opportunities in the environment. This is because they can take advantage of the lower sampling variance among larger samples due to the law of large numbers and central limit theorem. The mean value of opportunities from larger samples (searches) of the environment will more closely approach the average value in the environment as a whole. Smaller search areas (samples) by firms with fewer resources will tend to have greater variance, so that some will do well by chance and others not. This leads to firm strategies reflected in the principles of massed reserves or pooled risk, which were discussed in Chapter 2, whereby central stocks and reserves held against uncertain demands gain cost efficiencies, as in insurance.

Normative theory, propositions about what firms should do as opposed to what they can and do do, is limited in such conditions. There can be no experts with superior knowledge, and the only advice that can be offered is that firms should not waste time and effort trying to improve their strategies because any strategy is as good as any other and only size counts in absorbing the effects of the randomness. As already noted, financial markets appear to function in this way and random-walk investment strategies have proved to be as good as more sophisticated ones in some cases.

Note that random placid is not the same as a perfectly competitive market. In such a market consumers and suppliers are homogeneous and perfectly informed. But customers are randomly paired with suppliers, as there are no transaction costs to reduce or transaction benefits to gain from repeated transactions. Hence there is no value in forming relationships between customers and suppliers. Firms are price takers and can sell as much as they want at the prevailing price without affecting it. The optimal strategy is to produce the demanded good and offer as much as maximises profit, which occurs when marginal cost equals the price, and U-shaped cost curves are assumed so that there is a limit to a firm's size.

Type 2: Clustered Placid Environments

In clustered placid environments opportunities are not random but the environment is otherwise similar to the first type. The environment does not change in response to a firm's actions and it is neutral in the sense that it is not deliberately designed to prevent a firm's survival or to actively seek to harm it. The existence of non-random aspects to the environment makes learning possible and valuable. Adaptation focuses on the firm's ability to understand and respond in appropriate ways to its environment (L_{11} and L_{12}) through the identification of more and less preferred market positions and strategic moves. 'In an environment where things are clustered together in time and place it is possible for some things to act as cues for the co-occurrence or subsequent appearance of other things and for others to be seen as co-producers of certain desired effects' (Emery 1977, p. 7). The small fish in the big pond can now learn about its environment and move to preferred locations. In marketing terms, a consumer-orientated market strategy is called for in which firms seek to understand and respond to consumers' needs through market segmentation and positioning strategies. Sources of supply are also not randomly scattered and require similar differentiation and positioning strategies to gain access to those best suited to target customer segments. We are able to rely on market research for clues as to the actual behaviour of market actors, which contrasts with a random placid environment, where there would be no relation between research results and actual behaviour. In addition, because the environment is placid, forms of cooperation among complementary market actors with non-competing goals is possible, such as working with customers, suppliers or distributors to improve products and services. However, there are still potential conflicts with customers in terms of what is the best use of a firm's resources.

Such an environment corresponds to a situation in which firms can choose their strategies so as to optimise returns based on an evaluation of the relative value and likely outcome of different alternatives. Because firms operate in an environment that is potentially knowable, the resource-based theory of the firm (Barney 1991) can help explain why firms succeed or fail; the firm is limited only by its resources and competences in researching and responding to market opportunities. Forms of collaborative advantage are available, as firms can collaborate with each other and with their customers to better understand, use, combine and develop their resources. In principle, optimal strategies can be devised using various types of research, analytical and optimising techniques, which take into account the costs and benefits of alternatives. Much of neoclassical economics has evolved to solve these types of constrained optimisation problems (Denzau and North 1994).

As Lane and Maxfield (1996) point out, the methods for solving this type of strategic problem have been and still are the dominant modes of business training and strategic planning. In marketing these techniques are well represented in terms of marketing engineering (Lilien et al. 2002a), which includes methods to segment markets, to identify preferable market positions and to design profitable market offers (Lilien and Rangaswamy 1998, 1999). As Lilien et al. (2002a) argue, marketing engineering links the power of computers with data, knowledge and judgement to assist managers' decision making. Managers combine use of these techniques with their ability to identify acceptable tradeoffs among conflicting goals and the quality of their assumptions about aspects of the environment where research is too costly, limited or biased.

Type 3: Disturbed Reactive Environments

Disturbed reactive environments are clustered environments that are not placid. There are two or more competitors or firms of the same type, such that they cannot all simultaneously achieve their goals. It is a zero-sum game. The fish is no longer small or alone. A firm's actions affect its competitors directly or indirectly through its interactions with the environment, such that, for example, meeting the needs of customers means that these customers are not available to competitors (at least for the same needs and problems). The environment is not placid, as competitors exist who can gain at another's expense and who will directly or indirectly try to harm their rivals. Moves by a firm to a preferred location in a market can be disturbed by the reactions of other firms, as when two firms identify the same market niche as an opportunity. In this type of environment adaptation focuses on L_{11}, L_{12} and L_{21}. L_{21} becomes a focus of attention because of the need to respond to the intentions and capabilities of competitors.

The relevant theory of competitive advantage here is that of resource advantage theory (Hunt and Derozier 2004; Hunt and Morgan 1997), where resources are defined broadly to include any means by which valued products and services can be created and delivered. This is an extension of the resource-based theory of the firm and reflects the need for firms to offer products and services to customers that are preferred to competitors, i.e. they are perceived to offer more value or to cost less. A competitive as well as a consumer orientation is required. Thus it is not the existence and control of resources *per se* that leads to firms being able to serve customers better, but the extent to which they result in differential advantages. The importance of particular resources in generating competitive advantage depends on how valuable, rare, inimitable and non-substitutable they are (Barney 1991).

Resource advantage theory provides a framework for guiding firms in developing competitive advantage and for diagnosing sources of competitive disadvantage. To determine its strategy a firm has to understand the structure of the market, which is assumed to be stable and unaffected by competing firms' actions, including the resources that are important for creating and delivering value, the resources other firms have, and how they are likely to behave and respond.

The game of business here resembles a game of chess or war. At any stage in the game a player can assess their resource advantage in terms of the types of pieces they have compared to their opponent and the positions they occupy relative to opponents. This affects the types of moves that can be made. But even though the rules as well as the power and behaviour of individual pieces is fixed, there is no one best strategy; it depends on what other players' resources and strategies are. Competition, like chess or war, is a process of interaction that takes place over time. At the same time that player A is acting and responding to the resources and actions of player B, player B is doing the same concerning player A. Only if each perfectly predicts the behaviour of the other will expected outcomes occur. This tends only to occur in special circumstances, when the alternatives available are severely constrained, as in end games in chess. Usually, competitors have many possible alternatives to consider, and in these situations, as Brandenburger (1998) has pointed out, even in a simple two-person game the complexity is fundamentally infinite. Each player is responding to what they think the other will do and think, and what they think the other thinks they will do and think and so on in an infinite regress.

There is another dimension to competitive interaction in disturbed reactive environments. A new type of strategy emerges that involves out-manoeuvring a competitor in order to achieve a strategic end, what Emery (1977) calls 'operations'. Of course all can play the game and competitors engage in various types of misleading and deceptive conduct to confuse others about their actual strategies and intentions. In other words, competitor opportunism exists – self-seeking behaviour with guile (Williamson 1975).

As each firm is anticipating and responding to others, which are in turn anticipating and responding to them, complex patterns of behaviour emerge that are not predictable, resulting in unavoidable uncertainty in the Knightian sense. No firm is in control of how competition and outcomes develop. Outcomes are co-produced over time through the pattern of interaction among players' strategies, just as in a game of chess. There are no optimal strategies in such circumstances as they are contingent on the strategies of others. Instead, 'strategic options need to be formulated more in terms of power to meet competitive challenge than simply in terms of achieving optimal location' (Emery 1977, p. 9). The power to meet competitive challenge depends on the ability of firms to respond to different circumstances, and Wroe Alderson, one of the architects of modern marketing theory, identified a key normative principle relevant for guiding interactions in such conditions – the Power Principle. 'An individual or organisation, in order to prevail in the struggle for survival, must act in such a way as to promote the power to act' (1957, p. 51). In other words, a firm tries to take into account how current decisions enable or constrain future decisions, and tries to avoid committing resources in such a way that unduly narrows future options and flexibility. This principle is analogous to the type of dominant strategy that exists for all sophisticated competitive games such as chess or Go, which involve getting your opponent to commit themselves while remaining still flexible yourself (Padgett and Ansell 1993).

Marketing engineering and research techniques are still useful in this environment but they must be augmented by judgements about competitor and environmental responses, as well as the focal firm's own future responses. Here, the quality of management judgement becomes relevant and softer forms of data are likely to be important, such as rumour, espionage and gossip.

Competitive theory in type 3 environments is the realm of game theory, in which the actions of each player are modelled over time under different assumptions in order to identify better-performing strategies. Under various assumptions and game conditions, superior strategies may be identified, including Nash equilibria, in which each player is willing to persist with their strategy so long as others do. But such equilibria are not necessarily optimal or stable. Simulation experiments based on repeated prisoner's dilemma games, which involve a mix of competition and co-operation, show how different outcomes can emerge depending on the mix of strategies being played and the starting conditions (Dixit and Nalebuff 1991). Evolutionary models, such as those described in Chapter 6, that allow firms to learn and adapt their strategies over time based on the out-comes of earlier interactions, show some interesting results, including the potential emergence of cooperative behaviour among groups of competi-tors (e.g. Axelrod 1984, 1997; Lindgren 1997), although others are more sceptical (e.g. Binmore 1998). Such models are far from providing clear directions for management action except in particular types of market auc-tions, where behaviour is constrained by known rules.

Relations and networks can play an important role in type 3 environ-ments. Relations with customers, as well as other types of organisations, are potentially important resources that firms can use to create and sustain differential advantage, by reducing transaction and coordinating costs, designing and adapting products and services, protecting themselves against competition and gaining valuable information about competitors and the market environment (e.g. Dyer and Singh 1998; Gulati et al. 2000; Kanter 1997). Relationships as resources are particularly valuable because they are hard to duplicate or buy by competitors (Dyer and Singh 1998; Andersen et al. 2001). Developing relations with competitors is also poten-tially valuable in order to open up, control or suppress market competition and to develop acceptable market and industry standards (e.g. Gründstrom and Wilkinson 2005; Welch et al. 1996). `

Type 4: Turbulent Environments

Turbulent environments are dynamic environments like disturbed reactive environments, but the dynamics arises not only from the actions and reac-tions of competitors but from within the environment itself. The actions of firms not only affect competitors; they also have direct and indirect impacts on other aspects of the environment, including customers, sup-pliers and complementors. The environment comprises many types of purposeful, interconnected, interdependent, interacting systems and organisations, and evolves in response to the actions and interactions of those involved, leading to the emergence of new types of actors, relations and networks.

The game of business in turbulent environments is like a game of super-chess with many players who can compete as well as cooperate – a game with no fixed rules, in which the pieces have goals of their own and inter-action among pieces and players can change over time as a result of previous interactions, new types of pieces can arise from recombinations of existing pieces and through chance mutations, and where there is no set goal by which winners and losers are clearly defined. Today's winners may be tomorrow's losers and vice versa, and the game never ends. Over time there is a continuous co-evolution of players and patterns of interaction, where each player constitutes part of each other's environment, in which the fittest survive in the context of the environment that is co-created by the fittest, or as Stuart Kauffman (2000) describes it, 'The winning games are the games the winners play' (p. 79).

A turbulent environment is a complex adaptive system (CAS). Such systems arise in biochemical, biological, ecological and social systems, as well as in economic and business systems (Arthur et al. 1997). The behaviour of a CAS depends on the way the parts are interconnected, not just the characteristics of the parts. No participant is in control. Instead, order and large-scale structures emerge in a bottom-up self-organising way from the micro interactions taking place among individual actors, as well as top-down as macro structures are recognised and responded to locally. Interactions and interdependences among the parts of the overall system make its behaviour highly non-linear and impossible to predict. Outcomes are very sensitive to starting conditions and, because the outcomes of any actor's behaviour depend directly and indirectly on the behaviour and responses of many others, they cannot be traced back to the acts of individual actors. 'An organization reacts to the actions of others that are reacting to it. Much of what happens is attributable to those interactions and thus is not easily explicable as the consequence of autonomous action' (March 1996, p. 283).

People's intuitions regarding how to participate effectively in such non-linear systems may not serve them well, as traditional approaches to solving managers' problems are based on mathematical methods and approaches designed to deal with linear systems, that can be decomposed into independent subparts and studied and understood in isolation, and analytical solutions are possible. But as Robert May (1976, p. 467), a pioneer of non-linear systems analysis, points out:

> The mathematical intuition so developed, ill equips the student to confront the bizarre behaviour exhibited by the simplest of discrete nonlinear systems . . . Yet

such nonlinear systems are surely the rule, not the exception, outside the physical sciences.

In some ways this environment resembles the random placid environment and may appear to be so for an individual actor. But it is not random. It obeys rules of behaviour and interaction that defy closed-form solutions, even if we could write down the underlying behavioural equations. It is an example of strong uncertainty in the Knightian sense (Denzau and North 1994). The focus of adaptation now includes all types of firm and environment interactions, i.e. L_{11}, L_{12}, L_{21} and L_{22}. 'In turbulent environments adaptation is not possible unless somehow one comes to grips with the L_{22}' (Emery 1977, p. 10).

How does a firm come to grips with such a complex and dynamic environment, and what kinds of normative theories are relevant to guide the behaviour of participants in such systems? As I argue in the following section, one way this is accomplished is not through the planning and strategic actions of individual firms working in isolation, but through the sensing and response of networks of firms co-created and co-regulated through their actions, interactions and relationships over time. Such networks are more able to recognise and cope with the uncertainties involved, and they call for different types of competences and skills on the part of participant firms in order to contribute productively to and benefit from the processes by which such networks are co-created and co-regulated, and the way they co-evolve.

HOW CAN AND SHOULD FIRMS BEHAVE IN TURBULENT ENVIRONMENTS?

The term turbulence is used to describe environments in which individual firms face strong uncertainties because of their complex nature; this can result in rapid and unexpected change. Mintzberg (1993) points out that turbulence of this kind has tended to be ascribed to the current environment in every age, and that the patterns and directions of change only become clearer in hindsight.

The kind of turbulence we are interested in here is characteristic of type 4 environments. Whether a particular environment is type 4 is not determined simply by the degree of uncertainty firms face, as this can arise for various reasons. For example, hypercompetition is a source of extreme uncertainty that results from an accelerating pace of change in forms and types of competition and is confused with turbulence. Here, firms deliberately try to disrupt markets and undermine rivals' sources of competitive advantage in an ever-escalating race to achieve temporary rather than sustainable forms of competitive advantage. Temporary partnerships with other organisations can play a part in this process of seeking out and exploiting ways of disrupting competition for short-term advantage. But this is just an extreme form of a disturbed reactive environment, not a type 4 environment. The game of business is still a continuous succession of prisoner's dilemma-type games played among rivals and the focus is on ways to compete, not on any indirect consequences for other parts of the system.

Effective strategies in type 4 environments need to take into account second- and third-order effects of actions. However, the ability to recognise, understand and cope with these effects is beyond that of the individual organisation. It is also beyond the abilities of any centrally directed and coordinated networks of relationships, or what are referred to as strategic networks. Strategic networks and network forms of organisation are essentially a response to disturbed reactive environments (type 3). They focus on rivalry between networks as opposed to individual firms. But type 4 environments refer to conditions in which the environment is beyond the capacity of an individual firm to deal with, no matter how internally organised it may be and no matter how well it is able to orchestrate the behaviour and interactions of other organisations in its strategic network, because any centrally controlled and directed system lacks the requisite variety to match the variety in a type 4 environment. I have more to say about the concept of requisite variety shortly. In any period there will always be winners and losers as no one firm or strategic network is able to cope with all possible contingencies through time.

Type 4 environments are typified by periods of radical restructuring of industry and firm boundaries, and discontinuous change, such as were wrought by the coming of the railways, telephone, electricity and the Internet. In these cases technological developments disrupted previously established forms of interaction, competition and industry structure until new forms emerged to take their place. An illustration of this type of change is provided by Lane and Maxfield (1996) in terms of the evolution of the firm ROLM and PBX computer-based phone systems. They show how the impact of new technologies led to the emergence of new types of products, actors and relationships that could not be foreseen, planned or intended. Existing customer–supplier relations were undermined and new patterns of interaction, relations and networks formed within and between firms in the industry. The knowledge and learning that co-developed between firms as a result of these interactions led to radical and unexpected adaptations of strategy, including redirections in terms of both ends and means.

As already pointed out, environments of different types of causal tex-
tures coexist; there are environments within environments. Hence, for some
sectors and regions of industry and for some dimensions of a firm's strategic action space, non-type 4 environments may exist that allow a firm to
follow more clearly defined normative strategies born of these simpler environments or sub-environments. For example, in the PBX example referred
to above, competitive games were still played out between particular actors
over time (type 3 environment), customer preferences varied over time and
place calling for variations in systems, products and solutions adapted to
particular requirements (type 2 environment), and chance events dictated
why particular actors or relations gained or lost at particular times and
places (type 1 environment).

But how does a firm cope with a type 4 turbulent environment, which is
inherently unpredictable *a priori* and in which opportunities and outcomes
emerge in a self-organising way from the local patterns of interaction,
learning and adaptation taking place? Should they continue to try to construct, reconstruct and direct internal and external networks in order to
seek at least temporary competitive advantage? Or are new types of strategies called for? A key insight is that *the relevant unit of coping and response
is not the individual firm or lead actor but the network itself, i.e. the extended
enterprise*, which I referred to at the start of this chapter.

A useful analogy here is the way social insect colonies behave. In these
colonies there are no leaders. Instead, coordinated and directed action
takes place through the direct and indirect (e.g. via pheromones) interactions taking place among members of the colony and with their environment. These rules have evolved in the context of a particular environment
in order for the colony to survive, and are hardwired into their genes. Local
actions and responses produce macro patterns of behaviour for the colony,
including the way it houses itself, breeds, takes care of its young, searches
for and shares food, and how it recognises and responds to opportunities
and threats inside and outside the colony. All this is done without any
central direction.

If the environment changes so that existing rules of interaction do not
produce viable colony behaviour, a struggle for survival will take place.
Colonies will take different evolutionary paths in their 'search' for a new,
viable set of rules of interaction. The evolutionary searches are affected by
genetic variations among colonies that give them different starting conditions, by historical circumstances and by path dependences and random
mutations. Eventually, existing species become extinct or take on new
forms, and new types of species emerge that may redefine what we mean by
ants and bees. We and the ants and bees do not know how many evolutionary stable interaction strategies may exist; indeed, their number may

well be quite limited, as studies of evolutionary convergence suggest (Morris 2003).

Do we have any theories that help an individual ant or bee cope with these conditions? No, each ant does not have the resources or knowledge to cope alone; their behaviour and its outcomes for them and the colony are unknown and unknowable for the individual ant, as they depend on what other ants do and the conditions they face. Moreover, even for a fully informed outside observer, the outcomes of collective ant and bee behaviour and interactions are not knowable because the colony is a complex adaptive system – a non-linear system in which many possible equilibria exist to which the behaviour of the colony is attracted (hence the name attractors) depending on starting conditions, the type of stimuli experienced and random elements. And some of the attractors are strange, not simple static arrangements or cycles but more complex patterns of behaviour, interactions and responses.

While an ant or bee cannot alter its own rules of interaction, humans and firms actively seek to understand and manipulate their interactions with the environment and each other, and try to make sense of what is going on. They can change both their interpretation of themselves and their environment and – at least to some extent – the way they interact with others. Such adaptations to turbulent environments can be both maladaptive and adaptive. First we consider maladaptive responses.

Maladaptive Responses and Type 5 Environments

Coping with turbulence involves attempts to adapt to or reduce the level of relevant uncertainty. Emery (1977) identifies three types of responses that are maladaptive: superficiality, segmentation and dissociation. *Superficiality* involves reducing relevant uncertainty by lowering emotional investments in the ends being pursued. This is reflected in managers following ritualistic formal planning procedures they do not believe in, as they do not know what else to do. For example, Mintzberg (1993) points out how formal planning can become a substitute for control in large organisations rather than a means of control – an illusion that reduces management anxiety, allowing them to sleep better at night. Planning becomes an end in itself and a form of public relations that avoids dealing with the essential uncertainties confronting the firm.

Segmentation involves breaking the system into smaller, less complex systems insulated from each other. Emery (1977, p. 31) sees this in terms of 'the enhancement of ingroup–outgroup prejudices as people seek to simplify their choices'. In business, industry protection schemes, trade barriers and trade blocs are attempts to reduce interdependences and protect local business communities. The recent strong protests at world trade forums also reflect people's beliefs that reducing international interactions among economies and firms can reduce the complexities and uncertainties for individual nations and firms. Loyalty schemes, cooperatives and tied relationships can also be manifestations of segmentation.

Lastly, *dissociation* is a denial of any possible advantages to collaboration over individual selfish action and involves 'indifference, callousness and cynicism toward others and to existing institutional arrangements' (Emery 1977, p. 32). In business the 'greed is good' type slogan represents this, as does the callous and manipulative behaviour of executives, leading to some of the mighty firm collapses the world has been witness to of late – the Enrons, the OneTels, the HIHs. It is also reflected in a strategic focus on business relations from an exclusively adversarial and zero-sum perspective, in which the problem is primarily to reduce dependence, gain power, guard against opportunism and suppress conflict.

Such maladaptive responses have led some to propose a type 5 environment of hyperturbulence: 'the condition in which environmental demands finally exceed the collective adaptive capacities of members sharing an environment' (McCann and Selsky 1984, p. 460). Such an environment results from participants' attempts to reduce or avoid the inherent uncertainties, through one or more maladaptive strategies, that dampen turbulence and uncertainty by reducing the degree of interconnectivity in the environment. Research shows how even small changes in the degree of interconnectivity of a system have important effects on its behaviour and stability, moving it from regimes of ordered to chaotic behaviour. Maladaptive strategies reduce interdependence by partitioning the environment into separate subsystems with restricted interaction, or what McCann and Selsky (1984) call social enclaves and social vortices. Those able to cope collectively with a sub-environment, as defined by their own existence and separation, form social enclaves. Social vortices comprise those who cannot cope, out-groups relegated to the margins of society. Examples are South Africa before the end of apartheid and the decoupling of segments of US and other societies into ghettos, and survivalist communities. Today, as I write, the disengaged and disadvantaged worlds of the very poor in parts of Africa and the Middle East come to mind.

Adaptive Responses to Type 4 Environments

The challenge posed by turbulent environments has led to various proposals regarding appropriate ways for managers and firms to respond. These variously focus on the importance of participating, learning and knowledge development, adaptive strategies, effectuation and improvisation.

Such strategies recognise that firms are fallible, that they have limited information and operate in a complex adaptive system with unavoidable and profound uncertainties. A strategy is a kind of hypothesis to be changed, in terms of both targeted outcomes and means, in response to feedback as the firm muddles through. In this process of muddling through the firm changes its plans in a continuous way as new ends and new opportunities, as well as new means to reach existing ends, are discovered, recognised and responded to. The extended enterprise, the patterns of interactions and relations managers and firms have, directly and indirectly, with others in and outside the firm play a key role, as they are sources of learning, adaptation and response.

The role of relations and networks is exemplified in Lane and Maxfield's (1996) concept of generative relationships. These shape the way a manager or firm makes sense of their environment, including the relevance of different types of actors, their actual and potential roles and functions, and the way they act in relations to others. In the PBX case the example is given of the impact of interactions between technical managers (TMs) in customer firms and ROLM, a supplier of new types of computer-based systems. These interactions affected the way ROLM understood and approached the market in terms of target market segments, products and systems; it altered the position of TMs in their firms; it affected the interactions among TMs, leading to new customers for ROLM, and undermined relations between TMs and other suppliers. The problem is that such generative relations and their outcomes cannot be anticipated or predicted from knowledge of the participants; they emerge through participating in such relations over time. The firm's ongoing task is one of monitoring, interpreting and reinterpreting existing and potential patterns of interactions.

Fred Emery (1977) similarly focuses on the key role of relations and networks as the means of coping with turbulent environments. He explains this in terms of the emergence of widely shared values and ideals among organisations, and how these relate to fundamental dimensions of choice. Such values and ideals are not some new-age version of business philosophy and they are not achieved in the same way as other types of business goals, such as market share or profits. Instead, they act as a moral compass guiding choice and adaptation of goals in the face of the fundamental uncertainties of turbulent environments; they are kinds of shared mental models that help us to choose and adapt.

Ideals enable people:

1. To maintain continuity of direction and social cohesiveness by choosing another objective when one is achieved or the effort to achieve it has failed;

2. To sacrifice objectives in a manner consistent with the maintenance of direction and cohesion. (Emery 1977, p. 69)

Four dimensions of choice can be used as the basis for identifying appropriate values and ideals – probability of choice, probable effectiveness, probable outcome and relative value. The first is about improving the probability or range of choice by increasing *homony*. At a personal level this involves relating more closely to others, such as neighbours and workmates, through which people improve their range of choice. 'The experience of others is a prime source of "familiarity with" the world, and "the others" are usually best able to provide access to a wider range of course of action' (Emery 1977, p. 72). Humans naturally do this; they are able to learn from seeing others do things and solve problems in ways other animals cannot. In a similar way, improved coordination and cooperation between and within firms is a means for expanding the action possibilities for all – learning and co-learning from and with each other.

The second ideal, *nurturance*, focuses on resource creation and development through relations and networks by promoting the ability and effectiveness of our actions and responses. This is done through cultivating and developing our own as well as others' competences and resources. The concern is about growing the garden (productive relations and networks), not just picking the flowers (using relations to meet current objectives), and can be viewed as an extension of Wroe Alderson's Power Principle, i.e., involving others' actions and capabilities in promoting our own.

The third ideal is *humanity*. The probability of outcome derives from the first two components of choice and thus presumes homony and nurturance. Humanity focuses attention on the use of others as ends versus means or, as Norbert Wiener (1954) expressed it, 'Towards the human use of human beings'. At any time firms and people have many different objectives they may pursue. Choosing among them according to humanitarian ideals means not necessarily choosing the best in terms of achieving economic or technical goals, but those that fit our nature and place in the universe. The ultimate guide here is 'good for whom', how people generally are affected, not just firms. Firms are merely the local environments or habitats within which individuals seek out their ideals; organisations themselves are not ideal-seeking.

The last ideals, *beauty and relative value*, seem at first remote from the world of business but are not. The ideals deal with the interrelations of purposes or ends themselves, our place in the world and the survival of the world. Ideals only emerge in social systems in which inherent uncertainties arise from the interlocking purposes and goals of the actors involved; from the interdependences that exist among them. Beauty is used as a term for a higher-order rationality, which somehow rationalises and synthesises the inherent conflicts of interlocking purposes within a higher rationality or order of ends. In regard to business systems, higher-order logic includes the operations and maintenance of the overall market process itself and relates to the protection and maintenance of the material, biological and social environment. It is through market processes that winners and losers with conflicting purposes are sorted out so as to sustain and strengthen the process itself, i.e., the pursuit of interlocking purposes through market processes permits and stimulates the overall process to continue and enlarges our desires and possibilities. Fred Emery (1977, p. 76) expresses this in a more general way:

> men will increasingly choose and more consciously strive to choose those purposes that manifest intentions calculated to stimulate both themselves and others to expand their horizons of desire and to rationalize conflict.

Maladaptive strategies are examples of behaviour that constrain future desires and possibilities, whereas adaptive strategies open up possibilities. The principle is an extension of Alderson's Power Principle. It is not just the individual actor that seeks to act so as to maximise its own ability to act, but also to act and interact with others in such a way that enlarges the resources, capabilities and desires of all interacting market actors. Perhaps we should call this the *social power principle*.

The Extended Enterprise Again

The concept of generative relations and the values and ideals identified by Emery highlight the importance of relationships and networks in coping with type 4 turbulence. Further support for their role and importance comes from the 'Principle of Requisite Variety' advocated by Ross Ashby (1952). He argues that in order to respond to their environment, systems have to be able to match its variety or complexity; otherwise they will eventually confront conditions they cannot cope with. Over time environmental complexity in general has increased, due to the increasing number of people and organisations that are ever more interconnected and in which the frequency and speed of interaction and response are also increasing. We have moved from simpler hunter–gatherer societies, through early civilisations and the Industrial Revolution, to modern globalised industries and societies. Such changes lead to the emergence of different forms of organisation to cope with the increasing complexity.

A critical point is reached when the complexity of the environment exceeds that of an individual person or firm. This means that central direction from a single coordinator, no matter how well supported and informed they may be, cannot work because of the necessary limits to one individual's complexity. Similarly, single firms lack the requisite variety to cope with a highly complex environment. However, networks of organisations, in which knowledge, coordination and direction are distributed and behaviour emerges from the interactions taking place among those involved, have far greater intrinsic variety and therefore greater ability to cope with complexity. The business network itself functions as a kind of collective mind and body that is more 'intelligent' and able to adapt than the individual firms comprising it, yet it is formed out of those firms and the way they interact and respond to each other. The network mind and body is embedded in the patterns of interrelations within and among the actors. As an example, consider a description of the Toyota production system, which I also used in Chapter 2 to depict the intricate patterns of division of labour and specialisation existing in business networks:

> Toyota's knowledge of how to make cars lies embedded in highly specialized social and organizational relationships that have evolved through decades of common effort. It rests in routines, information flows, ways of making decisions, shared attitudes and expectations, and specialized knowledge that Toyota managers, workers, suppliers and purchasing agents, and others have about different aspects of their business, about each other, and about how they all can work together. (Badaracco 1991, p. 87)

Another example is the identification of productive technological partnerships from among a set of firms as described by Wolpert (2002). Here the aim is to bring together a set of firms with potentially valuable technological complementarities and facilitate the identification of productive relations within the group. The ability to do that depends on the assortment of firms in the group, from which potential collaborations can be identified. These are not properties of the individual members but a joint property of the group.[2]

EXTENDING RESOURCE-ADVANTAGE THEORY TO RELATIONS AND NETWORKS

Resource-advantage theory (R-AT) may be extended to incorporate the role of relations and networks. Let's start by considering the individual firm and its resources and how they contribute to its performance, then move on to consider the contribution of relations between firms. R-AT argues that a firm's market position is a function of the resources it controls, including tangible and intangible elements and the competences and skills embedded in the people, teams, relations and networks comprising the firm. These resources are combined in complex ways over time to produce the plans, actions and responses that characterise the firm and the way it responds to its environment, including competitors. In turn, these plans, actions and responses shape the firm's market position (Hunt and Derozier 2004).

The contribution of a particular resource to the firm's competitive position is not easy to assess for a number of reasons. First, its contribution varies over time and across markets depending on the type of value to be created and delivered, and the technologies available. Second, its value depends on how widely and easily available it is to others and the ease with which it may be appropriated, duplicated or substituted. Third, resources get used in combination and so the value and contribution of any one resource depends on the quality and availability of other resources within and among firms. Interaction effects occur among resources that affect their actual and potential contribution to a firm's competitive position. For example, a superior market research department is of limited value if the firm does not have the ability to translate this research into viable products and services. Lastly, a firm's actions and their results have feedback effects on the mix and value of their resources in the future. Some are used up or deteriorate; others grow and are enhanced – such as knowledge and learning.

The problem here is analogous to that of determining the effect of different genes on the characteristics of a resulting organism or phenotype. The organism's genome may be equated to the assortment of resources that a firm has that enable it to behave in particular ways in order to survive and prosper in its environment. The organism or phenotype that results from the expression of genes over time in an environment is equivalent to the organisation and behaviour of a firm that results from the expression of its resources over time in its environment. The use of resources reinforces or replicates their use to the extent they result in benefits or 'fitness' for the firm as a whole, and they are replenished or replaced by the actions of the firm. For example, the use of a firm's knowledge and research skills to produce competitive marketing strategies reinforces the use of and replenishes these knowledge and research skills.

Resources, like genes, do not act in isolation but interact over time as they are used in combination to create a type of firm with a particular organisation and behaviour repertoire. Firms are selected for based on the fitness of their behaviour in the relevant market environment; there is no absolute standard for judging the fitness contribution of a resource or gene. Fitness depends on the context, including the other resources of the firm and the resources of other firms and organisations, including competitors. Like genes, individual resources contribute to (or hinder) fitness and survival in the presence of other resources, which in turn contribute (or hinder) fitness in the presence of them. In one context a resource may be extremely valuable; in another irrelevant or harmful, such as the value of a market research department in a random placid environment or a perfectly competitive market compared to a clustered or disturbed reactive environment.

A simple example will serve to illustrate how resources are interconnected within and across firms. It is adapted from biological examples described by Richard Dawkins (1983). Resources can be used in various ways by firms, depending on their objectives and the other resources at their disposal. Consider how we might determine the effect of a particular resource, A, e.g. a design department, on the competitive market position of a firm. First, we might imagine comparing firms competing in similar markets with or without this resource and see how well they do in terms of market share, price premium, or customer loyalty. We may find that resource A is associated with gaining a price premium. Is resource A the resource 'for' price premiums? As Dawkins notes, we can only determine the effect of a proposed cause by comparison with another potential cause. Let us assume there are two firms with resources A1 and A2, which can be thought of as two kinds of design departments. To keep it simple, assume there are two kinds of firm outcomes – a price premium or a price discount (P1 and P2). In order to make the comparison, I will assume all the other resources of the firms are the same and the two firms are not competing against each other. If we find that, statistically, firms with A1 are more likely to get price premiums (P1 rather than P2) than firms with A2, we may conclude that A1 is a resource leading to price premiums. If price premiums are a key to a superior market position and success in the market, firms with A1 will prosper and other firms may try to build the same type of design department.

Although A1 appears to lead to P1, this may also depend on the other resources of the firm, which may suppress or enhance the likelihood of P1. There may be another resource B, the type of advertising department, that interacts with A1. Suppose there are two kinds of advertising departments, B1 and B2, and B1 may not get on well with design departments, particularly A1. The presence of B1 may interfere with the activities of A1 directly, or they may be unable to reflect the designs of A1 well in their campaigns. Hence, if all firms have A1 but do not get a price premium if they have B1, then B1 not A1 becomes the resource for gaining a price premium (P1). In other words, both resources A and B are potential causes of price premiums depending on the resource assortments that exist in the population of firms.

We may extend this argument to relationships and networks. The contribution of a resource not only depends on other firm resources; it also depends on the resources of other firms with whom a firm interacts. In this way one firm's resources may find their expression in a related firm's organisation and behaviour, not just their own organisation and behaviour. What we define as the phenotype associated with any genes, or in our case resources, is arbitrary as the chains of cause and effect links extend beyond individual bodies or organisations, to their behaviour and to other bodies and organisations – to what Richard Dawkins (1983) refers to as the *extended phenotype*.

A firm's resources are indirectly combined with the resources of connected other firms and organisations, resulting in impacts on the organisation and behaviour of these connected others. A firm's resource may not just affect its own competitive position but also the competitive position of others. This is clearly the case when firms outsource different functions to specialist firms in order to make use of their resources, as discussed in Chapter 2, and hence a supplier's resources contribute indirectly to the organisation, behaviour and competitive position of its customers. For example, a supplier's production and design department enhances or hinders the work of the customer's internal production and design department and, in turn, their relations with other departments such as advertising. The type of relationships a firm has with its suppliers affects the contribution of the supplier's skills and competences to the organisation and behaviour of the customer.

The networks of relationships in which firms are embedded may be viewed as extended phenotypes in which the resources of the firms comprising the network directly and indirectly contribute to its pattern of organisation and behaviour, as well as to the reinforcement and reproduction of the resources required to continue this pattern, depending on which patterns succeed. To use Richard Dawkins's phrase, this is *resource action at a distance* – not within one firm but within and across firms. Furthermore, the resources of other firms that influence a particular characteristic of the extended phenotype may be in conflict or support each other, just as they do in the case of genes. All the firms involved are not necessarily cooperating with each other; there is still room for conflict in terms of the resource impacts and interlocking objectives of those involved. The extended phenotype is jointly manipulated, not necessarily in a cooperative manner, by the resources, actions and interactions of directly and indirectly related firms who may span different types of industries and technologies and nations.

The important point is that the unit of analysis moves beyond the individual firm to the network of interconnected firms that together co-produce the behaviour and organisation of the network, and the outcomes. The survival and performance of individual firms is based on the organisation and behaviour of this extended phenotype in its environment. Richard Dawkins's central theorem is that 'An animal's behaviour tends to maximise the survival of the genes "for" that behaviour, whether or not those genes happen to be in the body of the particular animal performing it' (1983 p. 233). Analogously, a firm's behaviour tends to reinforce the resources that enable that behaviour, whether or not those resources happen to be part of that firm's resources or some other connected firm's resources.

Natural selection in the market works on the basis of outcomes. The outcomes of firms' plans, actions and responses have feedback effects on their resources, including their skills, competences and knowledge, as well as on their objectives and future plans and interactions. Firms, relations and networks are selected for and evolve based on the outcomes of their actions and interactions, which in turn affect the conglomeration of resources underlying network behaviour. The network, its membership and its resources change and evolve over time. New types of firms with different characteristic interaction and response patterns emerge as well as new types of relations.

Through extended phenotypic effects the interaction behaviour of firms can be indirectly affected by the resources and behaviour of connected firms, which can result in patterns of interaction becoming institutionalised in a network that facilitate or inhibit cooperative behaviour. Examples of this are to be found in studies of the evolution of cooperative behaviour among selfish actors in iterated prisoner's dilemma games and other types of interaction situations (see Chapter 6). The survival of such cooperative patterns of behaviour depends on whether it is evolutionarily stable, i.e. whether it can survive despite shocks such as 'invasion' by other types of strategies, including those that are more adversarial or non-cooperative.

The extended phenotype view of firms implies a need for a change in management philosophy, away from a focus on marketing engineering for the individual firm as an independent market actor and on adversarial relations, to one that presumes the existence of interdependent others and where trust and openness are strongly positively valued. This appears naïve at first. Surely, any firm openly espousing such ideals would be too easily taken advantage of because of the dependence that would be created on others. This is indeed the case because the ability of a firm to prosper through the pursuit of more cooperative strategies depends on the strategies of other firms in the population. So how can such ideals and strategies emerge in a population of firms?

GROUP SELECTION AND THE EMERGENCE OF COOPERATIVE STRATEGIES[3]

Three main types of theory have been offered to account for the emergence of cooperation in animal and human societies: kinship ties, signalling and repeated interaction or reciprocity. These theories are able to account for the emergence of cooperation in biologically related individuals and among those who repeatedly interact over time. But they are not able to account for the emergence of large-scale cooperation among people who are strangers, which is the kind characterising most types of business collaboration.

Kinship theories are based on the regard and care people have for others they are related to, such as children, parents and siblings, and studies show that the degree of altruistic, self-sacrificing or cooperative behaviour shown to others is proportional to how closely related they are. Social insects, such as ants and bees for example, are all half-sisters, which means they have many of their genes in common. This accounts for their extraordinary degree of collaboration and self-sacrifice for the common good of the colony. Similarly, parents make extraordinary sacrifices for their children that they would not do for strangers. Signalling theories are based on coop-erators being able to identify each other by signalling their cooperativeness, or what Richard Dawkins has called the green beard theory of cooperation. If all cooperators had green beards they could recognise each other and cooperate. Unfortunately this is a not a stable solution, as it would create opportunities for non-cooperators to evolve who had green beards, who could then exploit the cooperating greenies!

The third theory focuses on the effects of reciprocity or repeated inter-actions among individuals that can produce cooperation because of the shadow of the past and future it imposes on individual interactions. This has been demonstrated most famously in research by Robert Axelrod, who examined the development of cooperative strategies in iterated prisoner's dilemma games (more on this in a moment). I described these in some detail in Chapter 6. He showed how tit-for-tat, a cooperative strategy that co-operates in the first round of any interaction and then does whatever the other player did on the previous round, emerged as the winner of tourna-ments in which different strategies were made to play each other over several rounds, and how the same type of strategy emerged over time in an evolutionary simulation. Subsequent research has refined his results in various ways, but the central point, that repeated interaction, as well as the ability to choose and refuse partners, shapes the nature of the strategies that emerge and survive, still stands; and, further, that cooperative but not naïve strategies eventually do well and can win out.

While such theories help account for many forms of cooperation, they cannot account for large-scale cooperation among strangers. But such cooperation does occur, as has been demonstrated in much empirical research in human societies. For example, in a major international study, people from diverse cultures and backgrounds were asked to play the ultimatum game, which was suitably adapted to each particular context (Henrich et al. 2005). In this game people interact with others in an anonymous way in a one-shot deal. One is randomly given the task of proposer of the deal, which is to offer the other a share of $100 or the equivalent. If the proposal is accepted by the other, both parties get what is proposed. Suppose A offers B $10, keeping $90 for themselves. If B accepts, and why shouldn't they as they will be $10 better off, they get $10 and the proposer gets $90. What happens is that in all societies people make far more generous offers than would be suggested on purely selfish economic logic. And when offered a very unequal deal the proposal will be rejected, even though this will make the refuser less well off than they otherwise would be.

In other words, humans seem to have evolved instinctive pro-social, cooperative or altruistic tendencies that defy economic logic. They seem to care about the other, have some empathy for them, and even punish them if they behave badly, even when it is a one-shot deal with a stranger. Perhaps the presence of the researcher matters a bit here, but the overwhelming nature of the evidence is undeniable and has been featured in a major book and in articles in major scientific journals. So what is going on? How can this apparent cooperation among strangers be explained, and is it relevant to explaining cooperation in business?

Group selection mechanisms offer an old but recently rediscovered and powerful way of explaining such results. The development of cooperative business relations and networks can be explained in part by signalling theories and reciprocity, but group selection offers further insight into the way such cooperation can and does develop and the factors affecting its emergence.

Henrich (2004) points out that group-level factors of one form or another underlie all theories of the emergence of cooperation: '[A]ll solutions to the evolution of altruism – whether they are based on kinship, reciprocity or group selection . . . – are successful according to the degree in which "being an altruist" predicts that one's partners or group members are also altruistic' (p. 5). Thus being in a group of other cooperators is as important as being cooperative. But how do groups of cooperators emerge? Research in biological, social and business communities shows that competitive behaviour wins against cooperative behaviour within groups, but cooperative groups outperform competitive groups. A tension therefore arises between the evolution of competitive behaviour within groups and the evolution of cooperative groups.

Group selection mechanisms can be used to explain the emergence of cooperative groups, and they are relevant and important in explaining the emergence of collaboration in business because most business action is group or collective action. Within firms, people interact in groups of various size, from small teams, to departments, units and the firm as a whole. Business relations and networks are groups of firms that interact more with each other, and regional and national communities of people and firms are still other types of groups.

Group selection was ignored until recently because it was considered incorrect. This is strange, because the equations underlying it were proved and published by two researchers, Griffing (1967) and Price (1970), apparently working separately, in the 1960s. Based on these evolutionary equations, it can be shown that the expected change in frequency of a cooperative strategy over time depends on a combination of within-group and between-group selection processes, i.e. the effects of a cooperative strategy on an actor's performance, holding its local group composition constant, and the effects of the group on performance, holding the strategy fixed.

One interesting illustration of the operation of group selection mechanisms is the breeding of hens to lay more and larger eggs. Breeding from the fittest individual hens has been used for years to improve output in poultry farms and has evolved hens that lay more and bigger eggs. But the process also produces what might be described as 'psychopathic chickens' – hens that are very aggressive, who fight, kill and even eat each other. The result is high mortality rates that undermine the gains in laying ability. However, research by Muir (1996) showed that, by breeding from groups of hens, i.e. all those that lived in the cages producing the highest *average* egg mass, he was able to evolve hens that produced greater egg mass, were 'kind and friendly' towards each other and lived normal life spans. All this results in greater overall efficiency and improved animal welfare. Muir has shown that the same results occur in other types of animal and plant communities.

Do the same results apply to business? In order to investigate this, Dan Ladley, Louise Young and I did some computer experiments based on the earlier work of Robert Axelrod. His research focused only on individual selection; we compared this to group selection. An evolutionary simulation model was developed based around the iterated prisoner's dilemma (IPD) game with the payoff matrix shown in Figure 7.2. C is cooperate and D is defect. The IPD game involves a tension between cooperation and defection. If both cooperate, each gets a reward of 4, but if one cooperates and the other defects, the first gets the 'sucker's payoff' of 1 and the defector gains 5. If both defect, they get 2.

To simulate a game, players' strategies are represented in the form of a simple set of rules indicating what they will do in different situations. The technical details are not important. Strategies can differ in terms of how many past moves they remember and, for the simulations described here, only one-round and two-round memories were considered. The actors in

	C	D
C	4,4	1,5
D	5,1	2,2

Figure 7.2   Prisoner's dilemma payoff matrix

the simulation were divided into eight groups, and strategies in each group are at first randomly generated. Each player plays an IPD game over 200 rounds with each other member of its group, excluding itself, in a round-robin fashion. Then the performances of individuals and groups are calculated. Strategies are evolved for the next generation using either the fittest individuals in each group or all individuals in the group that is fittest on average. New strategies are produced by 'mating' or combining pairs of individuals selected. There is a low chance of a random mutation and of a player's strategy moving (being copied) from one group to another at the beginning of a generation. The same procedures are used for 1000 generations for individual and group selection separately, and the whole simulation is repeated 10 times for each.

Figure 7.3 shows the pattern of change in performance over time for group selection and individual selection averaged over all the 10 simulation runs. Results are shown when players are allowed to remember only two previous plays by their opponent. We can immediately see that average performance is greater for group selection and also produces the fittest, or highest-scoring, individuals. *Group selection produces fitter individuals than individual selection.* This happens because the extended phenotype or enterprise is selected for as well as individual player strategies. The outcomes of a strategy depend on the strategies of others a player confronts in their group, and in group selection the local group context is more conducive to superior performance by some.

An inspection of the mix of strategies resulting in the final round of the simulation shows that for group selection there is a much greater likelihood of players acting 'nice' or cooperating. In particular, cooperation is a frequent response when the opponent has defected in the previous two rounds, a strategy that does not emerge for individual selection. As a result, the mixes of strategies in groups evolved by group selection are less vulnerable to becoming locked into a cycle of defections. When the memory length of players was increased, differences also emerged in terms of the initial 'assumptions' players bring to a game, before they play an opponent. In

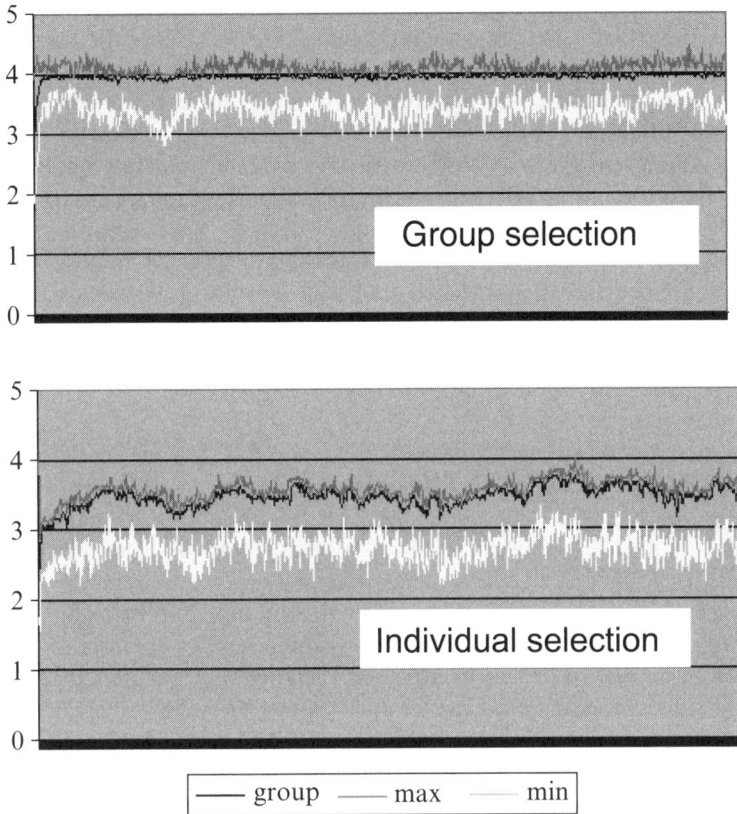

Source: Wilkinson et al. (2007, p. 6).

Figure 7.3   Performance over time: individual versus group selection

group selection, the players are more likely to think nice as well as act nice; they are much more likely to start interacting by assuming that the other player is cooperative.

In the IPD game the greatest total payoff is when both cooperate, which results in a payoff to each of 4 for a total of 8. If one cooperates and the other defects, the payoffs are 5 and 1, for a total of 6. In other interaction games the cooperate–defect combination can be set to produce a greater total payoff, even though one player does much worse than the other. Side payments could be made to induce this combination of plays, and this in effect happens under group selection, where ecologies of strategies evolve in a group that, in combination, produce superior payoffs for the group. But for individual selection such a mix cannot emerge, as those accepting lower individual payoffs 'for the common good' get eliminated – the tragedy of the commons.

Group selection theories have important implications for understanding and modelling the evolution of business relations and networks, and for examining when, why and how cooperative strategies emerge. The simulations show that group selection has important effects on the behaviour and performance of those involved. Group behaviour is what business is all about, and business relations and networks are types of groups. Group selection mechanisms must therefore be an important part of explaining the development and evolution of business. But to date only limited work has been done on this. In the next section I review some potentially productive concepts and theories that offer a way forward.

SOFT-ASSEMBLED STRATEGIES

Relationships involve joint choice and investment; firms need to be chosen as well as to choose partners, unless they are in very powerful positions. Part of the strategic problem for a firm is to compete to cooperate, to be able to join and remain in viable relations and networks. In order to do this it has to devote resources to attracting relationship partners, becoming attractive as a relationship partner and heading off rivals. I refer to this as *business mating* and I discussed it in Chapter 4. The rise of the markets-as-networks view, the development of relationship marketing theories and the concept of collaborative advantage reflect the increased attention being given to these issues in business.

The population of business firms and managers is changing in favour of those with more cooperative abilities, and more cooperative firms will survive in populations of cooperators. However, from an individual firm's perspective, adopting cooperative strategies is not easy, especially if they begin from a history of previously adversarial relations. But there are case studies reporting how firms have managed to change the nature of their relations with key partners to more collaborative forms. This usually involves taking small steps at first, facilitating stronger interaction among the parties involved, so they get to know and understand each other better, and putting in place incentive structures that reward and value attempts to gain from collaborative effort. As these cases make plain, relationship building takes time and is an area requiring more systematic research attention.

In order for firms to reach out beyond their boundaries and build relationships to access, build on and evolve collaborative advantage, they need help from each other. It is difficult if not impossible to do this alone – it is far easier to marry someone who wants to marry you! And, in turbulent environments, there is no guarantee that a particular firm will survive in the long term as a recognisable entity, even though, through its actions and responses, it will have played a part in shaping this future. The problem for the firm, as already noted, is to participate in the game of business through its interactions with and responses to others in such a way that it continues to be included as a viable player. But the evolution of business ecosystems cannot be foreseen; there are no magic strategies or prescriptions that can guarantee future survival.

This is not a very comfortable theory of business for managers to accept because it gives them no clear guidelines for action and results in a number of paradoxes. The very nature of the role of management and individual firm strategies comes into question. Our concepts of strategy and management have to change to reflect the realities of the complex adaptive systems of which firms are a part. One way forward is to embrace a concept of strategy described by the cognitive psychologist and philosopher Andy Clark – *soft assembled strategies*. Although developed in the context of individual behaviour and cognition, this concept has direct relevance in business and marketing.

The extended enterprise view of the firm is similar to the concept of the embodied mind in cognitive science, in which the mind, body and local environment are viewed as part of a dispersed and extended mind and body that is the sensing, thinking and responding system of a person. Thus we sense, think and respond with our brain, body and with parts of our local environment. We do not, for example, solve the problem of picking up a piece of paper by issuing commands to our muscles to act; we learn as we grow to enlist the innate characteristics of our arms and fingers to solve the problem. The technologies, tools and equipment we use, including language and other people, become part of our extended self in the same way that the stick of a blind person becomes part of them and the way they sense and respond to the world. They do not simply extend and enhance existing skills and abilities or remedy a defect; they provide new forms of functionality, creating new niches for action and intervention. For example, e-mail is not a replacement for face-to-face communication: 'It provides a *complementary functionality*, allowing people informally and rapidly to interact, while preserving an inspectable and revisitable space' (Clark 2003, p. 110, emphasis in original).

Andy Clark argues that humans are natural-born cyborgs, able to expand and reinvent our sense of body and action; that our body image and boundary is highly negotiable, and our brain's plasticity enables it to learn to exploit new kinds of feedback loops and action potential that come from being linked to external systems and technologies. We sense, think and act *with* and *through* our environment by learning from it and drawing on its intrinsic response tendencies, such that our body and the local environment become part of the means of solving problems, not their source:

> The job of the [central nervous system] . . . is *not* to bring the body increasingly 'into line' so that it can carry out detailed internally represented commands directly specifying e.g. arm trajectories. Rather the job is to learn to modulate parameters (such as stiffness), which will then *interact* with intrinsic bodily and environmental constraints so as to yield desired outcomes. In sum, the task is to learn how to soft-assemble adaptive behaviors in ways that respond to local context and exploit intrinsic dynamics. Mind, body, and world thus emerge as equal partners in the construction of robust, flexible behaviors. (Clark 1997, p. 45, emphasis in original)

In much the same way we can view the manager and firm expanding and reinventing their sensing, thinking and responding potential with and through their internal and external networks of relationships. To adapt Andy Clark's words to business:

> The job of the manager is *not* to bring the firm increasingly into line, so that it can carry out detailed plans centrally developed, such as how to position and carry out marketing activities for a product or service. Rather the manager's job is to learn to modulate parameters of the organisation, such as its customer responsiveness, its relationship and network competences, which will then *interact* with intrinsic firm, relationship and network constraints so as to yield desired outcomes. In sum, *the task is to learn how to soft-assemble adaptive behaviours* in ways that respond to local intra- and interfirm context and exploit intrinsic dynamics. Managers, firm and network thus emerge as equal partners in the construction of robust, flexible behaviours.

The example of ROLM referred to above and the way it identified and participated in various types of generative relations, as it felt its way forward in the PBX market, is an example of a soft-assembled strategy. The original strategies and interpretations of the market of ROLM and others changed in response to their participation in relations and networks and, at the same time, changed the pattern of relations and networks. Soft-assembled strategies are reflected also in the ways lead users have been incorporated into the innovation process, as discussed in Chapter 3. An example is the development of chef packs to enable meals designed by chefs to be easily mass-produced. The problem here was that of scaling up production of new types of meals designed by chefs in their kitchens for catering firms, airlines and packaged gourmet meals. Chefs work with ingredients that are not identical to the mass-produced ingredients used in the manufacturing process and so it became a major problem to reproduce what the chef did in their kitchen. The solution was to develop 'chef packs' of bulk ingredients, so that when chefs invented new meals using these ingredients – and they do this by tasting and experiment – the meals were immediately mass-producible. Similar types of solutions are to be found in the way the Apache public domain web site developer is developed by users and then incorporated into advanced versions of the software and in the way the Unix operating system Linux is developed (von Hippel 2005).

Iansiti and Levien (2004) use the term *business ecosystem* to describe the way firms play different roles in the industries and networks through which value is created and delivered to customers. One role is that of 'keystones', richly connected hubs providing the foundation for creating niches and increasing the diversity and productivity in their business ecosystems. TSMC is a keystone in the integrated circuit ecosystem and NVIDIA is a successful niche player. NVIDIA outsources all fabrication of its graphics processing units to TSMC, thereby leveraging the expertise of these suppliers. TSMC is based in Taiwan but enables its clients, like NVIDIA, to maintain close contact with the production system for its chips, to the extent that the client can make late engineering changes and even cancel orders at the last minute without a large penalty. TSMC uses the Internet to make information on designs and products available from its technology library all the time, so that the customer can access what they need without human intervention. They do not do any designs themselves or compete with their customers in design; its systems are set up to let its leading-edge customers lead. It would be impossible and impractical for the enabler to try to fully understand its customers' requirements and offer them potential solutions. Instead, it provides them with the necessary tools and means for others to use them effectively in solving their problems as they arise, and relies on them to understand their own problems.

In these examples firms attempt to develop relationships with customers and other firms that are generative, in which they can play both leadership and followership roles; allowing themselves to be planned by others as well as to plan for others, to change their interpretations of their environment and to harness their resources in ways they could not anticipate. It is impossible to capture the customer's or other organisation's understanding or 'mind' even with sophisticated marketing research and modelling methods, and to transfer this understanding to the 'mind' of the supplier.

Learning to soft-assemble strategies limits the need for managers to try explicitly to take into account all the direct and indirect relationship and network effects of their resources and actions. This is impossible and, even if it were possible, it would probably be counterproductive because it would make resources and networks even more richly interconnected and more unpredictable and chaotic. For this reason Stuart Kauffman (1994,

p. 84) has suggested that evolution has tended to produce organisms that are *optimally myopic strategists*: not because of costs of computation, but because, if we are individually too clever, we tend to transform the world in which we are adapting into a yet-more-chaotic world in which we fare less well.

Network Positioning and Exploitation versus Exploration

For firms, soft-assembled strategies involve two basic components: positioning and repositioning a firm in networks of relations; and exploiting and exploring relationship and network opportunities, threats and action potentials. The former focuses on the way a firm couples itself to other firms and organisations both directly and indirectly, and thereby extends the mind and resources of the network, i.e. the sensing, thinking and action potentials of the network – variety in Ross Ashby's sense. Positioning involves micro positioning in individual relations and macro positioning in networks of relations. The coupling process is not under the direct control of the firm because it involves, first, *business mating*, a double choice – choosing and being chosen by others. And, second, it involves *business dancing*, interacting, acting and responding, leading and following in a given relation.

In addition, the issue is as much about enabling others in the network as the focal firm (i.e. nurturance, as discussed above) because we cannot know in advance where new opportunities and threats will arise, who can and will recognise them and how to respond. There is no ideal network of relations. At any time a firm is involved in a portfolio of many types of relations with varying functions and connections to other relations, mixtures of cooperation and competition, and different strengths, which has evolved over time through the actions and interactions of those involved. Both strong and weak ties are important. Weak ties, because they are associated with structural holes, are potential sources of new types of information and play a key role in the discovery and development of new opportunities and ideas (see Chapter 3). Strong ties are also important because they are the means by which opportunities or threats can discover a firm as well as other functions already discussed. Strong cooperative ties are the means by which information about opportunities and threats are passed on to others or shared, and collaborative action and response are orchestrated.

Exploitation and exploration strategies involve trading off the gains to be made from working within existing relations and networks versus looking for and developing new potential relations and networks. Existing relations and networks both enable and constrain what can be sensed, understood and responded to by the network, and these capabilities

develop and evolve over time through the actions, interactions and outcomes. The way a network responds to particular challenges depends not
only on the nature of the current challenge but on its history and pattern
of relations, as these set the stage, the starting conditions, for encountering
and exploring the future. From a society's perspective a variety of networks
is needed in order to ensure that it is not locked into only one way of seeing
and responding to the future. The individual firm and its people have to be
sufficiently flexible to continually resculpture their network role and position to remain viable players in viable networks and, in so doing, contribute
to the evolvability of the networks in which they participate. I will explore
this more fully in Chapter 8.

CONCLUSIONS

This chapter shows how relationship and network strategies play different
roles according to the type of environment in which they operate. To date,
most attention has been focused on their nature and role in types 1, 2 and
3 environments. Here, the firm is the primary strategic actor, and relations
with customers and other organisations can be valuable means of creating
and sustaining competitive advantage. But the types of business problems
facing firms in type 4 environments are beyond the capacity of individual
managers and firms to sense, understand and respond to.

The increasing number, degree and speed of interconnectivity among
people and organisations in the world today has produced environments
that are complex and turbulent, in which firms face strong forms of uncertainty. The future is unknown and unknowable because it is produced by
complex patterns of interactions over time that defy traditional analytic
solutions. To survive and adapt in such environments requires a firm to
effectively participate in, help co-create and sustain networks of relations
in which no firm has control. This requires a change in management ideals,
values and strategies.

The forces that have produced this richly interconnected world provide
some of the means for people and firms to renegotiate their boundaries and
bring the manager, firm and network closer together. This includes developments in information and communication technologies that enrich network,
relationship and interrelating possibilities. Such developments not only
extend and enhance existing firm resources and functionalities; they create
new types of complementary functionalities, as managers learn to exploit
different kinds of feedback loops and action potentials that come from being
coupled to other firms and organisations in new ways. The network extends
more than the body of the participant firms, i.e. their resources and action

potential; it extends their minds and senses so that, through interactions with and through others, firms are able to recognise, comprehend and respond to opportunities and threats they otherwise could not.

There are signs that changes in business values and ideals are taking place, as firms are becoming more aware of and sensitive to the wider impacts of their actions, and are increasingly exploring the role of more collaborative strategies, by bringing suppliers, customers and other organisations earlier into strategy planning and development processes. But including other firms' thinking in your own planning and strategy development is only part of the problem. There is also the complementary need to be included in the planning and strategy development processes of relevant others. To achieve this requires of actors:

- an ability to adapt both goals and means (not just the means for achieving fixed goals) in response to others;
- to be an effective follower as well as leader; and
- to be prepared to be 'planned' by others as well as to plan for others.

Strategy becomes more about searching via interaction processes to discover and respond to opportunities and threats, rather than about designing and controlling resources to achieve desired outcomes. Network positioning and repositioning become key strategic issues, as firms seek to identify and engage in generative relations through which they sense, interpret and reinterpret their world, and act and respond to it. The relevant networks and relations here are not confined to a particular industry, place, or nation, although these may be important. Instead, they may span industries, technologies and nations, as I shall illustrate in Chapter 8.

Methods developed for guiding and solving management problems in other types of environments are of limited value in dealing with type 4 problems. Marketing engineering approaches may be able to solve part of the problem but, in turbulent environments, such optimisation problems are embedded in more complex problems that have no optimal solution and that relate to the broader environmental and strategic context in which the firm operates and in which the strategy will be understood and implemented. Local optima may be poor solutions for both the individual and their relationships and networks in a wider context, and may serve to limit a firm's understanding and ability to respond.

The focus of this chapter has been on the strategic problems confronting firms in different types of environments, particularly turbulent environments. In order to improve our understanding of this type of environment, to sensitise managers to the complexities involved and to give them better advice about identifying and responding to such environments, further research and theorising is needed. There is a fast-growing area of complexity science that focuses on the role and impact of interactions in shaping the dynamics and evolution of complex adaptive systems, such as type 4 environments. This offers both theories and methods to advance our understanding of and responses to such environments. While there are signs of a growing interest, this area is still underdeveloped in business and marketing. In the final chapter I offer suggestions as to how to advance theory and research building on these concepts and methods, but first I examine the implications for policy makers of a relationship and network view of business.

NOTES

1. This chapter is based largely on Wilkinson and Young (2005b).
2. Further details about this innovative innovation scheme may be found at the website www.ixc.com.au/.
3. This section is based on Wilkinson et al. (2007).

8. Strategies for policy makers in business relations and networks: evolving evolvable relations and networks

INTRODUCTION

The management implications of business research tend to receive centre-stage attention because most of it is done in business schools that train managers. Equally important are the implications for policy makers, those in government and industry regulatory organisations. They need to be informed by the realities of business life, not dead economists with idealistic notions of the way business life could and should work. In this chapter I consider the policy implications arising from a relationship and network perspective, what it means for the development of legal rules and regulations governing business. Policy makers are not outside the systems they regulate, monitor and control; they are part of the business system, they are the political actors in business networks, influencing it and being influenced by it, not part of the environment. They represent the interests of the third party involved in any and every business interaction – society. They influence business through the actions they take and through the rules and regulations they set and enforce, and they are influenced by business through lobbying, legal processes and through the direct interactions taking place between them in the marketplace.

Political actors can be very active and visible players in business networks. This is most obvious when they are key organisational customers, as in the case of defence equipment and public infrastructure development; when firms are monitored and controlled by various types of regulatory bodies such as investment boards, competition and industry watchdogs, trade promotion agencies and the like; and when formal legal processes are used to settle disputes and enforce rules and regulations. Policy makers also set and police the formal rules of the game regarding business relations and networks, and how firms interact. These include how powerful individual firms can become, who can buy and own whom, and the standards for communicating, competing and reporting.

In the first section of this chapter I discuss the political embeddedness of business networks, and the different ways in which governments and other political and legal actors are involved in them. In the final two sections I consider the implications for policy of taking a relationship and network perspective in two key areas – trade and industry policy and antitrust. I show how such a perspective offers fresh and valuable insights and suggests new and productive ways of thinking about, developing and implementing policy in these domains.

THE POLITICAL EMBEDDEDNESS OF BUSINESS NETWORKS[1]

Political embeddedness can take four forms: political institutions, political actors, political activities and political resources, and parallels the schemas, actors, activity and resource dimensions of business relations and networks that form the foundation of the Industrial Marketing and Purchasing (IMP) group's thinking. The role and impact of *political institutions* is most apparent when political ideologies and associated macropolitical structures change. The transitions of nations such as China, Russia, Vietnam and others in Eastern Europe to a market economy are the most striking examples in this period of history. The change has triggered a reconfiguration of business networks, with firms from other countries extending their networks into these markets for the first time; firms that were already exporting to the region rebuilding their existing networks in response to the new competitors and customers created by privatisation and the new rules for interaction. Less dramatic than these revolutions, though still involving significant transformations, is the disruption and restructuring of national and international networks caused by closer European integration. The ideological dimensions of political institutions are also revealed when new political and social values emerge and become embodied in changed rules and regulations. Environmentalism and climate change, and the rise of the 'green' movement, are having a profound effect on network activities, including the use of raw materials and product development.

The role of *political actors* in business networks includes bureaucrats, government ministers, members of parliament, political parties, interest groups and the media. Political actors can help form or change business networks through various kinds of facilitating and disrupting activities. For example, in their study of the Bofors scandal, Hadjikhani and Håkansson (1996) trace the interdependences that caused a crisis in the relationship between Bofors and the Indian government to spread to other firms in the network, notably other Swedish firms seeking contracts with the Indian government. Lars Hallén (1992) uses the term 'infrastructural networks' to refer to the facilitating role of non-business actors in business networks. These comprise the various social ties a particular firm or person has in a business network, including government officials, which are not directly related to a specific purchase or sale, but are important vehicles for information, communication and influence.

Political activities include the actions and interactions of political actors and firms as they intersect with business, as well as the political lobbying activities of business firms. Corporate political activities take place at all stages of the legislative process, from the formulation of policy to its implementation. Companies engage in lobbying efforts individually and join forces with competitors. One example is the setting of industry standards, such as the development of international industry standards for third-generation, 3G, mobile telephony, which merged mobile telecommunication with the Internet. The standards developed in the 1990s through a complex series of formal and informal discussions and meetings involving telecommunications operators, manufacturers and regulators as described in Gründstrom and Wilkinson (2004).

Political resources are what firms hope to gain through political activity, including public sector contracts, licences and approvals, favourable industry policies and regulation, tax concessions, tariffs and other protectionist measures and funding for R&D and regional development. Governments are also an important source of market-specific information, introductions and influence, especially when dealing with foreign governments. More fundamentally, firms act politically in order to achieve legitimacy, and in order to gain this firms invest in political relationships.

Three kinds of sub-networks may be distinguished in terms of the involvement of political actors, as depicted in Figure 8.1: (a) inter-business networks in which government actors play specific economic roles such as buyers, suppliers and intermediaries; (b) policy–business networks in which government and business interact through policy communities and issue networks in various ways to develop, influence and implement policy; and (c) inter- and intra-governmental networks involving ministries, departments, state and federal bodies and individuals within and across countries and multilateral agencies.

Political activities are undertaken for commercial outcomes, and business relationships are transformed as competitors, customers and suppliers take political action. Commercial relationships can be an important political resource and, at the same time, commercial resources are underpinned by political ones. In the postwar sugar industry studied by Catherine Welch and me (Welch and Wilkinson 2005), it was difficult to distinguish between a 'marketing' and a 'policy' exchange. Marketing arrangements were seen

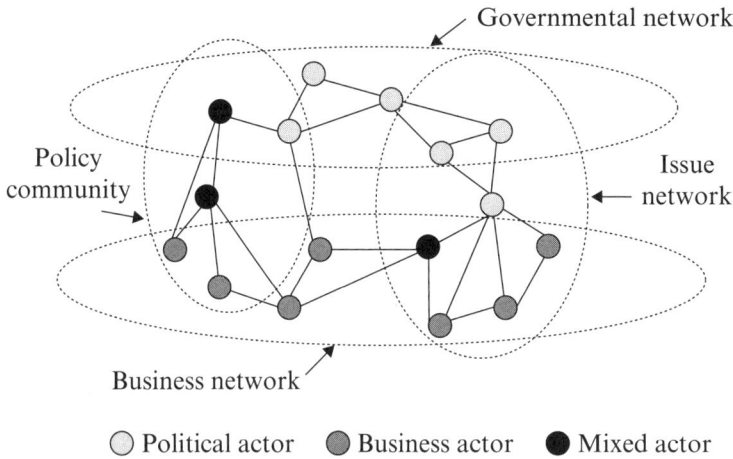

Source: Welch and Wilkinson (2004, p. 228).

Figure 8.1   Political and business networks

as a way of achieving particular policy objectives of government. At the same time, government involvement in marketing efforts was regarded as vital to commercial objectives. Analysis of interfirm relationships in this industry is impossible without reference to political relationships, and vice versa. Consequently, we can distinguish between policy communities and issue networks as two different forms of connection between political and business actors. Each of these has its own internal dynamic and unique history, which influences how actors, activities and resources are interconnected, and the position of different actors in the network. This in turn shapes the way the governmental network is affected by and responds to interactions with business networks, both directly and indirectly. At the same time, a firm's own network position, influenced by its network theory and political strategy, also has an impact on the evolution of its relationships with political actors.

Political and business processes are thus entwined and entangled in business networks. Political actors take economic positions and business actors take on policy-making roles. Political activities are undertaken for commercial purposes and business relationships are transformed as competitors, customers and suppliers take joint political action.

The way these networks function is part of the story told in the next two sections of the chapter, where I consider how taking a relationship and network perspective affects our understanding of trade and industry policy and antitrust policy. I build on the concepts and theories discussed in the previous chapters of this book. The issues and opportunities highlighted are not very different from those confronting the individual firm discussed in Chapter 7 because, as I have pointed out, policy makers do not stand outside the relevant networks looking in; they are participants in the networks they attempt to control, monitor and direct, contributing to and playing a part in the co-evolutionary processes.

TRADE AND INDUSTRY POLICY FROM A NETWORK PERSPECTIVE[2]

Nations around the world have employed a variety of policies to boost international trade performance and to make their industries and firms more competitive. These include various kinds of trade promotion activities, as well as more general macroeconomic, regulatory and environmental policies. In the main these policies focus on the characteristics of individual firms or industries and how to help them, and are informed by studies that have identified the problems, barriers and needs of firms in different industries and markets. The problem with such a 'user-oriented' approach is that it assumes existing firms know best the problems hampering their competitiveness and that this is an appropriate basis for policy development. But existing or potential exporters from a particular country and underperforming firms may not always understand what is required to succeed in international business operations and improve their performance. So, basing policies on what they think are the problems may be misleading.

From a trade policy perspective it is perhaps more appropriate to focus on the needs and problems of local and international customers rather than on actual or potential producers, suppliers and exporters. Helping international buyers buy from a nation's firms may be as important as helping domestic firms sell. This argument highlights the need to consider a supplier's needs in relation to the needs of its customers or, more generally, to take a relationship and network perspective. After all, value is not created and delivered to domestic and international customers by individual firms working alone. Value is co-produced through the actions and interactions of many firms, located in different industries which are spread all over the world – as has been explained in this book and depicted in the world product export network I included in the Introduction (Figure I.1).

Success in international and local markets depends on developing and managing successful relations and networks with local and overseas counterparts, including foreign customers. To be successful, a mix of different types of relations is needed, including some that are long-term, cooperative ones, involving mutual adaptations in which the needs and problems of the other are recognised and responded to; products and processes are thereby improved and mutual bonds and understandings are co-developed that facilitate such adaptation and learning. For trade and industry policy the implication is to shift from targeting individual firms as a way of enhancing performance, to a focus on the relationships and networks linking firms within and between industries.

Figure 8.2 illustrates the kind of inter-industry and interfirm connections that exist in a nation's economy. It depicts a hypothetical example of the value production and delivery systems associated with transforming raw materials into finished products and services for final consumption. Two types of networks of relations are distinguished: those associated with the *primary value system* and those associated with *ancillary value systems*. The *primary value system* is defined in terms of the sequence of relations involved in the transformation of raw materials through various production stages to the final distribution to end users. *Ancillary value systems* refer to the networks of relations involved in supplying various types of inputs to the primary value system at each production stage, including production equipment, sub-assemblies, technical know-how and specialised services required to carry out the activities performed by firms in the primary value system. They can be viewed as secondary network infrastructures supporting the primary network. The distinction between primary and ancillary networks is relative rather than absolute. There is not one primary value system but many that interpenetrate in the complex webs that make up economic systems, as is obvious from the world product export network figure shown in the Introduction. What is primary and ancillary depends on the focus of analysis; the distinction draws attention to the different kinds of relations between firms supplying materials, components and business services that will be incorporated in final and intermediate products and those supplying products and services that are not so incorporated.

In Figure 8.2, different types of trade flows and associated business relations are revealed, labelled A through D. Type A concerns international trade within the primary value system, as when semi-processed products such as textiles or processed materials are exported to other countries for further processing. Types B through D are various types of international trade involving ancillary networks in which inputs other than primary materials and components are traded to support, directly or indirectly, primary value system suppliers in other countries. Some ancillary networks in the figure are located entirely in the home country; others involve a mix of local and foreign firms.

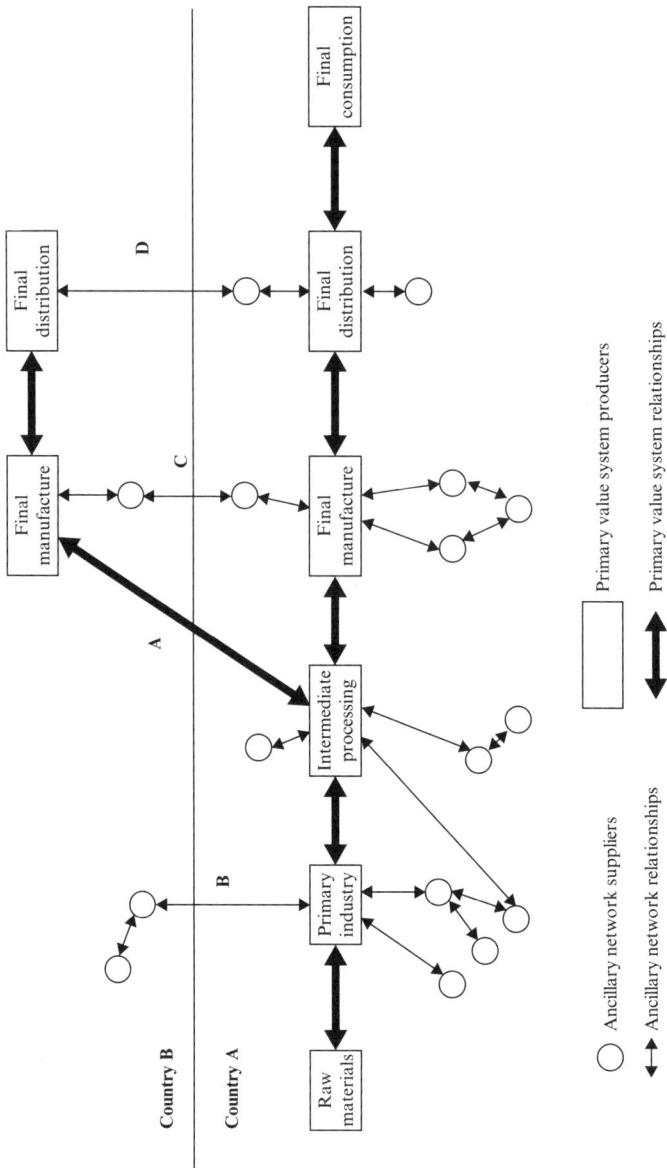

Country B

Country A

Final distribution

Final manufacture

Intermediate processing

Primary industry

Raw materials

Final consumption

Final distribution

Final manufacture

A

B

C

D

○ Ancillary network suppliers

◄► Ancillary network relationships

▭ Primary value system producers

◄► Primary value system relationships

Source: Wilkinson et al. (2000, p. 279).

Figure 8.2   A value production network

International Competitiveness in Primary and Ancillary Networks

An understanding of the structure and operations of a primary network and its associated ancillary networks provides a basis for developing and targeting trade and industry policies for enhancing a firm's competitiveness. Consider the case of Australia, a resource-based economy. Historically, most exports come from producers of less refined products located at the early stages of primary value systems for wool, wheat, meat and mineral products, for example. This has led some to argue that Australia should try to establish more internationally competitive value-added manufacturing industries further down primary value systems, such as exports of agricultural products in the form of processed food, wool in the form of textiles and clothing, and minerals in the form of more elaborately transformed manufactures. The development of Nestlé, a Swiss company, from a milk processor into many downstream processed food and beverage products, is an example of this. Through such developments, so the argument goes, Australia will capture a greater share of the revenues obtained from sales of higher-priced value-added products and services.

This argument focuses on the structure of the primary value system network and on one type of resource needed to establish value added manufacturing industry – raw materials. But further processing of primary products requires relationships and networks to be established and maintained with providers of many other types of resources and inputs in ancillary networks. These may not be available in a cost-effective manner in the same country. In addition, relationships have to be established with distributors and other organisations at subsequent stages of the primary network, in order to reach final customers at home and abroad. Without good access to such inputs, internationally competitive industries for more refined products may be very costly to establish and difficult to sustain. Nestlé's base in Switzerland is close to many developed European markets and provides it with ready access to other inputs. Economies such as Australia and New Zealand, South America and Africa have less easy access to such networks.

An alternative view is to focus on the ancillary networks that support primary production. The international competitiveness of primary production depends on the characteristics of these input networks and the relations within and between them. If a primary production stage is internationally competitive, firms in the input networks are likely to be internationally competitive as well, because they are the direct or indirect suppliers of these 'leading-edge' customers. This suggests an alternative policy focus: instead of looking further *down* the primary networks, look further *up* the ancillary networks supporting primary industries that are internationally competitive. In Sweden, for example, many internationally competitive firms emerged out of ancillary networks originally serving domestic-based primary producers in the mining industry (including rock drills and equipment, compressors, transport and loading machinery, elevators, mine hoists, pumps, crushing machinery, rubber components, explosives and consulting services), the pulp and paper industry, the car and truck industry, the shipbuilding industry and the steel industry. When some of these primary industries closed down or lost their international competitiveness, such as Swedish shipbuilding and mining industries, firms in the ancillary networks were still able to be internationally competitive and serve international customers.

In Australia, firms in the ancillary networks for various primary industries have become internationally competitive because of their relations with internationally competitive primary industries, including agriculture and mining. One example is the development of firms supporting the grain export industry to take advantage of opportunities arising from a major World Bank funded project in China. The trade promotion arm of the federal government, Austrade, formed a joint action group of relevant and interested firms from the ancillary network, including producers and designers of storage, handling and transport systems, control systems and training services. These firms were not generally internationally focused and the relations among them were underdeveloped. Joint promotion, inward and outward trade missions and various research activities were undertaken and they succeeded in gaining a sizeable share of the design work and some of the final contracts. What this example shows is how potential international competitiveness in ancillary networks may go unrecognised by policy makers and by the firms themselves, when they are seen only as suppliers to domestic industries and customers.

To develop this approach further I focus on two important characteristics of networks that impact on their international competitiveness: *location*, the extent to which the primary or ancillary network is domestically based or foreign based; and *the presence of internationally competitive firms in the network*.

Location affects trade and industry policy because important parts of the primary or ancillary network may lie outside the country and be less amenable to government intervention. Location also affects the ability of firms to build productive relations and networks, as relations between firms in different countries tend to be weaker and more difficult to develop than those among firms located closer to each other. This, in turn, affects the role they can play in developing and supporting international competitiveness. But close relations can be developed between counterparts in different countries in some situations. Examples are firms that are parts of a multinational

Table 8.1   Four types of networks

Internationally competitive firms?	Location	
	Mostly local	Mostly foreign
No	Case A: domestic focused	Case B: foreign focused
Yes	Case D: competitive	Case C: isolated

corporation, where direct foreign investment establishes overseas distributors and production units, or where historical, cultural or geographical circumstances conducive to relationship development exist. Canada and Mexico networks have strong links with industries in the USA, the Chinese diaspora links dispersed firms through family and cultural connections, and bonds exist in Commonwealth countries due to a shared colonial history, a love of cricket, and links to Britain.

The presence of internationally competitive firms in a network, together with their international connections and experience, is an indication of international competitiveness in other firms in the network because, as has been shown, the relations and networks a firm is involved in are an important source of a firm's competitiveness. Internationally competitive firms can play a role as leading-edge customers or suppliers, provide role models for others to emulate and be a source of business information and advice.

These two dimensions of networks can be used to classify them into four broad types, as shown in Table 8.1. Various policy options emerge from considering each of them.

Case A: Domestic-Focused Networks

In a fully localised and domestic-focused network the task of developing international competitiveness can be a major challenge. The domestic focus limits firms' abilities to conceive of, let alone exploit, international market opportunities. Firms have to be encouraged into the international arena through various types of familiarisation and education programmes. Because the base is so limited, general education programmes and broad incentives could be used to attract initial interest in foreign markets. In addition, to build foreign customer interest, government promotion of domestic firms, products and services in foreign markets is appropriate, to allow internationally competitive foreign-based customers to learn about and seek out new sources of supply. This can be done through trade missions, sponsoring participation in international trade fairs, and promotional literature describing the strengths and capability of domestic firms and networks.

There are many examples of government agencies facilitating business mating in these ways. One example is the aforementioned Australian government's joint action scheme to assist ancillary suppliers in the grain production and handling industry to gain a share of a major grain infrastructure project in China. As part of their assistance, a capability document detailing the ancillary network was prepared and provided to the Chinese government as part of an initial trade mission led by a high-ranking minister in the government. Because international firms are not present in the domestic network, government promotion activities may need to be tailored to and targeted at firms occupying central positions in the relevant networks because of the potential network impacts of changing their international competitiveness.

Another way of upgrading domestic-focused networks is to encourage internationally competitive firms to establish local operations. Japanese firms in the USA, Europe and Asia have led to changes in work practices, technology transfer, and the development of relations with domestic suppliers that have resulted in significant improvements in performance. In Australia, the deregulating of the financial system led to an influx of foreign players that boosted local competition and contributed to the internationalisation of domestic financial institutions, as well as some of their suppliers of software and technical services. In developing countries, the introduction of foreign firms through joint ventures is an important part of government policy and is in part designed to facilitate technology transfer which, it is hoped, has spillover effects for local suppliers and customers of these joint ventures.

The setting up of such internationally competitive firms can also attract additional network entrants. For example, Japanese multinationals are known to encourage their suppliers to establish a presence in the same or adjacent markets to support them. In this way the primary network is enhanced with potential spillover effects for local competitors and complementary suppliers, producing a positive spiral of development. The Australian government has been successful in attracting the regional headquarters of companies such as Cathay Pacific, DEC and American Express. In part this has been because of negotiated financial incentives, but more enduring are strengths in the telecommunication system, the time zone of Australia in relation to Asia, and the multicultural nature of Australia, i.e. relational and network issues. The multicultural strength lies in the ability to provide multilingual native speakers in nearly all languages, who have the cultural understanding and sensitivity to contribute to the development of international business operations, including the provision of high-quality communication and translation facilities (Wilkinson and Cheng 1999).

For policy makers and local firms the problem is how to facilitate the development of productive relations between the new firms and the local network. This may be done through offsets programmes, which encourage foreign-owned firms supplying the government to source some inputs locally. The danger is that such schemes only result in short-term relations that do not produce any sustained development of competitiveness. The foreign-owned firms may exclude local firms from their networks of suppliers and customers, or restrict them to non-core simpler tasks and inputs, meaning that they provide few opportunities for local firms to break into key networks and industries, and limit technological transfer to the host country.

The task for governments and firms is to find ways of breaking into such networks. These include setting initial conditions for entry, offset policies, and providing forums to facilitate the development of interpersonal and interfirm relationships. An example is the way MNC relations with domestic suppliers developed in the UK North Sea oil fields in the 1970s and 1980s. The primary producers (oil companies) brought the ancillary firms (e.g. drilling contractors) with them to Aberdeen in Scotland. However, local firms were to gain access to the primary producers via the help and expertise of Scottish-born managers who worked for the (mainly US-owned) oil companies.

In addition, immigration policy can play a role in introducing people into local networks with substantial international business experience, resources, knowledge and personal/professional networks. Australia and the USA are examples of countries that have benefited from a multicultural population. One of my favourite examples of this is Gateway Pharmaceuticals. This firm was established in Sydney by migrants from the Middle East, and began with some exports of vitamins and herbal remedies to the Middle East. They set up their operations in Australia in an area with a large Vietnamese community. Through personal and professional networks they identified opportunities in the Vietnamese market for various kinds of vitamins and mineral supplements and other herbal remedies. They participated in an early trade mission to Vietnam, began exporting and later set up a manufacturing and distribution operation in cooperation with the Vietnam government. Migrants from Lebanon come to Australia to learn about opportunities in Vietnam from other migrants and then succeed in developing business there. More generally, migration policies can be targeted at particular networks in terms of their international potential, and migrants can be selected based on the relevance of their experience, knowledge and personal/business networks.

Finally, domestic networks can become more internationally focused and competitive through sourcing as well as selling internationally. Firms are able to benefit from the experience and contacts gained from importing to build relations with foreign customers. Through extending their international links, opportunities in international markets are discovered and exploited.

Case B: Foreign-focused Networks

At the other extreme from Case A is the situation where most, if not all, of the primary and ancillary networks and customer base are located internationally. The problem for policy makers here is that there is little to build on in the home market. Some countries have been able to take advantage of this situation by becoming international tax havens and financial centres, which attract foreign companies to set up a notional base but, effectively, all of their actual value-adding operations are located outside the country. Examples are countries such as Bermuda and Luxembourg.

Case C: Isolated Networks

More typical are networks with a mix of local and internationally located players. Here more carefully targeted policies are required, adapted to the particular network configuration. To do this, policy makers require detailed maps of the network in order to identify where and how intervention may be appropriate. Links to international firms exist already, which can be built on through piggyback schemes or export groups in which foreign and local firms are brought together. One example is the Wisconsin 'indirect exporter' scheme, which focuses on suppliers to locally based exporting firms and encourages them to work with their local suppliers, to help them into international markets with which they were already familiar. One problem with this scheme was its success: some valuable managers in the exporters left the firm to take up senior positions in local supply firms because of the opportunities they could see and exploit.

Customer-focused trade promotion schemes need to be carefully targeted in order to deepen and extend existing international customer connections. This involves working more closely with particular customers in a more direct fashion, rather than more generic promotion. For example, trade promotion officers can help develop existing relations and establish new connections with members of the domestic networks. This happened in the China grain infrastructure project through the appointment of a local Chinese network facilitator. In Wisconsin, honorary commercial attachés were created among residents of foreign countries, who were traders experienced in dealing with Wisconsin firms.

Case D: Internationally Competitive Networks

Relevant policy objectives here are to facilitate the development and sharing of information with leading-edge firms and their foreign customers, similar to case C. The China grain infrastructure example mentioned above created, in effect, an action learning experience in which firms learned to dance with each other and with counterparts in China. Through this learning process relationships formed between ancillary suppliers and more internationally experienced firms, and personal and business relationships developed with each other and with Chinese firms and government officials that played an import role in winning a share of the business. Another joint action group facilitated the development of relations between hay producers in Australia and distributors and dairy farmers in Japan in order to boost trade. Another example is an industry-initiated joint action scheme, Fitout Australia, which is a network of firms interested in supplying various types of complementary products and services to hotels in international markets. They jointly promote and benefit from each other's experience and contacts.

One approach is to target particular leading-edge firms that have strong connections with many firms in the network. In this way they may become poles for the international development of the network as whole. Such firms may of their own volition be able to identify potential opportunities for facilitating exports and international ventures for firms in their input networks, as is the case with Japanese firms. But this is not without its problems, as discussed in case A above. Multinationals develop approved supplier lists of firms around the world and refer suppliers of one subsidiary to subsidiaries in other markets. For example, a supplier of car components in Australia was able to gain entry into the China market to supply a multinational's joint venture operation in part because of referrals from the Australia-based subsidiary for which it was an approved supplier.

Case D may be further developed in terms of the internationalisation of individual firms versus the network as a whole, as shown in Table 8.2. A *lonely international* is the only one that is highly internationalised and competitive. Firms in ancillary networks serving such a firm in the primary value system are indirect exporters because their inputs are incorporated into the outputs of the internationalised firm. If the internationalised firm is a sophisticated international player, it may have little need for government assistance, except for appropriate lobbying and representation of

Table 8.2   Internationalisation of the firm and network

Internationalisation of the firm	Internationalisation of the network	
	Low	High
High	Lonely international	International among others
Low	Early starter	Late starter

Source: Johanson and Mattsson (1988).

their interests to other governments and international bodies, and introductions to key decision makers in other countries. For policy makers an
important issue is sustaining the international competitiveness of such
firms as this requires continual upgrading of products and processes by
working with leading-edge firms. If this cannot be achieved with domestic
firms such firms will search for such networks abroad. Firms in relevant
ancillary networks may not be exporting because they do not contribute to
the international competitiveness of the internationalised firm. Low-cost
raw materials or export subsidies may be dominant factors, rather than any
inputs of specialised technology, components or other material. Here there
may be opportunities for the internationalised firm to work with suppliers
to upgrade inputs and thereby enhance their own competitiveness.

The international firm may be part of the ancillary network, not the
primary chain, but it can still assist local customers to internationalise. An
example is BHP Billiton, Australia's largest steel manufacturer, which has
tried to assist downstream users of its steel in Australia to expand and internationalise as a way of indirectly expanding its own business.

International among others are firms belonging to highly internationalised networks. Here, government policy can be designed to reduce or
eliminate any network-specific barriers to export development, in order to
let the full export potential of the network be realised. Research can be
directed to identify network-specific barriers to international trade. In
Australia such networks are likely to be linked to the mining and agricultural areas, and the government can play a role in facilitating relations with
overseas governments and multilateral agencies that play an important part
in initiating development projects in these areas. In the China grain
example, Australian aid funds were used to demonstrate Australian inputs,
and relations between Australian firms, the Chinese government and World
Bank were facilitated. Governments can also play a role in the early detec-
tion of international aid-funded projects and helping the formation of consortia to bid for them.

For three main reasons, it is important to develop and sustain the international competitiveness of both the primary and ancillary networks. First,
if the international competitiveness of primary firms comes to an end
because resources run out or they become more expensive, the input networks can still remain internationally competitive. This is because internationalised firms in ancillary networks can become less dependent on their
domestic customers, as happened in Sweden as the mining, steel and shipbuilding industries declined. Firms from those industries continue to be
highly internationalised and internationally competitive.

Second, in the 'international among others' case it is easier for internationalised firms in the primary value system to switch to non-domestic-based

suppliers than in the 'lonely international' situation. This is because there is already international trade in the inputs involved. Furthermore, frequently occurring mergers, acquisitions or strategic alliances between firms often influence their supplier structure. This poses both the threat of losing business for firms in the ancillary networks as well as the opportunity to gain business.

Third, an important part of international trade is linked to big projects, involving technology transfer and infrastructure development, for which firms or consortia are invited to bid. The choice of suppliers in such projects is influenced by the nationality of the main contractor and by the financial conditions offered. Government is often involved on the buying side, and successful bidders need some sort of political and financial backing from their own governments. It is easier for a main contractor or consortium from a particular country to have a high content from that country if the ancillary network is also internationally competitive.

Late starters are domestic-focused firms in highly internationalised networks. If they are members of the ancillary network, there are several reasons they may not export. First, the inputs might not make a significant contribution to the international competitiveness of other firms in the network. Second, barriers to trade for the products and service might exist, such as government prohibitions on sensitive military equipment. Third, growth opportunities in the domestic market may be more attractive. Fourth, they may not be internationally competitive or aware of international opportunities. Such firms run a high risk of becoming outcompeted in their own domestic market by foreign firms, unless they find some way to internationalise, because, by definition, many competitors (and customers) have been able to become internationally competitive. They might be a takeover target for a foreign firm and in this way become internationalised.

For policy makers, *late starters* pose a problem. Why are they late? If their outputs are of little significance, what types of advantage can they offer customers in international markets? If trade barriers are the reason, then their elimination is as likely to increase imports if there exists strong competition from foreign-based, highly internationalised suppliers. Policies relevant for lonely internationals may be appropriate, especially if late starters are unaware of export opportunities.

Early starters differ from late starters in that other members of their network are not internationalised. This can be for the same reasons as late starters but there are two important differences. First, there is little demonstrated internationalisation for this type of firm anywhere. One reason could be that the type of product or service supplied is not a tradable good or service, e.g. wholesaling, retailing, real-estate services, staff recruitment services. Hence these services are only exported embodied in other products or services. If such services have a significant impact on the competitiveness of firms using them, there is still a need to ensure that such firms are aware of their role and how they can work with their customers to enhance their exporting potential through upgrading service inputs.

The second difference is that, should this firm start to export, it may not meet internationally active competitors or customers, unless the domestic industry has been isolated from international trade. Since early starters are pioneers, it is likely that management attitudes to exporting are positive and that knowledge about internationalisation is limited. They need to be aware of the realities of international markets and competition; the time and resource commitments needed for sustainable international growth; and to establish relations with foreign distributors and customers. They also need to recognise that their international competitiveness depends not only on their own efforts and resources but also on others in their network and their relations with them. Because no one in the network is internationalised this may inhibit an early starter's international efforts. Tapping into the personal and professional relations and networks of individuals employed in firms in the network, as well as hiring such people, is one way of enhancing the international skills and resources of the firm and in developing international links.

Generic Network Approaches to International Competitiveness

Apart from the targeted initiatives discussed above, some general relationship- and network-oriented policies may be envisaged. The network approach focuses on the potential role and importance of establishing and managing cooperative relations among firms. Even competitors can have complementary interests.

Business education programmes need to focus attention on developing collaborative as well as competitive advantage, on the skills of business mating and business dancing described in earlier chapters, in order to harness the power of relations and networks. Part of this is the internationalisation of education courses and institutions, including course content and links, and exchange programmes with foreign universities. Also, courses designed to attract international students and study-abroad programmes can be important vehicles for improving cultural understanding and sensitivity, and they can help develop and strengthen personal and family links with foreign markets, which provide a potential base for future commercial activities. Policy makers and firms can assist in encouraging such developments in a number of ways, including: funding support for the development of international business education programmes; hosting international students in work experience programmes domestically and in overseas markets; setting up foreign-focused alumni associations, facilitating the development of and participating in study-abroad programmes; and assisting in international student recruiting through foreign-based agencies.

Likewise, research funding can be used as a tool to facilitate the development of international research and business networks, including international research collaborations between research organisations, business and government. International professional and personal connections among researchers and technologists, as well as international trade personnel, can lead to international technology transfer and to the development of networks that facilitates technological development. The exploitation of international market opportunities for domestic research can be facilitated through the development of such personal and professional relations, and governments can play a useful role here. Often, the technical aspects of R&D projects in industry may be sponsored by a government agency, but research on relevant international marketing issues concerning the outputs from such R&D projects are not, as when funding support is available for research on agriculture production issues but not for the development of refined products, distribution systems or international marketing. This inhibits the formation of relevant personal and business networks among researchers and business, and limits the exploitation of international market opportunities.

More generally, government policy needs to ensure that any barriers to the establishment and development of effective relationships are addressed. Governments should pay at least as much attention to transaction-cost-related policies as to production-cost-related policies in their efforts to create favourable conditions at home for internationally competitive industrial activities. This includes government antitrust policy, which needs to be reviewed in this context, and I discuss this in the next section.

A focus on transaction costs highlights the importance of removing or reducing trade barriers between nations that inhibit the development of internationally competitive industries and firms. In order to stimulate and enable firms to upgrade products and processes and to become more internationally competitive, reducing such barriers through tariff reductions, regional trading blocs and other means can have strong positive effects. It forces firms to face international competition at home and abroad, which increases learning and knowledge development, and boosts confidence. For example, the deregulation of the Australian finance industry showed some firms such as the Macquarie Investment Bank that they could compete with global players in particular markets, which in turn led management to internationalise.

Reducing such barriers prevents the growth of a dependence mentality among firms, relying on government policies to reduce threats of international competition. But more importantly, from a network perspective, trade barriers force firms into relations with customers and ancillary networks that are not conducive to developing or maintaining long-term international competitiveness. The case of New Zealand is instructive as many sectors of industry were protected from international competition, or their customers and suppliers were in such industries. After trade liberalisation, together with various assistance schemes, internationally competitive sectors of ancillary networks surfaced.

In an increasingly globalised marketplace, with easy and fast means of communication and access to people and organisations around the globe, the opportunity exists for firms to become truly international and to develop and manage effective personal and business relations and networks spanning international as well as industry borders. The continual upgrading of products and processes, and the growth in importance of created rather then inherited sources of competitive advantage, focuses attention on these relationship and network resources of firms and how they can be effectively harnessed and developed.

The network approach leads to a more wide-ranging, multi-pronged strategic and policy approach. The focus shifts from individual firms to networks of interconnected firms, both local and foreign. Adopting a network focus draws attention to the role played by a variety of government functions in influencing industry network development, including foreign investment policy, government purchasing policies, education and training, import policy, immigration policy and industry policy.

Policy and strategy development from a network perspective require an understanding of the structure and operations of business networks – more than typically emerges from government, industry and firm statistical reports. This is necessary in order to identify the network positions occupied by firms, the type of links they have with local and foreign networks, and the potential links that may exist that could significantly affect the international development of the network. It is also relevant for tracking the impact of policy and firm strategies on the evolution of the network.

For several reasons, governments can and should play only a limited role in facilitating network evolution. Most importantly, they are limited in their ability to respond to the increasingly rapid pace of technological and industrial development and restructuring that challenges business. Traditional forms of government bureaucracy are ill equipped to handle such a fast-changing landscape.

Second, the policies of more than one government are relevant to the structural development and operation of international business networks.

Each is trying to create and capture as many benefits as it can for its domestic economy and society, but the outcomes depend on what other governments are doing, in countries where existing or potential parts of the primary and ancillary networks are located. There is an opportunity for government trade policy agencies to develop effective relations and networks among themselves in order to co-create mutually supporting policies, rather than those that escalate the costs of competing for similar types of firms and networks.

Third, the primary role of government is not to pick winners but to help grow potential exporters in industrial networks – to create variety and rivalry in industrial networks. The winners will be selected by actual and potential counterparts in the networks, not by any government or a faceless market. The history of the development of networks in various countries shows that they are in a continuing process of structuring as new relations and opportunities become available. Governments cannot design them. Accounts of the structuring and restructuring of the Japanese industrial networks show how the government provided a framework within which networks developed naturally in a self-organising fashion. Relations need to form within a competitive framework in which there is some rivalry to negotiate relationships with key partners – not just forms of arranged marriages. Mutual commitment by individual network participants is necessary for their development. No amount of government incentives, encouragement and exhortation can substitute for a clearly perceived logic of relationship formation by the parties involved and identified beneficial outcomes. However, there *is* a role for government to play in facilitating the development of industrial networks and providing a framework that permits the self-organising process to operate effectively.

NETWORK EVOLVABILITY AND ANTITRUST POLICY[3]

To date, the main case for antitrust policy focuses on economising, including market power as a key filter for identifying suspect cases. Both production and transaction costs are considered as part of economising, and other factors are used to consider the benefits of different industry structures. A focus on the role and importance of business relations and networks, on how they underpin competitiveness and how they change and evolve, leads to an extension of the main case to a consideration of what I call 'evolvability'. This requires us to consider various types of direct and indirect network impacts in business that go beyond the traditional focus on production and transaction costs. These network impacts stem from the connections between transactions and relations over time and place, including how business arrangements at one time limit or enable arrangements in the future.

Antitrust policy is about influencing the rules of interaction and evolution of business systems, with the aim of avoiding pathological evolutionary paths and the emergence, survival and reproduction of undesirable firms, strategies and business systems. Current policies focus primarily on static market efficiency and price competition rather than dynamic market efficiency and value. Static market efficiency is reflected in rules to preserve price-competitive markets and to limit market power, which is interpreted in terms of the distribution of market shares in horizontally defined domestic markets for substitutable and similar products or services.

Dynamic market efficiency has to do with the development and evolution of new types of markets, firms and industries that create and deliver value to consumers. While there are links between static and dynamic market efficiency, these are problematic. For example, larger, more powerful firms may be able to devote more resources to innovation and thereby aid the evolutionary process. But they may also block or suppress undesirable (from their point of view) new competitors and be unable to recognise new types of opportunities that might undermine their existing position.

The topic of evolvability goes to the heart of the problem confronting antitrust policy makers. Evolvability is the essence of dynamic efficiency, whereas static efficiency is about tinkering with an existing business system to achieve improved outcomes, not with how this will affect its future evolution. The problem is that we cannot predict the future of business evolution, any more than we can predict the future of natural evolution. The history and existing nature of business systems affect how they can and cannot evolve but in ways we cannot fathom in advance because of the complex, non-linear, self-organising, adaptive nature of the systems involved. Complexity and evolutionary theories teach us how starting conditions and history matter and how micro interactions and adaptations lead to emergent macro patterns, and that systems gravitate towards different types of attractors depending on chance factors and tipping points that are only knowable with hindsight.

At first sight this seems to be an argument for 'anything goes' and for no antitrust policy at all, because anyone's guess about the future is as good as anyone else's. I disagree. The role of antitrust policy is to help encourage and select business systems for their evolvability, not to control or predict evolution. Antitrust policy makers and enforcers do not stand outside the world of business, observing it in some godlike manner, issuing edicts and making up rules and enforcing them; they are part of the system. They affect, through their actions and responses, what business does and how it evolves. Policy and issue networks involving interactions with business, various areas of government and academia take place all the time, through lobbying activities, informal and formal meetings, confrontations in the courts and in the way policy makers respond to what business and academics do and say. In short, a co-evolutionary process is going on involving antitrust policy makers and enforcers (including lawyers and law schools), other government agencies, business (including managers, workers, consumers and other stakeholders) and academia (including economists and business schools).

The problem for antitrust policy is not how to control and direct business in beneficial ways but to participate in the system of business so as to contribute to the productive evolution of the evolvability of business systems. Business systems are living systems, business ecosystems, and if they cannot evolve they will eventually stagnate and die, because they will be unable to cope with and contribute to changing business contexts, including new types of ideas, technologies, demands, competitors and natural conditions. In order to understand this more clearly, and what it means for antitrust, we need to understand the nature of evolutionary processes, starting with biology and then moving on to cultural systems, which include business systems.

Evolutionary Processes

Figure 8.3 depicts the main elements of evolution in terms of two key processes. First is the existence of entities that are capable of being reproduced over time. In biology the entities are the genes that are replicated, as genotypes are mixed and passed from generation to generation. Genes are essentially subroutines that become expressed and used in some kind of order over time as a plant or animal develops into its phenotype. In cultural evolution, including business culture, the entities that are replicated through time are called by different researchers cultural traits, routines or competences. These are acquired or modified by social learning, including teaching, imitation and other forms of social transmission and affect behaviour.

Richard Dawkins calls the basic entities of cultural evolution *memes*, which leap from mind to mind and are thereby reproduced, altered, reconfigured and diffused through time and space. Memes include ideas, knowledge, beliefs, values, skills, capacities, attitudes and orientations. But an individual idea is not really equivalent to a subroutine, as genes are, unless we define memes to include a related set of ideas that constitute a way of doing something. These could be called meme complexes, but to keep things simple I will use the term meme to refer to the subroutines expressed in cultural and business life.

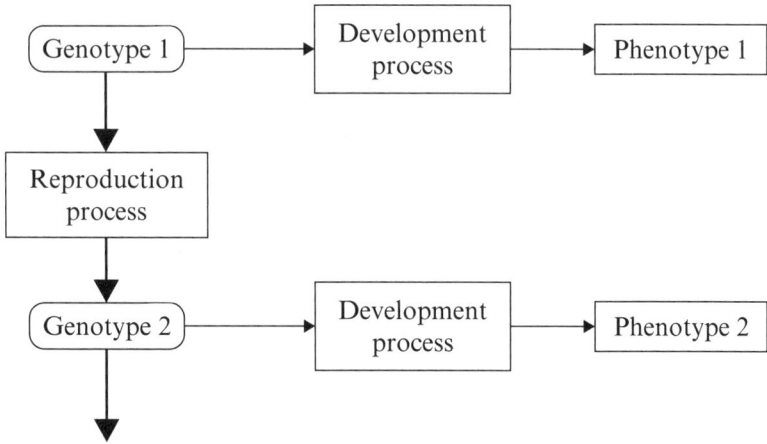

Source: Adapted from Dawkins (1989, p. 202).

Figure 8.3   The evolutionary process

Genes and memes do not exist in isolation but form genotypes or memotypes, assortments of cultural traits that characterise a particular
person, group or firm, and that govern the way a phenotype develops and
behaves. In biology, phenotypes are the myriad of types of flora and
fauna that develop from the existing population of genotypes. The
success of phenotypes affects whether or not the genes governing their
behaviour will be passed on to the next generation – whether they will
survive. In cultural evolution, phenotypes refer to the characteristic patterns of behaviour and responses of people and organisations that are
operating under the influence of different sets of memes or cultural
traits. The term 'business model' is sometimes used to refer to the mix of
traits characterising a particular type of firm's manner of operation and
response, and is a kind of business analogue to the concept of a genotype
in biology. Just as in biology, the success of a business model or memo-
type in its environment affects which memes or traits get reproduced over
time and place.

Genes and memes, as Richard Dawkins tells us, do two things – they
influence the development of the phenotype and they get themselves
reproduced. The success of different phenotypes depends on the environment in which they develop and operate, including the material world, the
world of physics, chemistry and biochemistry, as well as other phenotypes
that coexist and with which a phenotype interacts. Natural selection refers
to the struggle among phenotypes to develop and survive in a particular

Table 8.3   Components of evolution processes in biology and business

Dimension	Biology	Business
Replication unit	Genes	Memes
Transmission unit	Genotypes	Memotypes
Phenotype	Flora and fauna	Firms, households and organisations
Transmission process	Sex, division	Social and economic learning and copying
Adapting unit	Extended phenotype	Network
Variation	Mutation and recombination	Innovation, error and recombination

Source: Wilkinson (2006a, p. 119).

environment, independently or in cooperation. The same principle applies to biological and cultural evolution.

For genes to get themselves copied into the next generation, more than survival is required. Sexual selection, Darwin's other theory, as Dawkins refers to it, focuses on the struggle among males and females to find and secure mates with whom they can cooperate in passing on their genes to future generations. Genes that are useful for sexual selection may not be the same as and may even conflict with genes for natural selection, leading to some weird and wonderful sexual dynamics. The analogue to sexual selection in cultural and business evolution is business mating, which refers to the ability of firms to develop productive relations with other firms in achieving their goals. This was the subject of Chapter 4. The ability to form successful business relations requires competences that are different from but complementary because, as discussed in previous chapters, firms cooperate to compete and compete to cooperate.

Table 8.3 summarises the terms used to describe key components of the evolutionary process in biology and business. I now focus on cultural evolution, as this lies at the heart of our understanding of the development and spread of business systems and practices, and the development of appropriate antitrust policies.

The main processes that cause cultural change and evolution are *inertial forces* that tend to reproduce the same cultural variants over time and result from unbiased sampling and faithful copying of memes, and two forces for change: *transmission biases* that make people and firms more likely to encounter and adopt some memes rather than others and adapt their behaviour accordingly; and *natural selection*, which affects what happens to people and firms that have different cultural variants or memotypes, whether they succeed or not and hence whether their memes are perpetuated or not, and whether they become models to copy or not (Richerson and Boyd 2004).

For antitrust policy, the challenge is to influence transmission biases and natural selection processes so as to improve the evolvability of a nation's business systems, including: (a) weakening inertial forces that tend to reproduce the same business systems over time, when environmental variation calls for new business models; (b) shaping transmission biases to enhance productive entrepreneurial, innovation and imitation processes; and (c) influencing natural selection processes, including the birth and death of firms, to ensure that the pool of cultural variants in the business population remains viable and varied, such that it opens up rather than narrows future development opportunities and evolutionary paths.

The implication for antitrust policy of a relationship and network perspective is that the relevant units of adaptation and evolution are not individual firms competing in a focal market but networks of interconnected, interdependent, interacting firms and other organisations spanning various markets, industries and technologies, including the policy makers themselves. These networks, as has been shown in previous chapters, co-create and deliver value to intermediate and end consumers, and develop and evolve over time through their internal and external actions, responses and interactions. This involves a continual process of configuring and reconfiguring the connections between actors in the network, changes in the actors in the network and the role they play, and the creation and destruction of new types of actors and relations. This co-evolutionary process cannot be understood, the main forces that drive development and evolution cannot be identified, and the potential role and impact of antitrust policy cannot be fathomed without focusing on the structure and behaviour of business relations and networks.

Antitrust policy needs to focus attention more on the nature and functioning of market relations and networks if it is to participate meaningfully and productively in business systems development and evolution. This is a challenging undertaking, as the relevant interactions and relations are not under direct government control; governments have to learn how to sense and respond to different types of evolutionary pathways and tipping points, to help steer business away from pathological attractors. This, of course, is much easier to say than do, but research on complexity provides some guidelines.

Complexity theory directs our attention to the very nature and existence of the actors in complex adaptive systems such as business relations and networks. It makes the process primary, the continual flow of action and interaction, and economic actors such as firms are produced out of this ongoing flux. They come into existence as recognisable, reproduced patterns of action and interaction among people and objects over time, or what are called dissipative structures.

To illustrate what I mean let's use the analogy of a river. The continuous flow of water downstream in a river results in the formation of local patterns of repeated behaviour, such as eddies, whirlpools, ripples and rapids. These are local structures that are reproduced over time through an ever-changing stream of water molecules following the same patterns of behaviour. Eddies and whirlpools are mini-structures that arise, in a self-organising manner, from the ongoing local interactions taking place among an ever-changing stream of water molecules in a river bed. Over time, as conditions change, due to increased or decreased water flow, erosion and local environmental impacts, the pattern and location of eddies, whirlpools, ripples and rapids changes. Eddies, whirlpools, ripples and rapids are examples of what are called dissipative structures, a concept developed by Ilya Prigogine, for which he won a Nobel prize. Dissipative structures are what complexity is about. Business firms, relations and networks are dissipative structures, as indeed are people. They are continually reproduced and recognisable patterns of action and interaction taking place over time; they are produced and reproduced through the micro interactions taking place within and between the people and firms comprising them.

In this view, *non-change* rather than change becomes problematic. Organisations and networks exist because they are continually reproduced, not because they exist until they are destroyed. This perspective leads us to ask different kinds of questions that provide additional insights for guiding antitrust policy. Why do firms and networks with particular characteristic patterns of behaviour persist? How are these patterns reproduced over time amidst the constant flux of actions and interactions taking place?

Antitrust policy focuses on the structure and conduct of firms in markets as a means of improving overall economic performance. The underlying assumption is that firms organise the activities taking place in markets, and the number of firms in a market and the way they individually behave matters. After all, isn't it firms that make decisions about how and when to act and interact? The alternative perspective focuses on the ongoing processes taking place, the actions and interactions, and how these create and reproduce firms rather than the way firms create the patterns of actions and interactions. The business of antitrust is to help shape the kinds of interaction and feedback that lead to the right kinds of firms and networks evolving, rather than controlling the firms and networks that happen to exist at a particular time and place in order to produce the right kinds of interaction and feedbacks.

Research on the nature and formation of networks in complexity theory offers guidance. Different types of network structures have been identified including random, regular, small-world and scale-free or hub networks. Here, I focus on scale-free networks, as these are characteristic of living systems, including business. The underlying rule for the development of such networks is that 'the rich get richer'. As a network grows, new nodes are more likely to form links with and be attracted to, or find, nodes that are themselves already well connected. The probability of a new node linking with another node depends on how many links the other node already has. Thus people and firms are more likely to form links with people and firms who already have more links with other people and firms. Various psychological, social and economic mechanisms lead to this type of behaviour and they comprise various forms of positive feedback effects. In the case of Microsoft, for example, the network externalities involved in using a computer operating system that many already use is the main positive feedback mechanism.

Trading or business networks are likely to form scale-free networks because they grow by similar processes to those described. How should we deal with them and what are their benefits and dangers? Do they result in another form of natural monopoly, the hubs such as Microsoft, that require government antitrust regulation? First, it must be stressed that it is not the properties of the hub firm or person that cause them to become a hub; it is an outcome of the way networks grow and evolve. Hubs are a type of network role or position that emerges naturally in any living business or economic system.

What matters for network evolution and antitrust is how easy or difficult it is for rivals to take over hub positions from others if they can offer better value. The degree of competition for hub roles, by definition, is not indicated by the presence of many equally strong rival hub firms in a network, as this would not be a scale-free network. Hub competition is reflected in how contestable the markets for hub roles are. Potential rivals include existing minor hub firms in the network, which, in the case of Microsoft, would include alternative operating systems such as Apple, Linux and UNIX, as well as organisations occupying hub or keystone positions in related networks, such as Google, Amazon and PC or Internet connection providers.

Governments can move into hub roles by taking over and controlling hub firms in the public interest. However, it is not clear that government-managed hubs are desirable in evolutionary terms. If firms occupying hub roles are subject to government takeover and the free release of core technology, they have incentives to disguise their 'hubness' by promoting other hubs. This leads to a more visibly competitive hub market, but how efficient and effective is it, and how does this affect the evolution of the network over time? Another policy option is to break up hub firms. But, if scale-free networks are a natural result of interactions, breaking up Microsoft will just lead to the emergence of another operating system assuming the same powerful position. Is this the way to go or does it damage evolvability?

Can hubs become too powerful and control and direct the future evolution of the network in their own interests and against the larger good, or are there natural constraints that limit the power and reach of economic hubs or keystones such as Microsoft? I have already mentioned the contestability of hub positions as one limiting factor. There are limits also to how many relations one economic actor can have or how many friends an individual can have. Firm size, technology and geographic constraints affect how many customers or suppliers a firm can handle. In addition, firms and people are heterogeneous and there are forces of repulsion as well as attraction in networks, such that, at times, the rich may get poorer – at least for some in the network. For example, some people have strong negative feelings about using Microsoft and are committed to other operating systems such as Apple or UNIX.

Microsoft's role is similar to an organisation being in control of the development and evolution of the English language. You don't have to use English, but many people are using it because so many people already use it in business, science and social life around the world. We might argue about whether we all speak the same English, but let's not get into that. Languages evolve as new words are added, their meaning changes and the rules of grammar alter. All of us are free to use words to say, write and think what we want. No one controls the English language and regulates the core rules of grammar, spelling and meaning of words, although dictionaries and rules of good English are produced and taught. The living nature of a language is demonstrated by the way standards change over time and how innovations in language arise and spread. Attempts to control a language tend to fail or be counterproductive, as seems to have happened with the Latin and French languages.

What does all this mean for antitrust? Does it mean that a hub firm, such as Microsoft for example, is unable to control the evolution of the network in which it operates – in Microsoft's case the evolution of operating systems and the way they are used? From my limited understanding of the technicalities involved, Microsoft seems potentially more powerful than the French government is in controlling French. Its power comes from the core of its operating system, which is made available to developers only in machine code form so that it cannot be altered by anyone other than Microsoft. If this is so, evolvability is constrained. How serious this is and how difficult it is to work around this constraint is hard to say. Operating systems, like languages, evolve, and people and firms can switch operating systems and languages when the value of an alternative becomes greater and switching costs do not wipe out the benefits. The issue is whether the evolutionary biases currently existing as a result of Microsoft occupying a key hub role are worse than possible alternatives.

There are no simple answers to these questions and problems, but complexity theory and its associated methodologies help us to identify and address them more clearly. In the final section of this chapter I consider the good and bad characteristics of scale-free business networks, their evolution and evolvability and the role antitrust policy could play.

Nature, Role and Regulation of Scale-Free Business Networks

Scale-free networks are resilient because random failures of parts of the network do not affect its connectivity and functioning very much. However, if hubs can be identified, such networks are vulnerable to attack. This implies that we need to be worried about the failure of a Microsoft as well as its success, as failure could lead to rapid contagion and damage throughout the networks of organisations directly and indirectly linked to it. As a keystone, Microsoft is equally good at enabling value creation in others and in rapidly spreading damage by inhibiting and biasing the efforts of others. It is the latter possibility that lies at the heart of much discussion about regulating Microsoft, because its hub position gives it the power to do much good or evil, and economic theory tends to assume that monopolists like this will use their power in their own interests and against the interests of the many.

We need to distinguish here between the effects of regulating the behaviour or breaking up *existing* hubs on the performance and behaviour of others in the network, and the effects on the evolution and evolvability of the network as a whole. For example, will regulating a hub tend to ensure its continuation as a hub, preventing other forms of network evolution? Will breaking it up lead to the emergence of another hub with similar characteristics, which then has to be prosecuted all over again, or will it lead to some process of network evolution that will be better or worse? In order to answer these questions we need some idea of how networks evolve over time. After all, there were business networks before Microsoft and there will be afterwards.

Business networks evolve through a process of reconfiguring the links among actors (business, government, lawyers and educators), activities, resources and schemas. Incremental changes are taking place all the time through the ongoing flow of activities. Resources are being used and created, strengthened and weakened; learning and knowledge development and diffusion are taking place. Radical changes involve significant and novel types of reconfiguration. How does a scale-free network affect the evolutionary process? Innovations involve generating new ideas, which come from combining and recombining existing ideas – they are not exogenous manna from heaven (as discussed in Chapter 3). Ideas get recombined through the research effort of individual actors and through the communication and interaction taking place among and within actors, including people, firms, research institutions and governments.

Scale-free networks help preserve ideas, both good and bad, because ideas are hard to eliminate completely. This is shown by research on the spread of viruses in human and Internet environments. Although programmes targeted at hubs can significantly reduce their presence and spread in the network, they remain in parts of the network ready to spring into action when conditions permit. Scale-free networks also facilitate the recombining of ideas because of their small-world character. No matter where ideas are located, they are not very far from others in the network. This recombining is limited by the extent to which ideas are easily found, communicated and used by others, and by the way knowledge is distributed throughout the network. Some ideas are locked away by firms, protected by patents or not easily communicated or understood because they are tacit, sticky and embedded in relations and routines.

Hubs play an important part in facilitating the spread of ideas and therefore influence innovation through their impact on opportunity discovery and exploitation processes. As this is central to evolution and the evolvability of the network, this subject should play an important role in antitrust policy deliberations.

Potential targets for antitrust policy are various types of actual and potential transmission biases that could adversely affect evolvability. Some of these already form part of antitrust policy because they are related to issues of static efficiency and price competition. For example, misleading and deceptive practices result in biased transmission and affect the numbers and types of competitors, which in turn limit the cultural variants for the evolutionary processes to work on. Other ways in which potentially productive recombination of ideas can be inhibited include: entry barriers to new types of firms; obstacles to new types of relations and interactions forming among firms in and among different markets, industries and nations; the ability of workers to set up or move to new firms or nations in order to exploit innovations that their existing firms or nations are unwilling or unable to exploit; the limited exposure of some industries and parts of networks to international cooperative and competitive interactions; and the inability and unwillingness of firms to share information and ideas with other firms for fear of losing control of the ideas and/or damaging their own prospects compared to counterparts. These are perennial problems that shape the kinds of business networks that arise, the firms that eventually become hubs, how these change over time and how efficient a given network is at any given time.

The central issue is not to freeze business networks and antitrust policy in terms of a particular structure, pattern of conduct and/or regulation, but to ensure that many natural experiments can and do take place among and within firms and in different policy domains, in order to give evolution more to work with. In this way the requisite variety of network and business systems is preserved and many potential evolutionary pathways are opened up rather than closed off. Freezing a network or part of it is like killing off part of a living system, reducing it to be part of the environment rather than part of the living system and evolutionary process.

Tools to help us map and model the structure and evolution of business networks are now available to facilitate policy development and case analysis. Of particular relevance are agent-based models of business systems which offer ways of developing and testing our theories of business structure, conduct and evolution, including the impact of various types of antitrust policies. I consider them more fully in the final chapter.

We cannot conduct experiments about the impact of different types of antitrust policies on actual economic systems. It would be politically and managerially impossible to implement, extremely costly, likely to damage whole industries and economic sectors, and take a long time. Instead, we need to construct evolutionary models of business networks that can be used to conduct such experiments, that can be used to help us map out the potential range of outcomes implicit in particular network structures and processes and contexts, and that can help us understand what antitrust policy can and cannot do. Developments in computing systems and agent-based modelling methods enable us to represent key aspects of complex adaptive systems, such as economic and business systems, and the ways they develop and evolve, that hitherto have not been possible. These models can include antitrust policy development and enforcement as part of the model: they allow managers and policy makers to develop and hone their experience, sensitivity and understanding of the complex systems in which they operate, by providing realistic 'flight simulator' type interfaces for them to work with. Systematic experiments can be conducted in these artificial worlds to learn about the range of outcomes possible under different conditions, including different types of intervention mechanisms, in ways analogous to biological and chemical experiments.

An example of these kinds of model is an agent-based model of the wholesale electricity markets in the USA, which is being developed by Leigh Tesfatsion and her colleagues. It is designed to test the economic reliability of the Wholesale Market Power Platform proposed by the US Federal Energy Regulatory Commission in 2003 (Tesfatsion 2006). Such models will focus the attention of managers, policy makers and lawyers on key issues and assumptions that affect the development and evolution of business networks and their outcomes. In this way we can move beyond the existing narrow focus on static efficiency and price competition to considerations of dynamic efficiency, value and evolvability.

The aim here is not to develop models that accurately predict the future evolution of business systems – this is impossible. The aim is to develop agent-based models that enhance and extend our analysis, understanding and sensitivity to the behaviour and evolution of complex adaptive business systems; to extend our mind, brain and senses regarding the behaviour of such systems. They will not make antitrust policy makers masters of business destiny, only humble but valuable partners and participants in the ongoing game of business.

Conclusions

I have argued that the main case for antitrust policy should be extended beyond its current focus on static efficiency and economising to one embracing the realities of business relations and networks as complex adaptive systems. I suggest 'evolvability' as an important main case consideration, which leads to a focus on network costs and benefits over time and place. Network costs and benefits focus on the connections between transactions and relations over time and place, including how business arrangements at one time limit or enable arrangements in the future. Such considerations can be included in the rules of antitrust and in antitrust case analysis and decision making.

Incorporating such ideas into antitrust policy is not without its difficulties. In particular, it requires that they are made administratively and politically feasible. This has in part to do with the evolvability of the law, policy makers and lawyers, as well as business and law schools that are involved in the production and diffusion of relevant business and policy memes. Antitrust policy apparatus, business schools and law schools, as I have argued, do not stand outside business systems but are relevant and important actors in business ecosystems. They affect and are affected by business practice and ideas about business practice. Furthermore, in an increasingly globalised business system, issues of evolvability and economising are not confined to one nation but to interrelated networks of nations and their antitrust policies. US antitrust policy and decisions affect other countries' business systems and vice versa, which leads us into a much larger evolutionary arena.

By introducing a relations and networks perspective, and a complexity and evolutionary perspective, antitrust policies are seen in a new and helpful light and attention is directed to potential policy targets and mechanisms that may not otherwise be considered. In order to do this we need to make use of methods and theories of business and economics drawn from complexity and network research. We are at an exciting stage of development of these ideas, theories and methods, and need to draw from them and contribute to them.

NOTES

1. This section is based on Welch and Wilkinson (2004).
2. This section is based on Wilkinson et al. (2000).
3. This section is based on Wilkinson (2006a).

9. Reinventing the future of business relations and networks[1]

INTRODUCTION

This book has shown that, in business, interactions between the parts of a system (including people, firms, resources, activities and ideas) matter more than the characteristics of the parts themselves, and networks of interactions matter even more. This point of view brings aspects of business into clearer focus and is a source of insight that other, more narrowly focused, firm and management perspectives obscure. Interactions produce, reproduce or change the parts, the firms and other organisations involved in business and the way they are interconnected, including economic, social and political, and the activities, resources, bonds and schemas involved. In an important sense people and firms do not manage these interactions and networks of interactions within and across firm boundaries; the interactions 'manage' them.

I came to my views on business from a prior focus on systems theory and Aldersonian functionalist marketing theory, with a particular emphasis on the structure of marketing channels and the interactions taking place among firms in such systems. Business marketing allowed me to broaden this to encompass the structure and function of business networks more generally, including buyer–seller interactions and relations. I have written generally about the history of thought concerning business networks and channels in marketing elsewhere (Wilkinson 2001); in this chapter I summarise some of the key ideas in this book and how I think we can and should move forward in terms of our research and thinking.

MARKET TRANSACTIONS AND COLLABORATIVE ADVANTAGE

The analytical framework underlying this book may be summarised as follows. The primary unit of analysis in marketing is a market transaction, the means by which people, firms and other organisations exchange products and services creating value for each other. Market *trans*actions involve *inter*actions among the parties involved in order to bring the parties together and to work out and implement an exchange of values in the form of products and services and money. Each party contributes inputs to the transaction and receives outputs, both directly and indirectly, which may be summarised in the form of value equations. Because these inputs and outputs are differently valued by each party, transactions can and mostly do result in mutual gain. In business markets the parties involved are organisations, who themselves comprise interrelated and interacting people performing various roles, arranged in some type of formal and informal structure. Market transactions, as a result, may involve the efforts of a number of different people interacting across as well as within organisational boundaries. For convenience I use the word firm to refer to business firms and other types of organisations engaged in market transactions, such as government bodies, education institutions and social organisations of various kinds.

Market transactions do not take place in isolation. First, market transactions between firms interact with and depend on other types of transactions and interactions taking place within the firms involved, including buying and selling groups, interdepartmental and interfunctional interactions and relations. Second, market transactions between firms are linked to past transactions that have taken place between the people and firms involved and to potential future market transactions between them – the so-called shadows of the past and future. Relations between firms emerge over time as a result of market transactions and other types of interactions taking place between and within the firms involved. Third, market transactions between firms are connected, directly and indirectly, to other actual and potential transactions that have or could take place with other firms, which gives rise to networks of interrelated transactions and firms.

The strategic problem facing the firm may be depicted in terms of the market triangle of a firm, competitor and customer. A firm seeks to bring about market transactions with targeted customers that result in advantages to it, by offering products and services that have direct and indirect value to the customer. Competition comes in the form of rival firms seeking to bring about market transactions with the same customers by offering value in the form of different bundles of products and services. Customer value depends on the perceptions of the customer. Value is co-produced by customers and sellers who contribute various inputs and receive various outputs from market transactions which each evaluates in their own terms using their own standards of value. Which market transactions eventuate depends on the differential advantage each party is perceived to offer to the other, i.e. the value of the customer to the seller versus the competitor and the value of a supplier versus a competitor to the customer.

Much research in business marketing focuses on how firms do and should go about identifying potential target customers (including market segments) and how to efficiently and effectively create and deliver value to targeted customers that is superior to others. The resource-based and resource advantage theories of the firm focus on the way the resources and competences of firms affect how they can and do so compete. The potential value business suppliers and customers provide for each other has been an important focus of research attention and this has revealed how market transactions can have both direct and indirect functions or benefits as well dysfunctions and costs. The direct outcomes relate to the benefits and costs associated with carrying out the focal transaction itself. The indirect outcomes stem from the way the focal transaction is linked to other transactions with the same or different partners over time, creating opportunities for further business or leading to burdens and threats.

A focus on business markets shows how value is co-produced in relations through the interactions taking place. This is reflected in work on the nature and role of technological development in relations and networks, the concept of co-integration developed first in Germany and research on innovation in relations and networks. Research in business markets is ahead of that in consumer markets in this regard, as the development of relationship marketing and customer relationship management in consumer markets is more recent in origin and tends to focus primarily on the seller's activities in creating and delivering value. Services marketing is an exception because of the obvious nature of consumers' involvement in the value production process. But it is only recently that more general attention has begun to focus on the active role consumers in consumer markets can play in creating value.

The resources, competences and advantages that affect a firm's ability to compete stem not only from their own internal resources, knowledge and competences; they also stem from the market transactions and relations it develops, directly and indirectly, with others. Firms engage in market transactions with others and develop relations with other people and firms in order to access and create valuable resources, knowledge and competences that enable them to develop and sustain competitive advantage in the markets they serve. This makes market transactions and relations interconnected over time and place, as is reflected in the indirect functions and outcomes of market transactions and business relations.

The market triangle has to be extended to include connected transactions and relations through the inclusion of potential collaborators. Firms compete to cooperate and cooperate to compete. They compete to establish and maintain valuable relations with other organisations and targeted customers, and they cooperate to access and develop the means of so competing. Potential collaborators comprise both internal and external organisations of various types, including customers, competitors and complementors. Internally, a firm's ability to create and deliver value to customers depends on the relations and interactions that exist among the people and units of the firm, such as relations among different functional areas or among divisions or units dealing with different products and services.

Market transactions and other forms of interactions that take place over time among firms and other organisations in business markets shape the business networks that emerge: how and to what extent firms and other organisations are directly and indirectly connected and interdependent. Business networks are, I believe, central to our understanding of business markets; they have important implications for policy and practice and demand greater research attention. In order to see the full extent of these implications, we need to understand the structure, operation and evolution of these networks.

Business Networks and Business Strategy

Business networks pose problems for firms in conducting their affairs because business relations and networks are not under the control of any one firm, although, at times, some firms may assume powerful and leadership positions. Even if there are networks in which one firm is in control, the complexity of the problem of designing, implementing and adapting the network in an optimal manner is beyond the ability of one firm. All firms in a network have some degree of power and influence because they are more or less interdependent. The problem for a firm is how to access and use the resources, knowledge and competences available to it at a given time, so as to achieve its immediate goals and, at the same time, to protect and develop these resources, knowledge and competences for future access and use.

Much writing in business focuses on the problem depicted in terms of the market triangle. A firm is assumed to be operating in a given market and network structure, and the problem is couched in terms of what target market segments to aim at and how to allocate resources to marketing activities, the marketing mix, so as to best achieve the firm's goals given the nature of competition. Starting with the Industrial Marketing and Purchasing (IMP) group and their interaction approach, attention shifted away from this essentially one-way, stimulus–response view of marketing, to one in which the customer was viewed as active as well.

Marketing strategy in this view is not just something suppliers do to and for customers. First of all, customers can take the initiative in identifying required products and services and in bringing about market transactions. But, more importantly, market transactions involve various types of inter-actions and take place in the context of ongoing relations with a history of prior transactions and interactions. This history leads to the develop-ment of a relationship atmosphere, which comprises bonds between the actors involved, such as liking, trust, power-dependence, commitment and understanding, activity links, resource ties and schema couplings. The relationship is a quasi-organisation and the problem of business market-ing is one of developing and maintaining this organisation. The gover-nance of this quasi-organisation is not under the complete control of either party but is co-produced through their interactions over time and evolves as market conditions and the people involved change and due to changes taking place in transactions and relations involving other parts of the network.

There is an extensive literature on the subject of interfirm relationship governance, including both economic and behavioural dimensions, which, for the most part, takes the perspective of one actor in the relation. This research has contributed much to our understanding but is limited because it tends to ignore the essential interactive and dynamic nature of the issues at hand; each actor acts in the context of the actions and reactions of others that it does not and cannot fully control. In short, interfirm relations and networks involve co-regulated and co-produced behaviour.

A network approach incorporates the larger network of relations and interactions in which a particular market transaction and exchange is embedded, including both economic and social relations and interactions. The nature of the connections between business relations and the positive and negative effects, functions or value they create was first articulated and measured by those associated with the IMP group.

The central strategic problem confronting firms in networks is develop-ing, sustaining and protecting a firm's network position. Network position refers to the nature and pattern of relations a firm has with others in the network, both directly and indirectly, which both enable and constrain what it is able and required to do. Each firm occupies a position in a network, and network analysis concepts may be used to depict and measure various aspects of such positions. Positions are continually being made, remade or changed through the actions and interactions taking place; in patterns of market transactions, learning and knowledge flows, resources created and used, bonds created and used, and in plans developed and co-developed and their results.

The strategic problem goes beyond a focus on the market triangle. The process of acting and interacting in a market affects the market, and the speed and range of such effects are increasing with advances in telecommunication, speed of travel, the Internet and globalisation. The problem was well described many years ago by Wroe Alderson and Reavis Cox:

> a market changes day to day through the very fact that goods are bought and sold. While evaluation is taking place within a marketing structure, the structure itself is being rendered weaker or stronger, and the changes in organization which follow will have an impact on tomorrow's evaluations. Marketing theory will not provide an adequate approach if it ignores this interaction between the system and the processes which take place within it. (1948, p. 151)

In the act of developing and implementing a strategy in a network context, firms are necessarily affecting the network context giving rise to their actions. These feedback effects have largely been ignored in management and marketing because they are complex and admit of no easy solution. But important developments have taken place in the last decade or so that enable us to make headway in mapping, understanding and modelling such feedback mechanisms and their consequences. These developments stem from work on evolutionary theory in biological and social systems, work in the complexity sciences and developments in cognitive psychology. They also suggest a different perspective on the nature and meaning of management and strategy.

BUSINESS NETWORKS AS COMPLEX ADAPTIVE SYSTEMS

Business networks are examples of complex adaptive, self-organising systems. They comprise interacting people and firms that respond to each other and to the broader environment in which they operate. There is no network leader or captain in charge directing who should do what when and how. Instead, the overall structure and behaviour of the network arises in a self-organising bottom-up manner from the micro interactions taking place, and the overall or macro patterns of behaviour in turn exert a top-down effect on the micro interactions taking place. The overall structure and patterns of behaviour emerging shape the future development and evolution of the network and how it adapts to environmental events.

Such systems have various characteristics. Complex behaviour arises from the way the parts of the system are interconnected, not because the components of the system are themselves complex, although our components, being people and firms, are indeed complex because they are also complex adaptive systems. Because of these interconnections the behaviour of parts of the system cannot be studied in isolation and then added together to explain the system as a whole, such as examining the behaviour of each firm or relationship without taking into account the way behaviour and outcomes are linked to other firms and relations. Apparently unimportant events and circumstances can become important tipping points entraining a particular pattern of development and evolution of the system over time. There are many possible equilibria towards which a system may move over time (the system attractors), depending on starting conditions and circumstances along the way.

Implications for Management and Policy

Characterising business networks as complex adaptive systems is one thing, but developing theory to guide management and policy makers' actions is quite another. How should people and firms behave when they are participants in complex adaptive self-organising systems? Some simply ignore the problem and assume that networks are not complex adaptive systems or that there exist network commanders that design and direct the system. Firms seem to have survived without worrying about these issues much in the past, so what is the problem? This approach is but a convenient fiction, one that flies in the face of the emerging understanding of business and social systems and the way they are becoming more richly connected and faster paced. As a result, complex network issues and problems will confront us more and more, whether we like it or not. As Paul Ormerod in his delightful book *Butterfly Economics* observes, 'The complex systems world makes life more difficult, not just for policy makers but for scholars and businessmen alike. Unfortunately the world cannot be changed to suit our convenience' (2001, p. 183).

A second approach assumes that, by describing and characterising business relations and networks in better ways for managers and policy makers, we will necessarily improve practice. The IMP group originally subscribed to a belief like this. But now we can do better. Furthermore, providing richer understandings of the patterns of interconnections among firms and relations in business networks may not always be a good thing. It can lead firms to try to take into account more of these complex interconnections in developing and adapting their strategies, which can serve to make the world of business even more unpredictable and chaotic.

A third approach is to confront the reality of complex adaptive systems directly, to recognise the reasons for their existence, the potential benefits as well as problems they generate, and to rethink theories of management. In particular, we need to draw more on concepts of distributed, decentralised control, which is what complex adaptive systems are all about. Here we do not start with the assumption that firms can and do control the network in their own interests. The problem for a firm is how to manage its actions and interactions with others so as to preserve and promote a productive and valuable role for itself in the networks of which it is a part. Through these actions and interactions firms act, learn and adapt and thereby contribute to the self-organising process of the network. A network becomes an extended enterprise in which the firm is in the network and the network is in the firm.

We tend to have been brought up, at least in the West, to have a centralist mindset. If we see a pattern or design in nature we assume there must have been a designer, that it could not have occurred naturally; and when something goes wrong we look for someone to blame. But the 'blind watchmaker', as Richard Dawkins has characterised evolutionary processes, has led to the creation of complex organisms, senses and societies, without any need for a pre-given plan or objectives. Studies of the behaviour of complex systems also show how apparently coordinated and adaptive behaviour can arise from simple rules of interaction among system components, such as the flocking behaviour of birds or the foraging and nesting behaviour of social insects.

Distributed control has advantages over central control. Central control of a network faces the limitation imposed by one firm and its managers: their skills and understanding and their ability to design the network, including the way each part interacts with others and how the network adapts to changing external conditions. Complex adaptive systems such as networks and brains involve many interactions happening in parallel among partly independent, evolving entities, and such systems cannot be controlled through a serial bottleneck like a central planner, as Ross Ashby's concept of requisite variety makes plain, as well as Hayek's (1960) critique of centrally planned economies. This discussion leads to one of the paradoxes of networks: the more a firm is able to control a network, the less effective and innovative it will become.

How can firms and policy makers learn from distributed control systems? The answer to this leads us to a different way of thinking about management and policy making. Instead of focusing only on how firms can attempt to manage and lead others through their command and control of resources, we also need to consider the ways firms can attempt to be better managed by others; to be able to learn effectively from others and to co-develop knowledge, resources and competences they are unable to develop alone. The origins of my thinking here go back to the concept of 'business dancing'. Dancing, or at least ballroom dancing, involves both the skills of leading and following to dance well.

These ideas were developed further as a result of insights from studies of the way social animals, firms and people operate in complex adaptive systems and from theories of distributed cognition – in particular the work of Andy Clark. Studies of social insects reveal how complex and intelligent behaviour and responses arise from the swarm intelligence of a colony of insects. This intelligence is not in the ants or bees but in the way they respond to each other and to their local environment. Studies of how people interact within firms to solve complex problems and how firms interact within complex and dynamic networks show similar results in that the quality of the outcomes depends crucially on the way the parts interact with each other.

As Andy Clark shows, the brain does not act as a central controller of the body or the sole locus of our mind. It is not concerned with developing inner models of potential actions. Its job is *not* to bring the body into line to carry out detailed internally developed commands about how different parts of the body are to move. Its job is to learn to modulate and work with and through the intrinsic response characteristics of our body parts and local environment to achieve desired outcomes. People learn to exploit the reliable and intrinsic properties of their bodies and the ways they function as well as their local environment in order to *soft-assemble solutions* to their problems. Managers can and should learn to soft-assemble strategies by exploiting reliable properties of the way their firm behaves and the way this interacts with properties of their local environment, especially the relations and networks in which they operate. A firm is less complex, capable and intelligent than the relations and networks of which it is part. The relations and networks a firm is part of are extensions of its eyes, ears, resources, competences and mind. They help it to see, do, think and respond to opportunities and threats in ways it otherwise could not. They are not just a source of the problems firms confront; they are part of the solution.

Of course soft-assembled strategies and scaffolding on properties of the local environment and network are not without danger. Firms can be misled and confused by the actions and interests of others. But the alternative of relying only on a firm's own resources, competences and intelligence, and attempting to control the behaviour of others is also limiting and potentially misleading. Over time, firms, relations and networks evolve. Higher-performing and adaptive networks and relations survive and the patterns of thinking, behaviour and responses of the people and firms that co-produce such networks and relations persist and are imitated. Other patterns of behaviour and thinking are not reinforced and reproduced. An ecology of strategies evolves, not one best form, that mutually reinforce and challenge each other, including less cooperative and exploitative actors who help keep others on their toes and prevent a drift into naïve and vulnerable forms of cooperation and interaction.

A focus on the way firms manage their interactions with others and the theories in use underlying their actions highlight new areas of competence that affect the performance of firms. These relate to their ability to facilitate the development of productive relations with others and to their skills in recognising and developing productive connections among relations. The nature and dimensions of these skills are still being identified and measured, and include various concepts of relationship and network competence, including choosing and being chosen as relationship partners.

Such a focus has implications for policy makers as well as managers. Policy makers are not outside the systems they attempt to monitor and influence; they are part of the system. How they participate, including the rules they develop and how they are implemented, as well as the way they respond to others involved, affects how policy develops and how effective or not it is. As described in Chapter 7, these implications have been explored in research concerning the way governments can attempt to improve the international competitiveness of firms and industries by facilitating the development and evolution of interfirm relations and networks, and the way antitrust policy can make use of complexity and evolutionary perspectives in developing and implementing antitrust policies.

The Future

A focus on markets as complex, adaptive self-organising systems challenges our notions of management and strategy. But as I read the literature I see increasing attention being given to these issues by academics and practitioners alike. Practitioners increasingly talk about relations, alliances, partners, networks and supply chains, although they do so in a variety of ways that do not always fit with what I have been discussing here. The role and importance of relations and networks in business is increasingly the subject of research attention in the leading journals in management, organisation science, economics and economic sociology.

The complexity perspective is rich in terms of the theories and methodologies it brings with it to study the structure, processes and evolution of business markets and networks. The traditional focus of research on static, variance-based models of business markets, tested often with one-shot cross-sectional surveys, has reached the limits of its usefulness. The models developed and tested typically assume one-way causal processes among variables ripped from their contexts and the ongoing behavioural processes of which they are a part. While these methods have proved valuable in forcing us to spell out the logic of our models and to take care in the way we measure relevant variables, they cannot tell us much about the causal mechanisms at work and are a far cry from the ongoing actions, reactions and events characterising real markets, transactions, relations and networks.

I am excited about the possibilities associated with combining rich and systematic accounts of the histories of business relations and networks, which map the sequence of events taking place and how they are interwoven over time, and the power of agent-based models of complex systems that enable us to observe and experiment with alternative interaction logics and strategies and the way they evolve and interact over time. This will help researchers, managers and policy makers become more familiar with and sensitised to the often non-intuitive behaviour of the non-linear systems of which they are a part. As Steven Hawking has said, referring to the twenty-first century, 'I think the next century will be the century of complexity.' In the final section of the book I outline a programme of research to further develop and test theories of business relations and networks as complex adaptive systems, which, I believe, will greatly enrich our understanding of the way business works and provide new insights and guidance for managers and policy makers alike.

A RESEARCH AGENDA

A major gap in understanding business relations and networks is the way they develop and evolve over time, and the role managers and government can play in influencing this in productive ways. This gap exists because most research and theory to date is dominated by comparative-static, variance-based, survey-type approaches to describing and explaining relationship and network behaviour and performance, which ignore temporal processes, including development and evolution, interaction and order effects, and feedback effects. The overall aim must be, therefore, to build agent-based models (ABMs) of business relationship and network development and evolution as complex adaptive systems. These models must:

- integrate the main psychological, social, managerial, economic and other mechanisms operating, as identified in existing theories and through systematic narrative event history mapping of a sample of actual business relationship and network histories;
- be capable of reproducing the stylised patterns of development and evolution of actual business relations and networks;
- be able to systematically examine the kinds of relationship and network attractors that exist in different circumstances, the pathways to them, and their sensitivity to starting conditions and other factors;
- be able to be used to examine the role managers and government play in shaping patterns of development and evolution and to help design more effective intervention and participation strategies.

To explain, here, is in the sense described by Herbert Simon (Augier and March 2004, p. 5), the Nobel prize-winning economist and psychologist: 'to "explain" an empirical regularity is to discover a set of simple mechanisms that would produce the former in any system governed by the latter'. To grow (or generate) something is to explain. ABMs are a new way of doing research that emerged out of increased computer power and new programming methods that allow us to build, investigate and test models of systems that are beyond the reach of traditional analytical methods. To develop, analyse and test ABMs of business relations and networks, we need detailed and systematic accounts of the histories of actual relations and networks, and methods have been developed to assist us in doing this (for example, Buttriss and Wilkinson 2006).

Four types of theories exist for explaining relationship and network development and evolution. *Life-cycle theories* are based on an organic metaphor and characterise business relationship development in terms of a 'life' divided into a sequence of stages through which relations are assumed to progress or die. Such theories are of limited use since they assume implicitly that relationship development is some rigid, unfolding process, in which subsequent stages are determined from the start. They have limited predictive value and leave little room for management, ambiguity, uncertainty and external events in shaping relationship development. Second are *teleological theories*, which assume relationships and networks are controlled by central actors to achieve their purposes. But relations and networks comprise interdependent firms that self-organise in a bottom-up manner through the micro interactions taking place in and among firms. Third, *dialectic theories* focus on process and the way rival ideas, people and firms interact over time and the way such rivalries work themselves in a thesis–antithesis–synthesis manner. Such theories describe the process of change but not the forces driving the emergence of rival ideas and desires for change, and how power structures develop and evolve in support.

Last are *evolutionary theories*. These are more comprehensive and incorporate features of the other types of theories. They comprise the four generic processes of variation, selection, retention and diffusion. *Variation* concerns the mechanisms by which new forms of organisation emerge, which may be intentional or not; *selection* is the process by which internal or external forces support, develop or undermine new forms; *retention* refers to the way selected forms are preserved or reproduced over time; and *diffusion* is the process by which new forms are adopted or imitated by others in the relevant population. These processes are interrelated and together shape the pattern of evolution of relations and networks, which are forms of organisation.

There have been few in-depth studies of the way business relationships and/or networks develop and evolve, and these offer some insight into the kinds of mechanisms and processes operating, including:

- *business mixing and mating processes*, including finding and being found and mutual choice processes;
- *business dancing and interacting processes*, such as leading, following, collaborating, negotiating, communicating, influencing and conflict management;
- *business learning, and knowledge development processes*, including sense-making processes, imitation and knowledge sharing, and the flow of knowledge and ideas within and between firms;
- *business innovation and adaptation processes*, such as the way new ideas and opportunities are discovered, developed and exploited, and people and firms develop and adapt their activities, resources, feelings and ideas to each other;
- *business relation connecting processes*, the way ideas, bonds, resources and activities in one relation affect those in other relations.

The development and evolution of business relations and networks is a co-evolutionary process in which firms, relations and networks are each other's environment. At any moment, ongoing action is shaped by the relationship structure produced by history and, at the same time, the existing structure is being reproduced or changed by the experience and outcomes of ongoing interactions in the focal and connected relations. Many patterns of development are possible, and tipping points can alter the course of development in critical ways, as when a problem arises that challenges existing patterns of behaviour and thought, or when key individuals or connected relations change. Of particular interest in this research are the conditions under which forms of collaborative business relations can and do emerge and sustain themselves in ways that contribute to firms' competitive advantage.

Relations are interconnected because people and firms are involved in many at the same time, and what happens in one affects others. Several types of mechanism lead to positive and negative effects among relations, including comparisons that are made of the experience and outcomes in different relations, which can lead to changes in other relations; the way learning and adaptation taking place in one relation is communicated to and has spillover effects in other relations; and the way resources developed or depleted in one relation affect the resources available for use in others. Two such mechanisms that are receiving increased attention in the literature of late are structural or social balance and group selection. These are discussed in other chapters of this book.

What this all shows is that business relations and networks are multiply complex. They involve many types of interpersonal, interdepartmental and interfirm relations and interactions, and emerge from the simultaneous and ongoing operation of a diverse and interconnected set of underlying generative or driving mechanisms, including interaction, exchange and market mechanisms, communication and learning mechanisms, power and influence mechanisms, trust and commitment mechanisms, innovation, imitation and adaptation mechanisms, ageing and maturation processes, teleological processes, cyclical and timing effects, cohort effects, structural balance mechanisms, multi-level evolutionary selection mechanisms, and environmental change mechanisms and so on. The pace of action and change varies for different aspects of business, with slower dynamics constraining and influencing faster dynamics. Changes in technology and resource structures take time, as machines and people age at different rates, decision-making and planning cycles have their own timing; attitudes and perceptions change at different rates, and daily, weekly, yearly and longer routines and cycles of behaviour influence the timing of events.

In order to analyse such systems, resort must be made to simulation methods in which the behaviour of the system is played out over time under various conditions and assumptions.

Agent-Based Models (ABMs)

ABMs are new ways of doing research that allow us to build, investigate and test models of complex adaptive systems (CASs) that are beyond the reach of traditional analytical methods, of which business relations and networks are an example (for example, Tesfatsion and Judd 2006). Such systems are not centrally controlled and directed; control is distributed and systems self-organise through the micro interactions taking place in a bottom-up way, and the macro structures arising exert forms of top-down influence. CASs are highly non-linear, sensitive to starting conditions and tipping points. ABMs are means of gaining traction in analysing and understanding such systems, as they can capture key aspects of their evolutionary and development mechanisms and processes.

ABMs are a type of theory, in the form of the equations of motion and interaction of the system represented in a computer program, as well as a means of analysis, experimentation and testing the theories. They are not based on a set of general driving equations, as in system dynamics simulation methods, but allow for bottom-up control, via a heterogeneous set of interacting agents. These agents could represent people and firms, as well as other actors and objects such as markets, environments and resources, each with their own characteristics, predispositions and rules of behaviour.

The rules can and do change as a result of learning via interaction and feedback effects. Such models offer a middle ground between 'thick' and 'thin' descriptions. Thick descriptions result from in-depth case studies of actual histories, which reveal the complex causal processes involved but cannot be easily generalised. Thin descriptions result from sample survey-type research that is more generalisable but abstracts away from any examination of the processes, events or choices by which different types of variables are interrelated and affect outcomes.

Instead of being limited to a study of what has happened, the types of business relations and networks that do or have existed, ABMs allow us to test counterfactuals, in effect to *synthesise new business life*. As Chris Langton, one of the founders of such research, explains (Langton 1996), synthesis has played an important part in the development of many scientific disciplines 'because it extends the empirical database upon which the theory of the discipline is built beyond the often highly accidental set of entities that nature happened to leave around for us to study'. We cannot go back and rerun history to see how sensitive outcomes are to different factors and interventions, but ABMs enable us to capture important features of the process, identify tipping points, and to conduct computer experiments of the impact of different factors. Different theories or assumptions about the system can be implemented and examined.

Final Words

The research agenda addresses key issues underlying the international competitiveness, efficiency and performance of firms and industries – the development of collaborative advantage to enhance competitive advantage. The role and importance of business relations and networks as a major driver of firm competitiveness is now being increasingly recognised. But the processes by which such collaborative relationships develop and can or cannot be managed are not well understood or studied because of the complexity of the systems involved.

Examining and modelling the processes by which domestic and international business relations develop and more collaborative forms emerge will contribute to the identification, understanding and development of improved management techniques and government policies to facilitate these processes. In particular, it will generate models for managers and policy makers to test the effectiveness of different intervention and policy initiatives, and to hone their intuitions and understanding of the dynamics of business relations and networks.

Methodologies, software and computer resources now exist to realise this research agenda. ABMs provide the methodology and software systems, and programming languages have been developed to facilitate the development, calibration and testing of these types of models. Methodologies, narrative event history methods, also exist to develop systematic histories of the processes, mechanisms and events shaping relationship and network development. These can inform the modelling work and help validate the resulting models. They also deal with the ongoing messy reality of actual day-to-day interactions, practice and operations, and so come much closer to dealing with the problems and issues in the way managers and policy makers experience their world: not the abstract wiggling of disembodied variables, ripped from their contexts. Actors act, not variables, and it is through action that things change and develop.

NOTE

1. This chapter is largely based on a restrospective essay I wrote for the anniversary issue of the *Journal of Business and Industrial Marketing* (Wilkinson 2006b) plus a research proposal written with two colleagues, Robert Marks and Louise Young (Wilkinson et al. 2006), to develop agent-based models of the dynamics and evolution of business relations and networks.

Bibliography

The bibliography includes additional sources which have not been directly cited.

Abbott, Andrew (1992), 'From causes to events', *Sociological Methods Research*, **20**, 428–55.

Abell, P. (2004), 'Narrative explanation: an alternative to variable-centred explanation?', *Annual Review of Sociology*, **30**, 287–310.

Achrol, Ravi S. and Kotler, Philip (1999), 'Marketing in the network economy', *Journal of Marketing*, **63** (special issue), 146–63.

Ackoff, Russell and Emery, Fred (1972), *On Purposeful Systems*, Chicago, IL: Aldine-Atherton.

Alderson, Wroe (1957), *Marketing Behavior and Executive Action*, Homewood, IL: Irwin.

Alderson, Wroe (1965), *Dynamic Marketing Behaviour*, Homewood, IL: Richard D. Irwin.

Alderson, Wroe and Cox, Reavis (1948), 'Towards a theory in marketing', *Journal of Marketing*, **13** (October), 137–52.

Aldrich, H. (1999), *Organizations Evolving*, London: Sage Publications.

Anderson, H., Havila, V. and Salmi, A. (2001), 'Can you buy a business relationship?', *Industrial Marketing Management*, **30** (October), 575–86.

Anderson, James C., Håkansson, Håkan and Johanson, Jan (1994), 'Dyadic business relationships within a business network context', *Journal of Marketing*, **58**, (October), 1–15.

Antal, T., Krapivsky, P. and Redner, L.S. (2006), 'Social balance on networks: the dynamics of friendship and enmity', *Physica D*, **224**, 130–36.

Arthur, W. Brian, Durlauf, Steven N. and Lane, David A. (eds) (1997), *The Economy as an Evolving Complex System II*, Santa Fe Studies in the Sciences of Complexity, Reading, MA: Addison Wesley, pp. 337–69.

Ashby, W. Ross (1952), *Design for a Brain*, London: Chapman and Hall Ltd and Science Paperbacks.

Augier, M. and March, J.G. (2004), *Models of a Man: Essays in Memory of Herbert A. Simon*, Cambridge, MA: MIT Press.

Axelrod, Robert (1984), *Evolution of Cooperation*, New York: Basic Books.

Axelrod, Robert (1997), *The Complexity of Cooperation: Agent-based Models of Competition and Cooperation*, Princeton, NJ: Princeton University Press.

Badaracco, J.L. (1991), *The Knowledge Link: How Firms Compete through Strategic Alliances*, Cambridge, MA: Harvard Business School Press.

Baligh, H.H. and Richartz, L.E. (1967), *Vertical Market Structures*, Boston: Allyn and Bacon.

Barney, J. (1991), 'Firm resources and sustained competitive advantage', *Journal of Management*, **17** (1), 99–120.

Bar-Yam, Yaneer (1997), *Dynamics of Complex Systems*, Reading, MA: Addison-Wesley.

Bar-Yam, Yaneer (2001), *Introducing Complex Systems*, Boston, MA: New England Complexity Science Institute Press.

Baxter, Leslie A. (1985), 'Accomplishing relationship disengagement', in Steven W. Duck and Daniel Perlman (eds), *Understanding Personal Relationships*, Beverly Hills, CA: Sage Publications, pp. 243–65.

Beekman, M. and Wilkinson, I.F. (2004), 'What can social insects teach us about marketing?', Australia–New Zealand Marketing Academy Annual Conference, Victoria University, Wellington, December.

Bensaou, M. (1999), 'Portfolios of buyer–supplier relationships', *Sloan Management Review*, **40** (4), 35–44.

Binmore, Ken (1998), 'Review of Robert Axelrod, *Complexity and Cooperation*', *Journal of Artificial Societies and Social Simulation*, **1** (1) online, http://jasss.soc.surrey.ac.uk.

Blenkhorn, D. and Noori, A.H. (1990), 'What it takes to supply Japanese OEMs', *Industrial Marketing Management*, **19** (1), 21–30.

Blois, Keith (2002), 'Business to business exchanges: a rich descriptive apparatus derived from MacNeil's and Menger's analysis', *Journal of Management Studies*, **39** (4), 523–51.

Bonabeau, Eric, Dorigo, Marco and Theraulaz, Guy (1999), *Swarm Intelligence: From Natural to Artifical Systems*, Oxford: Oxford University Press.

Boulding, Kenneth (1953), 'Towards a general theory of growth', *The Canadian Journal of Economics and Political Science*, **19** (August), 326–40.

Brandenburger, Adam (1998), *Embracing Complexity: Exploring the Application of Complex Adaptive Systems to Business*, Cambridge, MA: Ernst and Young Center for Business Innovation.

Brandenburger, Adam M. and Nalebuff, Barry J. (1997), *Co-opetition*, New York: Doubleday.

Breyer, Ralph (1931), *Commodity Marketing*, New York: McGraw-Hill.

Burt, Ronald (1992), *Structural Holes: The Social Structure of Competition*, Cambridge, MA: Harvard University Press.

Burt, Ronald (2004), 'Structural holes and good ideas', *American Journal of Sociology*, **110** (2), 349–99.

Buttriss, G. and Wilkinson, I.F. (2006), 'Using narrative sequence methods to advance international entrepreneurship theory', *Journal of International Entrepreneurship*, **4**, 157–74.

Cameron, Ross and Wilkinson, Ian F. (1997), 'Influence processes in household purchase decisions: an empirical investigation', *Asian Journal of Marketing*, January, 7–27.

Cannon, J.P. and Perreault, W.D. (1999), 'Buyer–seller relationships in business markets', *Journal of Marketing Research*, **36** (4), 439–60.

Casti, John L. (1997), *Would-Be Worlds: How Simulation is Changing the Frontiers of Science*, New York: John Wiley.

Chandra, Yanto (2007), *Internationalization as an Entrepreneurial Process*, Ph.D. Thesis, University of New South Wales.

Chandra, Yanto, Styles, Chris and Wilkinson, Ian F. (2005), 'The discovery of international entrepreneurial opportunities: insights from knowledge-based industries' Second AGSE International Entrepreneurship and Innovation Research Exchange, Swinburne University of Technology, Melbourne, 10–11 February.

Cheng, Constant and Wilkinson, Ian F. (1999), 'Multicultural marketing in Australia: synergy in diversity', *Journal of International Marketing*, **7** (3), September, 106–25.

Christensen, Clayton M. (1997), *The Innovator's Dilemma*, Cambridge: Harvard Business School Press.

Clark, Andy (1997), *Being There: Putting Brain, Body and the World Together*, Cambridge, MA: MIT Press.

Clark, A. (2003), *Natural-born Cyborgs: Minds, Technologies, and the Future of Human Intelligence*, Oxford: Oxford University Press.

Collander, David (2003), 'Complexity, muddling through, and sustainable forest management', Middlebury College Economics Discussion Paper No. 03-20, August.

Corbett, C.J., Blackburn, J.D. and van Wassenhove, L.K. (1999), 'Case study: partnerships to improve supply chains', *Sloan Management Review*, **40** (4), 71–82.

Cox, Reavis and Goodman, Charles S. (1956), 'Marketing of housebuilding materials', *Journal of Marketing*, **21**, July, 36–61.

D'Aveni, R. (1994), *Hypercompetition: The Dynamics of Strategic Maneuvering*, New York: Free Press.

D'Aveni, R. (1999), 'Strategic supremacy through disruption and dominance', *Sloan Management Review*, **40**, 127–35.

Darwin, C.R. (1859), *On the Origin of the Species*, London: John Murray.

Darwin, C.R. (1871), *The Descent of Man; and Selection in Relation to Sex*, London: John Murray.

Dawkins, Richard (1983), *The Extended Phenotype*, Oxford: Oxford University Press.

Dawkins, Richard (1989), 'The evolution of evolvability', in Chris Langton (ed.), *Artificial Life*, Redwood City, CA: Addison-Wesley, pp. 201–20.

Denzau, Arthur T. and North, Douglass C. (1994), 'Shared mental models: ideologies and institutions', *Kyklos*, **47** (1), 3–31.

Diamond, Jared (1991), *The Rise and Fall of the Third Chimpanzee*, London: Vintage.

Diamond, Jared (1999), *Guns, Germs and Steel: A Short History of Everybody for the Last 13,000 Years*, New York: W.W. Norton and Co.

Diamond, Jared (2005), *Collapse: How Societies Choose to Fail or Survive*, London: Allen Lane.

Dixit, A.K. and Nalebuff, B.J. (1991), *Thinking Strategically: The Competitive Edge in Business, Politics and Everyday Life*, New York: W.W. Norton and Co.

Dixon, Donald F. (2002), 'Emerging macromarketing concepts: from Socrates to Alfred Marshall', *Journal of Business Research*, **55** (9), February, 737–45.

Dixon, Donald F. and Wilkinson, Ian F. (1982), *The Marketing System*, Melbourne: Longman Cheshire.

Dixon, Donald F. and Wilkinson, Ian F. (1985), 'An alternative paradigm for marketing theory', *European Journal of Marketing*, **18** (3), 40–50. (Reprinted in special issue *The Best from the European Journal of Marketing*, **23** (8), 1989, 59–69.)

Dixon, Donald F. and Wilkinson, Ian F. (1986), 'Toward a theory of channel structure', in Louis P. Bucklin and James Carmen (eds), *Research in Marketing: Distribution Channels and Institutions*, Vol. 8, Greenwich, CT: JAI Press, pp. 27–70.

Doney, P.M. and Cannon, J.P. (1997), 'An examination of the nature of trust in buyer–seller relationships', *Journal of Marketing*, **51**, 35–51.

Dwyer, F. Robert, Schurr, Paul H. and Oh, Sejo (1988), 'A transaction cost perspective on vertical contractual structure and interchannel competitive strategies', *Journal of Marketing*, **52** (April), 21–34.

Dyer, Jeffrey and Singh, Harbir (1998), 'The relational view: cooperative strategy and sources of interorganizational competitive advantage', *Academy of Management Review*, **23**, 660–79.

Emery, F.E. and Trist, E.L. (1965), 'The causal texture of organisational environments', *Human Relations*, **18**, 21–32.

Emery, F.E. (1977), *Futures We Are In*, Leiden: Martinus Nijhoff.

Emery, Merrelyn (1999), *Searching: The Theory and Practice of Making Cultural Change*, Amsterdam: John Benjamins Publishing.

Epstein, J.M. (2006), *Generative Social Science*, Princeton, NJ: Princeton University Press.

Fallows, James (1982), *National Defense*, New York: Random House.

Fites, Donald V. (1996), 'Make your dealers your partners', *Harvard Business Review*, **74** (2), 84–97.

Fligstein, Neil (2001), *The Architecture of Markets*, Princeton, NJ: Princeton University Press.

Florence, P. Sargant (1953), *The Logic of British and American Industry*, London: Routledge and Kegan Paul (reprinted by Routledge 2003).

Ford, David (1980), 'The development of buyer–seller relationships in industrial markets', *European Journal of Marketing*, **15** (5/6), 339–54.

Ford, David, Gadde, Lars-Erik, Håkansson, Håkan, Lundgren, Anders, Snehota, Ivan, Turnbull, Peter and Wilson, David (1998), *Managing Business Relationships*, Chichester, John Wiley.

Ford, D., Berthon, P., Brown, S., Gadde, L.-E., Håkansson, H., Naude, P., Ritter, T. and Snehota, I. (2002), *The Business Marketing Course: Managing in Complex Networks*, Chichester: Wiley.

Forrester, Jay W. (1961), *Industrial Dynamics*, Cambridge, MA: MIT Press.

Franke, N. and Shah, S. (2003), 'How communities support innovative activities: an exploration of assistance and sharing among end-users', *Research Policy*, **32** (1), 157–78.

Franke, N. and von Hippel, E. (2003), 'Satisfying heterogenous user needs via innovation toolkits: the case of Apache Security Software', *Research Policy*, **32** (1), 157–78.

French, John and Raven, Bertram (1959), 'The bases of social power', in Dorwin Cartwright (ed.), *Studies in Social Power*, Ann Arbor, Michigan: Institute for Social Research.

Gadde, Lars-Erik and Mattsson, Lars-Gunnar (1987), 'Stability and change in network relationships', *International Journal of Research in Marketing*, **4**, 29–41.

Gadde, Lars-Erik, Huemer, Lars and Håkansson, Hakan (2003), 'Strategizing in industrial networks', *Industrial Marketing Management*, **32**, 357–64.

Ganesan, Shanker (1994), 'Determinants of long-term orientation in buyer–seller relationships', *Journal of Marketing*, **58** (2), 1–19.

Gardner, M.R. and Ashby, W. Ross (1970), 'Connectance of large dynamic (cybernetic) systems: critical values for stability', *Nature*, **228**, 794.

Ghoshal, Sumantra and Bartlett, Christopher A. (1990), 'The multinational as an interorganizational network', *Academy of Management Review*, **15** (4), 603–25.

Granovetter, Mark (1973), 'The strength of weak ties', *American Journal of Sociology*, **78** (May), 1360–80.

Granovetter Mark (1985), 'Economic action and social structure: the problem of embeddedness', *American Journal of Sociology*, **91**, 481–5.

Griffing, B. (1967), 'Selection in reference to biological groups. I. Individual and group selection applied to populations of un-ordered groups', *Australian Journal of Biological Science*, **10**, 127–39.

Grönroos, Christian (1994), 'From marketing mix to relationship marketing: towards a paradigm shift in marketing', *Asia–Australia Marketing Journal* (now *Australasian Marketing Journal*), **2** (1), 9–29.

Gründstrom, Christina and Wilkinson, Ian F. (2004), 'The role of personal networks in the development of industry standards: a case study of 3G mobile telephony', *Journal of Business and Industrial Marketing*, **19** (4), 283–93.

Gulati, R., Nohria, N. and Zaheer, A. (2000), 'Strategic networks', *Strategic Management Journal*, **21**, 203–15.

Gummesson, E. (2006), *Many-to-Many Marketing*, Stockholm: Niche Information.

Hadjikhani, A. and Håkansson, H. (1996), 'Political actions in business networks: Swedish case', *International Journal of Research in Marketing*, **13** (5), 431–47.

Hagel III, John and Brown, John Seely (2005), 'Productive friction: how difficult business partnerships can accelerate innovation', *Harvard Business Review*, **83**, February, 82–91.

Håkansson, Håkan (1982), *International Marketing and Purchasing of Industrial Goods: An Interaction Approach*, Chichester: John Wiley.

Håkansson, Håkan and Ford, David I. (2002), 'How should companies interact in business networks?', *Journal of Business Research*, **55**, February, 133–40.

Håkansson, Håkan and Snehota, Ivan (1995), *Developing Relationships in Business Networks*, London: Routledge.

Håkansson, Håkan and Snehota, Ivan (1998), 'The burden of relationships or who's next', in Peter Naude and Peter W. Turnbull (eds), *Network Dynamics in International Marketing*, Oxford: Pergamon, pp. 16–25.

Håkansson, Håkan, Harrison, Debbie and Waluszewski, Alexandra (2004), *Rethinking Marketing: Developing a New Understanding of Markets*, New York: Wiley.

Hall, Margaret (1949), *Distributive Trading*, London: Hutchinson's University Library.

Hallén, Lars (1992), 'Infrastructural networks in international business', in Mats Forsgren and Jan Johanson (eds), *Managing Networks in International Business*, Philadelphia, PA: Gordon & Breach, pp. 77–92.

Hamilton, Gary G. (ed.) (1996), *Asian Business Networks*, Berlin and New York: de Gruyter.

Hargadon, Andrew (2003), *How Breakthroughs Happen*, Cambridge, MA: Harvard Business School Press.

Hatch, W. and Yamamura, K. (1996), *Asia in Japan's Embrace: Building a Regional Production Alliance*, Cambridge: Cambridge University Press.

Hayek, F.A. (1960), *The Constitution of Liberty*, New York: Wiley.

Heider, Fritz (1958), *The Psychology of Interpersonal Relations*, New York: Wiley.

Henrich, J. (2004), 'Cultural group selection, coevolutionary processes and large-scale cooperation', *Journal of Economic Behaviour and Organisation*, **53**, 3–35.

Henrich, J., Boyd, R., Bowles, S., Gintis, H., Fehr, E. and Camerer, C. (eds) (2005), *Cooperation, Punishment and Self Interest: Experimental and Ethnographic Evidence from 15 Small Scale Societies*, New York: Oxford University Press and University of Michigan.

Herstatt, C. and von Hippel, E. (1992), 'From experience: developing new product concepts via the Lead User Method', *Journal of Product Innovation Management*, **9** (3), 213–22.

Hibbert, D.B. and Wilkinson, Ian F. (1994), 'Chaos in the dynamics of markets', *Journal of the Academy of Marketing Science*, **22** (3), 218–33.

Hidalgo, C.A., Klinger, B., Barabási, A.-L. and Hausmann, R. (2007), 'The product space conditions the development of nations', *Science*, **317**, 482–7.

Holmen, E., Håkansson, H. and Pedersen, A.-C. (2003), 'Design and monitoring a supply network', paper presented at the Industrial Marketing and Purchasing Conference, Lugarno, September (www.impgroup.org).

Huang, Yimin and Wilkinson, Ian F. (2006), 'Understanding power and trust in interfirm relationships: a dynamic perspective', IMP Conference, University of Bocconi, Milan, 6–9 September.

Hummon, N.P. and Doreian, P. (2003), 'Some dynamics of social balance processes: bringing Heider back into balance theory', *Social Networks*, **25** (1), 17–49.

Hunt, Shelby D. (1997), 'Competing through relationships: grounding relationship marketing in resource advantage theory', *Journal of Marketing Management*, **13**, 431–45.

Hunt, Shelby D. and Derozier, C. (2004), 'The normative imperatives of business and marketing strategy: grounding theory in resource-advantage theory', *Journal of Business and Industrial Marketing*, **19** (1), 5–22.

Hunt, Shelby D. and Morgan, R.M. (1997), 'Resource-advantage theory: a snake swallowing its tail or a general theory of competition', *Journal of Marketing*, **61**, October, 74–82.

Hunt, Shelby D. and Nevin, Jack (1974), 'Power in a channel of distribution: sources and consequences', *Journal of Marketing Research*, **11**, 186–93.

Iansiti, Marco and Levien, Roy (2004), *The Keystone Advantage: What the New Dynamics of Business Ecosystems Mean for Strategy, Innovation, and Sustainability*, Boston, MA: Harvard Business School Press.

James, David (1994), 'When losing control can put you in the driver's seat', *Business Review Weekly*, February, 58–60.

Jarrillo, J.C. (1988), 'On strategic networks', *Strategic Management Journal*, **9** (1), 31–41.

Johanson, Jan and Mattsson, Lars-Gunnar (1988), Internationalisation in industrial systems – a network approach', in N. Hood and J.E. Vahlne (eds), *Strategies in Global Competition*, New York: Croom Helm, pp. 287–314.

Johanson, Jan and Mattsson, Lars-Gunnar (1992), 'Network positions and strategic actions – an analytical framework', in B. Axelsson and G. Easton (eds), *Industrial Networks: A New View of Reality*, London: Routledge, pp. 205–17.

Johanson, J. and Mattsson, Lars-Gunnar (1994), 'The markets-as-networks tradition in Sweden', in G. Laurent, G. Lillen and B. Prass (eds), *Research Traditions in Marketing*, Boston, MA: Kluwer, pp. 321–42.

Kanter, Rosabeth Moss (1994), 'Collaborative advantage: the art of alliances', *Harvard Business Review*, July–August, 96–108.

Kanter, Rosabeth Moss (1997), *World Class: Thriving Locally in the Global Economy*, New York: Touchstone.

Kauffman, S. (1992), *Origins of Order: Self Organisation and Selection in Evolution*, New York: Oxford University Press.

Kauffman, S. (1994), 'Whispers from Carnot: the origins of order and principles of adaptation in complex nonequilibrium systems', in G.A. Cowan, D. Pines and D. Meltzer (eds), *Complexity: Metaphors, Models, and Reality*, Sante Fe, NM: Addison Wesley and the Santa Fe Institute, pp. 83–136.

Kauffman, S. (2000), *Investigations*, Oxford: Oxford University Press.

Kim, Kesuyek and Oh, Changho (2002), 'On distributor commitment in marketing channels for industrial products: contrast between the United States and Japan', *Journal of International Marketing*, **10** (1), 72–97.

Kinch, N. (1987), 'Emerging strategies in a network context: the Volvo case', *Scandinavian Journal of Management*, **3** (May), 167–84.

Kipnis, David (1976), *The Powerholders*, Chicago: University of Chicago Press.

Kipnis, David, Schmidt, Stuart M. and Wilkinson, Ian F. (1980), 'Intraorganizational influence tactics: explorations in getting one's way', *Journal of Applied Psychology*, **65** (4), 440–52.

Kipnis, David and Schmidt, Stuart M. (1982), *Profiles of Organization Influence Strategies*, Form M., San Diego, CA: University Associates.

Kirzner, I. (1997), 'Entrepreneurial discovery and the competitive market process: an Austrian approach', *Journal of Economic Literature*, **35**, 60–85.

Knight, Frank (1921), *Risk, Uncertainty and Profit*, Boston, MA: Houghton Mifflin.

Koesrindartoto, Deddy, Sun, Junjie and Tesfatsion, Leigh (2005), 'An agent-based computational laboratory for testing the economic reliability of wholesale market designs', paper presented at Society for Computational Economics, 11th International Conference on Computing in Economics and Finance.

Kraljic, Peter (1983), 'Purchasing must become supply management', *Harvard Business Review*, **61** (5), 109–17.

Kumar, N. (1996), 'The power of trust in manufacturer–retailer relationships', *Harvard Business Review*, November–December, 92–106.

Lane, David and Maxfield, Robert (1996), 'Strategy under complexity: fostering generative relationships', *Long Range Planning*, **29** (2), 215–31.

Lane, David, Malerba, Franco, Maxfield, Robert and Orsenigo, Luigi (1996), 'Choice and action', *Journal of Evolutionary Economics*, **6**, 43–76.

Langton, Christopher G. (ed.) (1996), *Artificial Life: An Overview*, Boston, MA: MIT Press.

Leonard, Dorothy and Swap, Walter (1999), *When Sparks Fly: Igniting Creativity in Groups*, Boston, MA: Harvard University Press.

Leonard-Barton, Dorothy (1993), 'Developer–user interaction and user satisfaction in internal technology transfer', *Academy of Management Journal*, **36** (5), 1125–39.

Leonard-Barton, Dorothy (ed.) (1995), *Wellsprings of Knowledge-Building and Sustaining the Sources of Innovation*, Boston, MA: Harvard Business School Press.

Levitt, T. (1986), *The Marketing Imagination*, New York: The Free Press.

Lilien, Gary L. and Rangaswamy, Arvind (1998), *Marketing Engineering: Computer-Assisted Marketing Analysis and Planning*, Reading, MA: Addison-Wesley.

Lilien, Gary L. and Rangaswamy, Arvind (1999), *New Product and Brand Management: Marketing Engineering Applications*, Reading, MA: Addison-Wesley.

Lilien, Gary L., Rangaswamy, Arvind, van Bruggen, Gerrit H. and Wierenga, Berend (2002a), 'Bridging the marketing theory–practice gap with marketing engineering', *Journal of Business Research*, **55**, February, 111–22.

Lilien, Gary L., Morrison, Pamela D., Searls, Kathleen, Sonnack, Mary and von Hippel, Eric (2002b), 'Performance assessment of the lead user idea generation process', *Management Science*, **48** (8), 1042–59.

Lilien, Gary L., Rangaswamy, Arvind, van Bruggen, Gerrit H. and Starke, Katrin (2004), 'DSS effectiveness in marketing resource allocation decisions: perception vs reality', *Information Systems Research*, **15** (3), 216–35.

Lindblom, Charles E. (1959), 'The science of "muddling through"', reprinted in Andreas Faludi, *A Reader in Planning Theory*, Oxford: Pergamon Press, 1973.

Linder, Jane (2004), 'Transformational outsourcing', *MIT Sloan Management Review*, Winter, 52–8.

Lindgren, Kristian (1997), 'Evolutionary dynamics in game theoretic models', in W. Brian Arthur, Steven N. Durlauf and David A. Lane (eds), *The Economy as an Evolving Complex System II*, Santa Fe Studies in the Sciences of Complexity, Reading, MA: Addison-Wesley, pp. 337–69.

Lonergan, W. (1998), *The Valuation of Businesses, Shares and Other Equity*, 3rd edn, Warriewood, NSW, Australia: Business and Professional Publishing.

Lüthje, C. (2003), 'Customers as co-inventors: an empirical analysis of the antecedents of customer-driven innovation in the field of medical equipment', in *Proceedings of the 32nd European Marketing Academy Conference*, Glasgow: European Marketing Academy.

Lüthje, C. (2004), 'Characteristics of innovating users in a consumer goods field: an empirical study of sport-related product consumers', *Technovation*, **24** (9), 683–95.

Lüthje, C., Herstatt, C. and von Hippel, E. (2002), 'The dominant role of local information in user innovation: the case of mountain biking', working paper, MIT Sloan School of Management.

March, James G. (1991), 'Exploration and exploitation in organizational learning', *Organizational Science*, **2**, February, 71–87.

March, James G. (1996), 'Continuity and change in theories of organizational action', *Administrative Science Quarterly*, **41**, June, 278–87.

May, Robert (1972), 'Will a large complex system be stable?', *Nature*, **238**, 413–14.

May, Robert (1974), *Stability and Complexity in Model Ecosystems*, Princeton, NJ: Princeton University Press.

May, R. (1976), 'Simple mathematical models with very complicated dynamics', *Nature*, **261**, 459–67.

McCann, J.E. and Selsky, John (1984), 'Hyperturbulence and the emergence of type 5 environments', *Academy of Management Review*, **9**, 460–70.

McKelvey, Bill (2004), 'Toward a complexity science of entrepreneurship', *Journal of Business Venturing*, **19**, 313–41.

Mercer, G.A., Monier, J.-H.J. and Satpathy, A. (2004), 'The right restructuring for US automotive suppliers', *The McKinsey Quarterly*, October.

Miller, Geoffrey (2001), *The Mating Mind*, New York: Anchor Books.

Mintzberg, H. (1993), 'The pitfalls of strategic planning', *California Management Review*, Fall, 32–47.

Mirowski, Philip (2002), *Machine Dreams: Economics Becomes a Cyborg Science*, Cambridge: Cambridge University Press.

Moorman, Christine and Miner, Anne S. (1998), 'Organizational improvisation and organizational memory', *Academy of Management Review*, **23**, October, 698–723.

Morgan, Robert M. and Hunt, Shelby D. (1994), 'The commitment–trust theory of relationship marketing', *Journal of Marketing*, **58** (July), 20–38.

Morris, Simon C. (2003), *Life's Solution: Inevitable Humans in a Lonely Universe*, Cambridge, UK: Cambridge University Press.

Morrison, P.D., Roberts, J.H. and von Hippel, E. (2000), 'Determinants of user innovation and innovation sharing in a local market', *Management Science*, **46** (12), 1513–27.

Muir, W.M. (1996), 'Group selection for adaptation to multiple-hen cages: selection program and direct responses', *Poultry Science*, **75**, 447–58.

Nahapiet, J. and Ghoshal, S. (1998), 'Social capital, intellectual capital and the organizational advantage', *Academy of Management Review*, **23** (2), 242–66.

Nelson, P. (1970), 'Information and consumer behavior', *Journal of Political Economy*, **78**, 311–29.

Nelson, Richard R. and Winter, Sidney (1982), *An Evolutionary Theory of Economic Change*, Cambridge, MA: Harvard University Press.

North, Douglass (2005), *Understanding the Process of Economic Change*, Princeton, NJ: Princeton University Press.

Ohmae, K. (1982), *The Mind of the Strategist*, Middlesex, UK: Penguin Books.

Ormerod, Paul (2001), *Butterfly Economics: A New General Theory of Social and Economic Behaviour*, London: Basic Books.

Padgett, John F. (1997), 'The emergence of simple ecologies of skill: a hypercycle approach to economic organization', in W. Brian Arthur, Steven N. Durlauf and David A. Lane (eds), *The Economy as a Complex Evolving System II*, Reading, MA: Addison Wesley, pp. 199–222.

Padgett, John F. and Ansell, C.K. (1993), 'Robust action and the rise of the Medici, 1400–1434', *American Journal of Sociology*, **98** (6), 1259–319.

Podolny, Joel M. (2001), 'Networks as the pipes and prisms of the market', *American Journal of Sociology*, **107**, July, 33–60.

Porter, Michael E. (1980), *Competitive Strategy*, New York: The Free Press.

Porter, Michael E. (1985), *Competitive Advantage: Creating and Sustaining Superior Performance*, New York: The Free Press.

Porter, Michael E. (1990), *The Competitive Advantage of Nations*, New York: The Free Press.

Powell, W.W. (1998), 'Learning from collaboration: knowledge and networks in the biotechnology and pharmaceutical industries', *California Management Review*, **40** (3), 228–40.

Price, G. (1970), 'Selection and covariance', *Nature*, **227**, 520–21.

Rao, Asha, and Schmidt, Stuart M. (1998), 'A behavioural perspective on negotiating international alliances', *Journal of International Business Studies*, **29** (4), 665–93.

Redding, S. Gordon (1990), *The Spirit of Chinese Capitalism*, Berlin and New York: de Gruyter.

Richardson, G.B. (1972), 'The organisation of industry', *The Economic Journal*, **80** (September), 883–96.

Richerson, Peter J. and Boyd, Robert (2004), *Not By Genes Alone: How Culture Transformed Human Evolution*, Chicago: Chicago University Press.

Ritter, Thomas, Wilkinson, Ian F. and Johnston, Wesley J. (2002), 'Measuring network competence: some international evidence', *Journal of Business and Industrial Marketing*, **17** (2/3), 119–38.

Ritter, Thomas, Wilkinson, Ian F. and Johnston, Wesley J. (2004), 'Firms' ability to manage in business networks: a review of concepts', *Industrial Marketing Management*, **33**, April, 175–83.

Rosenberg, Larry J. and Stern, Louis W. (1970), 'Toward the analysis of conflict in distribution channels: a descriptive model', *Journal of Marketing*, **34** (October), 40–46.

Sako, Mari (1992), *Prices, Quality and Trust: Inter-Firm Relations in Britain and Japan*, Cambridge: Cambridge University Press.

Sanchez, Angel and Cuesta, Jose A. (2004), 'Altruism may arise from individual selection', *arXiv*, 1 1, 16 March q-bio.PE/0403023.

Saravathy, S.D. (2003), 'Entrepreneurships as a science of the artificial', *Journal of Economic Psychology*, **24**, 203–20.

Seabright, Mark A., Levinthal, Daniel A. and Fichman, Mark (1992), 'Role of individual attachments in the dissolution of interorganizational relationships', *Academy of Management Journal*, **35** (1), 122–60.

Selsky, John W., Goes, James B. and Baburoglu, Oguz N. (2003), 'A socio-ecological logic of strategy making: interrogating the "hyper" environment', Working Paper 2003/10014, Department of Management, University of Melbourne, Australia.

Senge, Peter M. (1990), *The Fifth Discipline: The Art and Science of the Learning Organization*, New York: Doubleday.

Shane, Scott (2000), 'Prior knowledge and the discovery of entrepreneurial opportunities', *Organization Science*, **11**, 448–69.

Sharma, Neeru, Young, Louise C. and Wilkinson, Ian F. (2006), 'The commitment mix: dimensions of commitment in international trading relationships with India', *Journal of International Marketing*, **14** (3), 64–91.

Sheth, Jagdish N. and Parvatiyar, Atul (eds) (2000), *Handbook of Relationship Marketing*, London and Thousand Oaks, CA: Sage.

Shove, G.S. (1930), 'The representative firm and increased returns', *The Economic Journal*, **40** (March), 94–116.

Stacey, Ralph D. (1996), *Complexity, Creativity and Management*, San Francisco, CA: Berrett-Koehler.

Stacey, Ralph D., Griffin, Douglas and Shaw, Patricia (2000), *Complexity and Management: Fad or Radical Challenge?*, London: Routledge.

Stern, Louis (ed.) (1969), *Distribution Channels: Behavioral Dimensions*, Boston, MA: Houghton Mifflin.

Stigler, George J. (1946), *The Theory of Price*, New York: Macmillan.

Stigler, George J. (1951), 'The division of labour is limited by the extent of the market', *Journal of Political Economy*, **45** (June), 185–93.

Taleb, Nassim (2005), *Fooled by Randomness: The Hidden Role of Chance in Life and in the Markets*, New York: Random House.

Tesfatsion, L. (2006), 'Agent-based computational economics: a constructive approach to economic theory', in L. Tesfatsion and K.L. Judd (eds), *Handbook of Computational Economics*, Vol. 2, Amsterdam: Elsevier/North-Holland.

Tesfatsion, L. and Judd, K.L. (eds) (2006), *Handbook of Computational Economics*, Vol. 2, Amsterdam: Elsevier/North-Holland.

Thomas, Kenneth W. (1992), 'Conflict and conflict management: reflections and update', *Journal of Organizational Behaviour*, **13** (3), 265–74.

Urban, G.L. and von Hippel, Eric (1988), 'Lead user analyses for the development of new industrial products', *Management Science*, **34** (5), 569–82.

Vaile, R., Grether, E.T. and Cox, R. (1952), *Marketing in the American Economy*, New York: Ronald Press Coy.

von Hippel, Eric (1988), *The Sources of Innovation*, New York: Oxford University Press.

von Hippel, Eric (1994), '"Sticky information" and the locus of problem solving: implications for innovation', *Management Science*, **40** (April) (4), 429–39.

von Hippel, Eric (2005), *Democratizing Innovation*, Cambridge: MIT Press.

Walter, A., Ritter, Thomas and Gemunden, Hans Georg (2001), 'Value creation in buyer–seller relations', *Industrial Marketing Management*, **30**, 365–77.

Walter, Achim, Muller, Thilo A., Helfert, Gabriel and Ritter, Thomas (2003), 'Functions of industrial supplier relationships and their impact on relationship quality', *Industrial Marketing Management*, **32**, 159–69.

Weick, Karl and Sutcliffe, Kathleen (2001), *Managing the Unexpected: Assuring High Performance in an Age of Complexity*, San Francisco: Jossey-Bass.

Welch, Catherine and Wilkinson, Ian F. (2002), 'Idea logics and network theory in business marketing', *Journal of Business to Business Marketing*, **8** (3), 27–48.

Welch, Catherine and Wilkinson, Ian F. (2004), 'The political embeddedness of international business networks', *International Marketing Review*, **21** (2), 216–31.

Welch, Catherine and Wilkinson, Ian F. (2005), 'A network interpretation of international interfirm conflict', *Journal of Business Research*, **58** (February), 205–13.

Welch, Denice, Welch, Lawrence, Wilkinson, Ian F. and Young, Louise (1996), 'Export grouping relationships and networks: evidence from an Australian Scheme', *International Journal of Research in Marketing*, **13**, 463–77.

Welch, Denice, Welch, Lawrence, Wilkinson, Ian F. and Young, Louise (1998), 'The importance of networks in export promotion: policy issues', *Journal of International Marketing*, **6** (4), 66–82.

Wiener, Norbert (1954), *The Human Use of Human Beings: Cybernetics and Society*, Boston: Houghton Mifflin.

Wiley, James, Wilkinson, Ian F. and Young, Louise C. (2006), 'The nature, role and impact of connected relations: a comparison of European and Chinese suppliers' perspectives', *Journal of Business and Industrial Marketing*, **21** (1), 3–13.

Wilkinson, Ian F. (1973), 'Power and influence structures in distribution channels', *European Journal of Marketing*, **7** (2), 119–29.

Wilkinson, Ian F. (1974a), 'Researching the distribution channels for industrial and consumer goods', *Journal of the British Market Research Society*, **16** (1), 12–32.

Wilkinson, Ian F. (1974b), 'Distribution channel management: power considerations', *International Journal of Physical Distribution*, **4** (1), 4–15.

Wilkinson, Ian F. (1979), 'Power and satisfaction in channels of distribution', *Journal of Retailing*, **55** (1), 79–94.

Wilkinson, Ian F. (1981), 'Power, conflict and satisfaction in distribution channels: an empirical study', *International Journal of Physical Distribution and Materials Management*, **11** (7), 20–31.

Wilkinson, Ian F. (2001), 'History of channels and network thinking in marketing in the 20th century', *Australasian Marketing Journal*, **9** (2), 23–53.

Wilkinson, Ian F. (2006a), 'The evolvability of business and the role of antitrust', *Antitrust Bulletin*, **51** (1), 111–41.

Wilkinson, Ian F. (2006b), 'The evolution of an evolutionary perspective on B2B business', *Journal of Business and Industrial Marketing*, **21** (7), 458–65.

Wilkinson, Ian F. and Cheng, Constant (1999), 'Multicultural marketing in Australia: synergy in diversity', *Journal of International Marketing*, **1** (3), 106–25.

Wilkinson, Ian F. and Kipnis, David (1978), 'Interfirm use of power', *Journal of Applied Psychology*, **63** (3), 315–20.

Wilkinson, Ian F. and Nguyen, Van (2003), 'A contingency model of export entry mode performance: the role of production and transaction costs', *Australasian Marketing Journal*, **11** (3), 44–60.

Wilkinson, Ian and Yeoh, Kevin (2005), 'Value creation in Chinese and European business relationships', in David Brown and Alistair McBean (eds), *Economy and Business in China*, London: Routledge, pp. 87–101.

Wilkinson, Ian F. and Young, Louise C. (1994), 'Business dancing: an alternative paradigm for relationship marketing', *Australasian Marketing Journal*, **2** (1), 67–80.

Wilkinson, Ian F. and Young, Louise (2002), 'On cooperating: firms, relations and networks', *Journal of Business Research* 55 (February), 123–132.

Wilkinson, Ian F. and Young, Louise C. (2005a), 'A planning framework for relationship and network management', in P. Andersson, S. Hertz and S. Sweet (eds), *Perspectives on Market Networks – Boundaries and New Connections*, Economic Research Institute, Stockholm School of Economics, pp. 39–52.

Wilkinson, Ian F. and Young, Louise C. (2005b), 'Toward a normative theory of normative marketing theory', *Marketing Theory*, **5** (4), 363–96.

Wilkinson, Ian F., Freytag, Per and Young, Louise (2005), 'Business mating: who chooses whom and gets chosen?', *Industrial Marketing Management*, **34** (7), 669–680.

Wilkinson, Ian F., Marks, R. and Young, L. (2006), 'Toward agent-based models of the development and evolution of business relations and networks', International Conference on Complex Systems (ICCS 2006), Boston, MA.

Wilkinson, Ian F., Mattsson, L.-G. and Easton, G. (2000), 'International competitiveness and trade promotion policy from a network perspective', *Journal of World Business*, **35** (3), 275–99.

Wilkinson, Ian F., Young, L.C. and Ladley, D. (2007), 'Group selection versus individual selection and the evolution of cooperation in business networks', IMP Conference, University of Manchester, UK, 29 August–1 September.

Williamson, Oliver E. (1975), *Markets and Hierachies: Analysis and Antitrust Implications*, New York: Free Press.

Wolpert, J. (2002), 'Breaking out of the innovation box', *Harvard Business Review*, August, 77–83.

Wong, C.K.L. (2006), 'Towards an empirical taxonomy of business market relations: an atmospheric approach', B.Com. Honours thesis, School of Marketing, University of New South Wales, Australia.

Young, Louise C. and Denize, Sara (1995), 'A concept of commitment: alternative views of relational continuity in business service relationships', *Journal of Business and Industrial Marketing*, **10** (5), 22–37.

Young, Louise C. and Wilkinson, Ian F. (1989), 'The role of trust and co-operation in marketing channels: a preliminary study', *European Journal of Marketing*, **23** (2), 109–22.

Young, Louise C. and Wilkinson, Ian F. (1997), 'The space between: towards a typology of interfirm relations', *Journal of Business to Business Marketing*, **13** (6), December, 53–96.

Yukl, Gary (2001), *Leadership in Organizations*, Englewood Cliffs, NJ: Prentice Hall.

Index

repeated interaction 209
requisite variety 203, 204
resource-advantage theory (R-AT) 26,
    27, 204–5
  assessing contribution of resources
      to competitiveness 205, 206,
      207
  interconnection of resources within
      and across firms 205, 206, 207
resource ties 72, 73, 74
Richardson, G. 45, 56
Richartz, L. 64
Ritter, T. 106
Rosenberg, L. 158

Sako, M. 160
Santema, S. 103
Saravathy, S. 86
scale-free networks 248
  antitrust policy 248–50, 251, 252
  evolutionary process 251
  vulnerabilities 250
schemas 72, 73, 74, 75
Schmidt, S. 155, 156
Seabright, M. 174
sellers' perspectives
  classification of business
      relationships 124, 125, 127–8,
      137, 138, 139
Selsky, J. 200
sexual selection 89–90, 92, 245; *see also*
    business mating
shadow of the future 8, 55, 56, 209,
    256
shadow of the past 8, 55, 114–15, 118,
    139, 209, 256
Shah, S. 81
Shane, S. 77
Sharma, N. 163
Shove, G. 40
signalling 209
similar activities 45, 51–2
  coordination situations 52, 53
  see also economies of specialisation
Simon, H. 266
simultaneous involvement in numerous
    relationships 185
Singh, H. 194
Smith, A. 32, 38
Snehota, I. 1, 72

social animals
  humans as 22, 89
social balance processes 74, 75
social enclaves 200
social vortices 200
soft assembled strategies 215, 216, 217,
    263
  exploitation and exploration
      218–19
  network positioning 218
sorting activities
  types of 31, 32
specialisation, *see* division of labour
stabilising effect of relations and
    networks 22
stage models
  relationship development 96–100
  starting conditions 101, 102
    complementarity and compatibility
        of resources 107–8
    connected relations 108–9
    market and environmental
        conditions 109
    relative dependence and power
        105–7
    role and purpose of the relation
        102–5
Stern, L. 147, 158
Stigler, G. 39, 43
strategic triangle 25–6
  collaborative advantage 27, 28
  cooperators 27
  customer advantage 26, 27
  supplier advantage 26, 27
strong ties 218
  business mating 95, 96
  innovation 83, 84, 85
structural holes 218
  innovation 83, 84
structure of networks and relations 72,
    101, 102
  activity links 73, 74
  actor bonds 72, 73, 74
  continuously changing 73
  relationship with functions 73
    constructive effects 73, 74
    deleterious effects 73, 74, 75
  resource ties 72, 73, 74
  schemas 72, 73, 74, 75
succession 182